JFK and His Enemies

JFK and His Enemies

A Portrait of Power

Thomas J. Whalen

ROWMAN & LITTLEFIELD
Lanham • Boulder • New York • Toronto • Plymouth, UK

Published by Rowman & Littlefield
4501 Forbes Boulevard, Suite 200, Lanham, Maryland 20706
www.rowman.com

10 Thornbury Road, Plymouth PL6 7PP, United Kingdom

British Library Cataloguing in Publication Information Available

Library of Congress Cataloging-in-Publication Data

Whalen, Thomas J.
JFK and his enemies : a portrait of power / by Thomas J. Whalen
p. cm.
Includes bibliographical references and index.
ISBN 978-1-4422-1374-6 (cloth : alk. paper) -- ISBN 978-1-4422-1376-0 (electronic)
1. 2. I. Whalen, Thomas J. Title.
BH39.H445 2011
111'.85--dc22
2014037457

Author's note: Portions of this book have been repurposed from my earlier works *Kennedy Versus Lodge: The 1952 Massachusetts Senate Race* (2000) and *A Higher Purpose: Profiles in Presidential Courage* (2007). I have also provided original source citations where appropriate.

™ The paper used in this publication meets the minimum requirements of American National Standard for Information Sciences Permanence of Paper for Printed Library Materials, ANSI/NISO Z39.48-1992.

Printed in the United States of America

In loving memory of Herman T. Whalen, 1928–1982

Contents

Introduction

The famed nineteenth-century humorist Finley Peter Dunne once commented that life "would not be worth living if we didn't keep our enemies."[1] Certainly John F. Kennedy could appreciate the wisdom behind this observation. At nearly every stage of his noteworthy political career, which stretched from the dank, run-down tenement houses of Charlestown, Massachusetts, in 1946 to the gleaming downtown skyscrapers of Dallas, Texas, in 1963, Kennedy had collected his fair share of enemies.

Some, like Henry Cabot Lodge Jr. in 1952 and Lyndon Johnson in 1960, presented formidable political obstacles to his attaining higher office. Others, like Nikita Khrushchev during the Cuban Missile Crisis of 1962, threatened the very survival of the human race itself.

Regardless of the stakes, Kennedy always seemed to rise to the level of the domestic or international challenge presented. "Our problems are man-made, therefore they may be solved by man," he said.[2] To those who knew him best, this single-mindedness was not surprising. "He clearly wanted to establish a place in history," insisted Robert McNamara, Kennedy's Secretary of Defense.[3] But being a historian himself, Kennedy realized that political success did not come easily or cheaply. It required individual strength of character, clarity of thought, and the ability to act decisively. "There are risks and costs to action," he allowed. "But they are far less than the long range risks of comfortable inaction."[4] Kennedy "had a steely core," acknowledged Donald Wilson, former Deputy Director of the US Information Agency. "I don't remember any occasions where he was cold, but I can remember many occasions where he was strong, and even abrupt, in making decisions, he was not polite all the time."[5]

Consistent with this attitude was the hardball way in which Kennedy often dealt with his adversaries. Richard M. Nixon, his GOP opponent for the presidency in 1960, was a prime example. Although the two had been on opposite sides of the political aisle from the time they had arrived in Washington together in the late 1940s, Nixon admitted he was unprepared for the kind of rough personal treatment he received from Kennedy during the campaign. Indeed, Kennedy hammered away at his opponent for being "soft" on communism, a distortion of Nixon's record that left the Republican reeling. "I had been through some pretty rough campaigns in the past, but compared to the others, going into the 1960 campaign was like moving from the minor to the major leagues," Nixon complained in his memoirs. [6]

Nixon would not be the last to underestimate Kennedy's mettle. After Kennedy failed to topple Cuba's Fidel Castro during the spectacularly mismanaged Bay of Pigs invasion of 1961, Soviet Premier Nikita Khrushchev could not resist viewing Kennedy as an inept "young man in short pants." Accordingly, he directly challenged the young president on a number of key geopolitical fronts, including Berlin. Only when Kennedy stood his ground against Khrushchev's clandestine attempt to place offensive nuclear missiles in Cuba and threaten World War III in the process, did the Russian leader back down and begin to take his Cold War counterpart seriously. "He showed himself to be sober-minded and determined to avoid war," Khrushchev later wrote. "He didn't become frightened, nor did he become reckless." [7]

In 1963 Alabama Governor George Wallace sought to thwart Kennedy's attempt to integrate the University of Alabama at Tuscaloosa by standing "at the schoolhouse door" and blocking the entry of two African American students. But Wallace's act of defiance was foiled by a strong federal response led by Kennedy that forced the governor to step aside and allow the students admission. "Today we are committed to a worldwide struggle to promote and protect the rights of all who wish to be free," Kennedy said. "And when Americans are sent to Viet-Nam or West Berlin, we do not ask for whites only. It ought to be possible, therefore, for American students of any color to attend any institution they select. . . . This is one country. It has become one country because all the people who came here had an equal chance to develop their talents." [8]

Success did not always follow Kennedy in his dealings with other opponents. When confronted with the formidable bureaucratic infighting skills of J. Edgar Hoover, Kennedy found himself overmatched. The FBI Director had a thick file of embarrassing revelations about Kennedy's personal life in his possession, including explosive proof that the chief executive was carrying on an illicit sexual affair with a Capitol Hill prostitute. Hoover used such information to coerce Kennedy into allowing a bureau wiretap of civil rights leader Martin Luther King Jr., whom the director believed was under the thrall of international communism. Kennedy likewise failed to remove Fidel Castro from power, despite his approval of the Bay of Pigs and several CIA assassination attempts to bump off the Cuban dictator. "We were doing almost everything you could dream up," revealed one administration insider. [9]

Ironically, it would be an obscure but fanatical American supporter of Castro, Lee Harvey Oswald, who finally put an end to Kennedy's presidency in a hail of gunfire on November 22, 1963. That this twenty-four-year-old former high school dropout on his own was able to brutally snuff out one of the leading lights of postwar American society has always filled Kennedy admirers with incredulity. Yet the fact remains: Oswald was a disturbed lone assassin who changed the entire course of history. "On November 22 [Kennedy's] future merged with his past, and we will never know what might have been," noted the late presidential speechwriter Theodore C. Sorensen.[10] Amen.

Over the years a number of superb scholarly works on Kennedy have appeared, including James MacGregor Burns's *John Kennedy: A Political Profile* (1960), Joan and Clay Blair Jr.'s *The Search for J.F.K.* (1976), Herbert S. Parmet's *Jack: The Struggles of John F. Kennedy* (1980), Doris Kearns Goodwin's *The Fitzgeralds and Kennedys: An American Saga* (1987), Nigel Hamilton's *JFK: Reckless Youth* (1993), Robert Dallek's *Unfinished Life: John F. Kennedy, 1917–1963* (2003), and Michael O'Brien's *John F. Kennedy: A Biography* (2005). None, however, have taken a detailed historic look at the conflict-laden relationships Kennedy had with his political enemies or the ramifications they held for his times. The following pages hope to rectify that situation, for one cannot hope to fully understand America in the crucial period between V-J Day and Vietnam without first understanding these fractured ties. As Kennedy said, "Things don't happen, they are made to happen."[11]

NOTES

Author's Note: Portions of this book have been repurposed from my earlier works *Kennedy Versus Lodge: The 1952 Massachusetts Senate Race* (Boston, 2000) and *A Higher Purpose: Profiles in Presidential Courage* (Chicago, 2007). I have also provided original source citations where appropriate.

1. *The Daily Herald* (Utah), July 10, 1959.

2. John F. Kennedy, "Commencement Address at American University in Washington" (June 10, 1963) in *Public Papers of the Presidents of the United States: John F. Kennedy, 1963* (Washington, DC, 1964), 461.

3. Ralph G. Martin, *A Hero for Our Time: An Intimate Story of the Kennedy Years* (New York, 1983), 276.

4. *Manila-US Times*, August 2, 2008, http://manilaustimes.blogspot.com/2008/08/wheres-pelosi_02.html.

5. Gerald S. Strober and Deborah H. Strober, *"Let Us Begin Anew": An Oral History of the Kennedy Presidency* (New York, 1993), 53.

6. Richard Nixon, *RN: The Memoirs of Richard Nixon* (New York, 1978), 225.

7. Nikita Khrushchev, *Khrushchev Remembers* (Boston, 1979), 500.

8. Kennedy, "Radio and Television Report to the American People on Civil Rights" (June 11, 1963), *Public Papers of the Presidents: John F. Kennedy 1963*, 468, 470.

9. Alex Von Tunzelmann, *Red Heat: Conspiracy, Murder, and the Cold War in the Caribbean* (New York, 2011), 253.

10. Theodore C. Sorenson, *Kennedy* (New York, 1965), 756.

11. John F. Kennedy, "Address at the University of North Dakota," September 25, 1963, in *Public Papers of the Presidents of the United States: John F. Kennedy, 1963*, 718.

ONE

Prelude to Power

Growing Up Kennedy

George Smathers was a proverbial man about town. The longtime Florida politician enjoyed fine cigars, the company of attractive young women, and partaking in the bracing pleasures of the Washington, DC, social scene. But when he first met John F. Kennedy in the late 1940s, he felt strangely underwhelmed. Despite sharing the same pleasure-seeking, cosmopolitan outlook, Kennedy came across as off-puttingly different. "In those days Jack was a rather sickly fellow," Smathers explained. "In addition to his bad back . . . he was constantly plagued with colds and one thing or another which kept him constantly laid up." If these weren't enough strikes against him, Kennedy also exhibited a somewhat remote and diffident personality. "He was so shy he could hardly tell you his name," Smathers said. "One of the shyest fellows I'd ever seen." Little did Smathers realize that this seemingly unimpressive young man would go on to become the 35th President of the United States. But then, Kennedy had always surprised people.[1]

The second oldest of nine children of Irish Catholic parents, Kennedy was born on May 29, 1917, in Brookline, Massachusetts. His father, Joseph P. Kennedy, was a Harvard-educated business entrepreneur on his way to making the first of many millions on Wall Street and in Hollywood. His mother, Rose Fitzgerald Kennedy, was the daughter of former US congressman and Boston mayor John F. "Honey Fitz" Fitzgerald, one of the most colorful Irish American politicians of the early twentieth century.

Although he once claimed in an interview to have been raised in a struggling, run-down district (in actuality, Brookline was an upper-middle-class community), John Kennedy did not lack for any material comforts growing up. For sure, he dressed in the finest clothes, attended the best schools, and was driven around town by a chauffeur. Emotionally, his needs were tended to by his mother. "She's not as forceful as my father," he later recalled, "but she was the glue." This quality notwithstanding, Rose could come across as distant and aloof at times, preferring matters of the soul to matters of the heart. "She was deeply religious, highly devout," Kennedy explained. "She wasn't interested in politics so much [but she] was interested in things like the Pilgrims' landing at Plymouth Rock, things like that."[2]

While Rose's influence was unquestionably strong, it still did not compare to that of Joseph P. Kennedy, whom many regarded as the "architect" of his children's lives. Proud, ambitious, overbearing, and unscrupulous, the "Founding Father" exerted a "savage domination" over his sons and daughters. "I don't think you can have nine children in a house without there being some rigid authority," John Kennedy later commented, "and I think my father supplied that. But not unnecessarily so, and I think it did us all good."[3]

Not everyone agreed with this assessment. "He disciplined Jack like a Jesuit," complained Boston friend Norman MacDonald. "When the father was around, Jack couldn't invite any of his friends he wanted to their summer home in Hyannis Port. He had to submit a guest list and schedule to his father, and could invite only people who were useful."[4]

Viewing his children as extensions of himself, Joseph Kennedy sought to instill in them a burning desire to succeed. "The father particularly laid it on hard trying to make the boys, and the girls, excellent in something," Supreme Court Justice William O. Douglas later recalled, "whether it was touch football, or tennis, or boating, or something else." Sometimes the emphasis on competition bordered on the extreme. When Joe Junior lost a sailboat race one summer, his father ordered a new mainsail be made that was nine inches longer than the rules of competition allowed. The notion of fair play did not enter the equation. All that mattered was Joe Junior winning his next race. "For the Kennedys," Joseph Kennedy once said, "it is the castle or the outhouse—nothing in between."[5]

This obsession with winning stemmed from a deep-seated sense of personal frustration. Barred from entering Brahmin society on account of his Irish Catholic heritage ("When are the nice people of Boston going to accept us?" his wife asked an acquaintance), the elder Kennedy vowed his children would be accepted into elite circles. To this end he packed up his family and moved them to tony Riverdale, New York, in an attempt to "show" his supposed Brahmin betters he needed neither their acceptance nor approval. "I was born here," he said. "My children were born here. What the hell do I have to do to be an American?" Not satisfied with having his children receive a public or parochial school education, he sent them off to select boarding schools where they could rub elbows with other sons and daughters of the rich and famous. "Joe was a hard-nosed fella," said George Smathers, "but there was no question that Joe was the driving force behind that family. He was the guy that made them all ambitious and in some respects [this competitive attitude] almost became pugnacious."[6]

If there was a model for what Joseph Kennedy wanted his children to become, one could look no further than Joe Junior. Tall, handsome, athletically gifted, and smart, the eldest son represented "the best and the brightest" of the Kennedy clan. In him Joe Senior invested all his hopes and dreams. "Joe Junior was the doer," wrote the historian Herbert S. Parmet, "the gregarious charmer who, backed by enormous money and a powerful father, was guaranteed to turn his attributes toward the leadership of others." Joe Junior also possessed a violent temper that could unexpectedly boil over at times. He once tossed his baby brother overboard when the latter made a critical error in a sailboat race that cost their side a victory. "I was scared to death," Ted Kennedy wrote years later. Other family members endured even worse physical abuse. "I used to lie in my bed at night sometimes," younger brother Robert Kennedy remembered, "and hear the sound of Joe banging Jack's head against the wall." Needless to say, this kind of bullying behavior left a deep impression. "It wasn't the father [the Kennedy children] were afraid of," noted one observer. "It was Joe Junior."[7]

In contrast, John Kennedy was the so-called "runt" of the litter. Thin, bookish, and sickly, he did not cut a particularly striking figure. "He was too slight, too frail, too brittle to make the varsity in any contact sport," recalled one prep school instructor. "He tried them all only to wind up with broken fingers, wrists or ankles or whatever. Through both school and college he was frustrated by his failure to measure up to his older brother, but he never stopped trying." More times than not, however, these efforts proved unsuccessful. "My brother is the efficient one in the family," young Jack conceded, "and I'm the boy who doesn't get things done. . . . If my brother were not so efficient, it would be easier for me to be efficient. He does it so much better than I do."[8]

To compensate for these perceived shortcomings and carve out his own sense of identity, Kennedy became something of an "archetypal rebel." At Choate School in Wallingford, Connecticut, for instance, he specialized in having fun and antagonizing the school's administration. "Well, I have two things to do," complained headmaster George St. John to Joe Senior. "One to run the school, another to run Jack Kennedy and his friends."[9] Indeed, so unruly did Kennedy's behavior become that he came within a hair of being permanently expelled.

The precipitating incident involved the formation of a clandestine student prankster group known as the "Mucker's Club." So named for the term St. John used to describe undisciplined boys, the group flourished on the all-male campus, threatening even to surpass the popularity of the football team. "Why were we so devilish?" remarked one member. "Maybe we didn't like to be structured. Each of those guys had a pretty darn good sense of humor. Jack had a very, very keen wit. We just liked fooling people. . . . We were just nonorganization in some ways."[10]

Concerned that the Muckers were undermining his authority as headmaster, St. John rounded up the club's ringleaders, including Kennedy, and proceeded to inform them that they were no longer welcome as students at the school. "I don't blame them," said Mucker Maurice Shea years later. "He thought we were not quite the boys he wanted to have the stamp of Choate on." Only through the timely intervention of his father, who reportedly made a generous financial contribution to the school, were the future Massachusetts politician and his friends able to avoid expulsion. "If that crazy Mucker's Club had been mine," Joseph Kennedy told his son, "you can be sure it wouldn't have started with an M."[11]

Despite such levity, Joe Senior was disturbed enough by the affair to pen his son the following warning: "Don't let me lose confidence in you again because it will be pretty nearly an impossible task to restore it—I am sure it will be a loss for you and a distinct loss for me." Thus chastened, John Kennedy spent the remainder of his Choate career staying out of trouble and improving upon his mediocre academic record. Still, he could not resist the temptation of pulling off one final prank. As class elections got under way, he convinced friends to stuff enough ballot boxes on his behalf to become "Most Likely to Succeed."[12]

Upon graduation from Choate in 1935, Kennedy entered Princeton University, but a hepatitis attack forced him to leave the school after only six weeks of classes. By attending the prestigious Ivy League institution, the former Mucker had hoped to escape the shadow of his older brother, Joe, who had become a star student athlete at Harvard. It didn't work out that way. News of his brother's triumphs continued to reach him at Princeton, thanks to letters from old Choate schoolmates and family members.

Determined to match his brother's success, Kennedy gave in to pressure from his father to matriculate into his alma mater. "Jack," Joseph P. Kennedy wrote a Harvard dean at the time, "has a very brilliant mind for the things he is interested in, but is careless and lacks application in those in which he is not interested. This is, of course, a bad fault."[13] As if to prove his father's point, the younger Kennedy spent most of his freshman year pursuing the two activities he enjoyed the most: socializing and playing football. While he could hold his own against his brother in the former, he did not stand a chance against him in the latter.

"Joe was physically more rugged," remembered Torbert MacDonald, Kennedy's Harvard roommate and later a US Congressman. "Jack played [junior varsity] offensive end and was a very good pass receiver. He had great desire, wanted to play very much, but his physical makeup was not that of an end who could block tackles which in those days were the biggest defensive linemen that the opponent ever had. His greatest success was in catching passes, shall we say."[14]

It wasn't until his sophomore year that Kennedy's intellectual curiosity became aroused. Although his grades showed scant improvement, he began to read more and ask questions about the world around him. "I don't know what to attribute it to," he later told a journalist. "No, not professors. I guess I was getting older. . . . It was during my junior year that I went to England for six months, which meant taking six courses as a senior and hard work. I had to work like hell."[15]

He took a semester off and went to England with his father, the ambassador to the Court of St. James appointed by President Franklin Roosevelt. FDR had made the move on strictly political grounds; he wanted to shore up support within his Irish Catholic constituency. "The office," surmised historians David Burner and Thomas R. West, "would make him the social superior of Boston's 'best people'; it was an achievement by which one generation of Kennedys could extend the reach to the next."[16]

The Kennedys did, in fact, for a time become the toast of London society, and while young Jack shared in the excitement of the seemingly endless rounds of embassy parties and royal galas, he spent an equal amount of time familiarizing himself with the problems that would soon plunge the Continent into World War II. "It was a great chance to go because it certainly was Europe on the eve," he later told an interviewer, "and the tempo was heightened because of it. It was a great opportunity to see a period of history which was one of the most significant."[17]

What he observed in Europe was later incorporated into his senior thesis, "Appeasement at Munich," which earned him magna cum laude honors. The 150-page study, an analysis of the reasons why British prime minister Neville Chamberlain "appeased" German leader Adolf Hitler at the Munich Conference of 1938, placed heavy emphasis on the role of public opinion in determining national policy. Arguing that the overwhelming pacifist sentiment of the country forced Chamberlain to make unwise concessions to the Nazi dictator, he proceeded to exonerate the British leader of any blame.

He concluded that the Munich Pact, which pledged British acquiescence to Germany's seizure of the Sudetenland from Czechoslovakia, was inevitable given the conditions of democratic government. Although there were some reservations about the quality of the writing, Kennedy's thesis advisor, Henry A. Yeomans, determined that, on the whole, the work represented "a laborious and intelligent discussion of a difficult question."[18]

Pleased by his son's effort and the thesis's mirroring of his own sympathetic attitude toward Chamberlain, Joseph Kennedy sent a copy to Pulitzer Prize–winning columnist Arthur Krock of the *New York Times*. Finding the author's argument persuasive, the longtime Kennedy family friend recommended the work be refashioned into a book. "I was an editor, an advisor," Krock later admitted to Kennedy biographer Clay Blair, "and I may have supplied some of the material as far as prose is concerned, but it was [Kennedy's] book. So we got it published and you know the rest."[19]

Retitled *Why England Slept*, a clever take on Winston Churchill's widely acclaimed *While England Slept*, the book soared to the top of most national best-seller lists. But things were not as they appeared. Fearing poor book sales would reflect badly on his son's budding literary reputation, the elder Kennedy clandestinely purchased hundreds of copies to give the impression the work was a runaway success. "You would be surprised how a book that really makes the grade with high-class people stands you in good stead for years to come," the ambassador wrote his author-son.[20]

After his graduation from Harvard in June 1940, John Kennedy spent the next year and a half largely adrift and unfocused. He enrolled at Stanford University in California to do graduate work in business and political science, but the slow pace of academic life bored him. Putting aside his studies, the wealthy Ivy Leaguer spent most of his time visiting popular beachfront hideaways and dating socially eligible Stanford coeds and Hollywood actresses. "I've known many of the great Hollywood stars, and only a very few of them seemed to hold the attraction for women that JFK did, even before he entered the political arena," recalled Robert Stack, the popular film and television actor who befriended Kennedy during this period. "He'd just look at them and they'd tumble. I often wondered (in subsequent years) why he wasted his time on politics when he could have made it big in an important business like motion pictures."[21]

Only occasionally did the outside world intrude upon Kennedy's thoughts. That occurred in December 1940, when his father sought his advice for a radio speech he intended to give on American neutrality. A staunch isolationist and defeatist ("I'll bet you five to one—any sum— that Hitler will be at Buckingham Palace in two weeks," he once told an aide), the now former ambassador sought to keep America out of World War II.[22]

Although he had expressed support of his father's isolationism as a college undergrad, even going so far as advocating "considerable concessions to Hitlerdom" in an unsigned *Harvard Crimson* editorial, John Kennedy had in the interim experienced a political transformation. Reasoning that a triumphant Nazi Germany in Europe would endanger the security of the entire Western Hemisphere, the future commander in chief urged his father to back policies aimed at militarily propping up a besieged Great Britain. "We should see," he wrote, "that our immediate menace is not invasion, but that England may fall—through our lack of support."[23] Adhering to his son's advice, Joseph P. Kennedy came out in favor of the Lend-Lease Act, which empowered the president to sell, lend, or lease defense materials to Britain and her allies.

When American entry into the war became more likely in 1941, John Kennedy decided to sign up for military duty. Again, as was the case with his decision to enter Harvard, sibling rivalry played a key role. Envious of his brother Joe's acceptance into the prestigious US Naval Aviation program, the ex-ambassador's son tried to enlist in both the Army and Navy, but a bad back brought on by an earlier football injury convinced service officials that he lacked the physical health to be inducted.

Unwilling to see Joe Junior have a monopoly on all the military glory, he got his father to arrange for a second Navy physical, this time with a friendly doctor the elder Kennedy knew.[24] The ruse worked; he passed the examination without difficulty and received an ensign's commission in the US Naval Reserves. Several weeks later, while returning from a regular Sunday morning touch football session with friends, he heard the news of the Japanese attack on Pearl Harbor. His life, as well as the lives of millions of other Americans, would never be the same.

Kennedy's naval career began with an unglamorous desk job at the Office of Naval Intelligence in Washington, DC. His assigned duties involved preparing a daily intelligence bulletin for the Secretary of the Navy and other top officials. "We never dealt in anything higher than 'secret,'" remembered one contemporary, "and if we had code-breaking information, it came up to us disguised, so we didn't know its source." Bored by the tedious work, Kennedy sought diversion by carrying on a romantic tryst with a former Danish movie actress turned Washington newspaper reporter named Inga Marie Arvad. "There was something adventurous about her," said Kennedy friend and journalist Charles Spalding. "She'd done so much, been involved in so much. She was a fictional character almost, walking around."[25]

Yet the fact that she had once been on friendly terms with Adolf Hitler and other top Nazi leaders raised red flags among Kennedy's superiors. They believed Arvad was a potential security risk, so Kennedy was reassigned to another naval base in Charleston, South Carolina, where his duties would be less sensitive. Here he languished unhappily until he persuaded his father to "pull strings" and get him transferred to sea duty.[26] Freed from the drudgery of desk work, Kennedy entered midshipman's school at Northwestern University, where he signed up for patrol torpedo boat duty. Otherwise known as PT boats, these small but maneuverable craft had gained considerable publicity at the start of the war for whisking Douglas MacArthur to safety during the Japanese invasion of the Philippines.

Lured by the hype, Kennedy, along with several other Ivy Leaguers with sailing or yachting experience, could not resist the temptation of commanding so glamorous a vessel. Assigned to the Solomon Islands of the South Pacific, the now lieutenant junior grade got more action than he could have reasonably expected. On the night of August 1, 1943, Kennedy's boat, the PT-109, was sliced in two by a Japanese destroyer while on a routine patrol of the Blackett Strait. "How it felt?" he later mused. "I can best compare it to the onrushing trains in the old-time movies. They seemed to come right over you. Well, the feeling was the same, only the destroyer didn't come over us, it went right through us."[27] Two crewmen, Andrew Kirksey and Harold Marney, lost their lives in the crash while another, forty-one-year-old machinist Patrick McHahan, was badly burned. "We were fortunate the destroyer was very narrow and sharp, because only two of us were killed, I guess, or disappeared anyway," remembered Barney Ross, the PT-109's forward lookout that evening. "And the next thing I know, the boat is at about a 45–50 angle and everything seems to be lit up [by the ignited gasoline from the ship's fuel tanks]."[28]

Thrown into the sea by the impact of the collision, Kennedy cajoled the surviving thirteen members of his crew into swimming to a nearby atoll about three and a half miles away. "I have nothing to lose," he told them, "but some of you have wives and children, and I'm not going to order you to try to swim to that shore. You'll have to make your own decision on that."[29]

With Kennedy leading the way, all of his men arrived safely on the deserted atoll. "During the week we spent on the island," he later recounted, "the men never beefed as they did when a request for going to town in the states was refused them. I never could praise them enough." The feeling was mutual. "Kennedy was the hero," remembered crew member Charles "Bucky" Harris. He "saved our lives. I owed him my life. I tell everybody that. If it wasn't for him I wouldn't be here—I really feel that . . . Everybody on the crew thought he was top-notch."[30]

What prompted such praise was the extent to which Kennedy was willing to place his own life at risk for the sake of his men. In a desperate attempt to signal a passing PT boat, the young lieutenant swam out to an island passage with a blinking lantern in one hand. "In the first place," recalled a fellow survivor, "it was a hell of a long way out to the passage. He'd go out there and float. Now in my mind if the boats had seen a light in the water, they'd have blown the light out of the water!"[31]

After several failed attempts, including one in which his men had given him up for dead, the former Harvard athlete stumbled across some friendly natives who agreed to alert Allied authorities about the whereabouts of him and his crew. The now legendary message he gave them to deliver was written on the husk of a green coconut and read as follows: "NAURO ISL NATIVE KNOWS POSIT HE CAN PILOT 11 ALIVE NEED SMLL BOAT KENNEDY."[32]

In the immediate aftermath of his rescue, Kennedy tried to downplay any talk of being a hero. "None of that hero stuff about me," he declared in a newspaper article afterward. "Real heroes are not the men who return but those who stay out there like plenty of them do, two of my men included."[33] His reluctance to see himself in this light was understandable.

Though he displayed great courage and personal leadership in keeping his men together following the sinking, he had nonetheless showed questionable command judgment in allowing his ship to be sunk in the first place. Indeed, he had only one of his three engines engaged when the Japanese destroyer was spotted, making escape a highly unlikely prospect. "Kennedy," a naval commander later remarked, "had the most maneuverable vessel in the world. All that power and yet this knight in white armor managed to have his PT boat rammed by a destroyer. Everybody in the fleet laughed about that." Joe Junior couldn't help but get in a few digs too. "What I really want to know," he asked his brother in a letter, "is where the hell were you when the destroyer hove into sight, and exactly what were your moves?"[34]

Such ridicule, however, did not prevent Joe Senior from successfully lobbying Undersecretary of the Navy James Forrestal into awarding his second son the Navy and Marine Corps Medal for valor. "Unmindful of personal danger," Forrestal's citation read, "Lieutenant Kennedy unhesitatingly braved the difficulties and hazards of darkness to direct rescue operations, swimming many hours to secure aid and food after he had succeeded in getting his crew ashore."[35]

Picking up on this heroic theme, the *New Yorker* magazine commissioned future Pulitzer Prize–winning author John Hersey, a personal friend of the Kennedy family, to write about the PT-109 affair for a mid-1944 issue. Entitled "Survival" and later republished in a condensed form for the more widely circulated *Reader's Digest*, the article depicted John Kennedy in Hemingwayesque terms: "He thought he had never known such deep trouble. . . . His mind seemed to float away from his body. Darkness and time took the place of a mind in his skull. For a long time he slept, or was crazy or floated in a chill trance." For his part, the now famous junior officer felt uncomfortable about such embellishment. When he became president two decades later, he privately conceded that the entire PT-109 episode was "more fucked up" than his efforts to unseat Fidel Castro in Cuba.[36]

To put the incident behind him, Kennedy took command of another vessel, the PT-59. "Jack felt very strongly about losing those two men and his ship in the Solomons," recalled fellow naval officer and friend Alvin Cluster. "He . . . wanted to pay the Japanese back. I think he wanted to recover his self-esteem." He thus became involved in several combat engagements, including one involving two other PT boats in the desperate rescue of a company of Marine paratroopers trapped on the Japanese-held island of Choiseul. "The PTs arrived about 6:15 P.M., November 2," remembered Marine commanding officer Victor "Brute" Krulak, who later served as a military advisor to the Kennedy White House. "There were only three [landing craft] to load the company and they were going to overload the boats. The Japs were pushing them, firing with machine guns and rifles."[37]

Somehow Kennedy and most of the Marines survived. "I myself am completely and thoroughly convinced that nothing is going to happen to me," he had earlier written his parents. "I think this is probably the way everyone feels—someone else, yes, themselves, no. Feeling that way makes me anxious to see as much [combat action] as possible and then get out of here and get back home. The more you see here, the quickest you get out—or so they tell us."[38]

Kennedy's combat career came to a close in early December as persistent back troubles and a bout with malaria sidelined him permanently from active duty. He returned home a war hero, albeit a weary one. "I met Jack in Palm Beach after he came back from the Pacific," Charles Spalding said. "I can still see him sitting there [at a local restaurant], the war running through his head, and certainly through a lot of his body— he was pretty well banged up. He just sat there, looking and thinking. And you could just tell what was going through his head—the terrific discrepancy between people at home dressed in white jackets with bow ties, looking like asses . . . and then thinking of the nonsense of people being killed, somebody having his leg blown off. You could see the anguish in his face as he was trying to put it together. We stayed there an hour and I don't think he said one word, not one word."[39]

Meanwhile, Joe Junior had his own personal issues to contend with. Since earning his wings as a naval flier, he had spent most of his time patrolling European waters on the lookout for German submarines. Yet for all his dedicated service, he had no medals of valor—and this irked him. "It looks like I shall return home with the European campaign medal if I'm lucky," he groused.[40]

Joe Junior wanted to secure his own share of family military glory and had just about given up all hope when a unique opportunity arose in early July. Fortified German bunker installations along the northern French coast had been launching deadly V-1 rocket or "buzz bomb" attacks on London. To prevent any further carnage, a top-secret Allied plan was developed to take out the rocket sites, involving remote-controlled PB4Y and B-17 bombers packed with several tons of explosives. Volunteers were needed to pilot the planes until they reached the requisite height and distance after takeoff. Then, as the pilot and copilot parachuted to safety, two accompanying "mother" aircraft would electronically guide "the flying bombs" to their intended targets.

Joe Junior could hardly believe his good fortune. If successful, the operation, code named Anvil, would make him an even bigger war hero than John. He enthusiastically volunteered on the spot. "I am going to do something different for the next three weeks," he cryptically wrote his

Figure 1.1.   JFK with his PT-109 crew. His wartime heroism in the South Pacific would greatly add to his political appeal in the years to follow. JFK Library PC100

parents on July 26. "It is secret, and I am not allowed to say what it is, but it isn't dangerous so don't worry."[41] Of course, the opposite was true. It was an extremely dangerous mission, as Joe Junior and his fellow copilot Wilford Willy of Texas would tragically discover on August 12. For twenty-eight minutes into the flight, their PB4Y plane mysteriously malfunctioned and exploded into a large orange fireball, leaving no traces of either Kennedy or Willy. "The biggest explosion I ever saw until pictures of the atomic bomb," noted one observer.[42]

Official word of Joe Junior's death arrived at the Kennedy family's summer residence in Hyannis Port on August 13. Most of the clan was present, including John, who had traveled down from the Chelsea Naval Hospital near Boston, where he was being treated for war-related injuries. "We were listening to a recording of Bing Crosby singing the number-one tune of that year, 'I'll Be Seeing You,' when a strange dark car pulled into the front driving circle and stopped," remembered Ted Kennedy, the youngest family member and future US Senator. "Two naval chaplains got out, walked up the steps to the porch, and knocked on the screen door. Mother looked up from the Sunday paper she'd been reading in a tiny rocking chair that only she could fit into. As she received the clerics, we could hear a few words: 'missing-lost.' All of us froze." Joe Senior, who had been taking a nap upstairs, was immediately stirred from his sleep by his wife and taken to confer with the two chaplains in a private room downstairs. "When they emerged," Ted later wrote in his memoirs, "Dad's face was twisted. He got the words out that confirmed what we already suspected, Joe Junior was dead." A flood of tears ensued, but Joe Senior extricated himself from the emotion-laden scene. He did not want his children to "witness his own dissolution into sobs."[43]

Ted's older sister Kathleen, who next to John was perhaps Joe Junior's closest sibling, had no such trepidation in expressing her own sense of loss. "Without Joe there will be always a gap in the Kennedy circle," she wrote, "but we are far, far luckier than most because there are so many of us. And I know Joe would always feel that Jack could easily take over the responsibility of being the oldest. I know the one thing Joe would never want is that we should feel sad and gloomy about life without him. Instead, he'd laugh with that wonderful twinkle shining out of his Irish eyes and say, 'Gee, can't you all learn to get along without me?'"[44]

Kathleen received an added jolt of grief three weeks later when she learned that her British husband, Lord William Cavendish, had been killed by a German sniper's bullet while advancing with his Coldstream Guards unit in Belgium. "Now I understand your sorrow for Joe much better," she wrote her parents. "When a brother dies, a sister is very sad but she doesn't have the gnawing pain which one gets when one loses a part of oneself—that was Joe to you both—And Billy to me." Kathleen would meet a tragic end herself in 1948 as the small twin-engine plane she was traveling in with her new lover, the married British aristocrat Peter Fitzwilliam, crashed in the Cévennes Mountains of southern France. Interred at the Cavendish family plot in Chatsworth, England, her stone grave marker reads, "Joy she gave—Joy she has found."[45]

Joe Junior's passing impacted John Kennedy particularly hard. His whole life up to this point had been largely shaped and defined by how well he stacked up against his "Golden Boy" older brother. "Now Joe was gone and Jack did not know where to turn," noted biographer Doris Kearns Goodwin. "After years of being the underdog, Jack had just begun to outperform his brother—first at Harvard and then in the Navy. But now the possibility of eventual victory was forever closed."[46] In an attempt to come to terms with these unresolved emotions, John Kennedy began compiling a book of remembrances about Joe Junior from various family members and friends.

Entitled *As We Remember Joe*, the finished work did not ignore the unremitting sense of unease and frustration that John had felt toward his eldest sibling in life. In his own introductory essay he made special note of the latter's abrasive nature and unfortunate penchant for smiling sardonically during social gatherings. That smile "could cut and prod more sharply than words," Kennedy maintained. Still, the decorated World War II veteran found it within himself to forgive these unflattering personality traits and celebrate what he considered to be "an extraordinarily full and varied life. "[Joe Junior's] worldly success was so assured and inevitable that his death seems to have cut into the natural order of things," he wrote.[47]

This thoughtful personal gesture did little to relieve the debilitating grief Joseph Kennedy was feeling. He later said he could never summon the inner emotional strength to finish the book. "Joe's death has shocked me beyond belief," he confided to future Secretary of Defense James Forrestal, a longtime personal acquaintance. "All of my children are equally dear to me, but there is something about the first born that sets him a little apart—he is always a bit of a miracle and never quite cut off from his mother's heart. He represents our youth, its joys, and problems." Always something of a loner, Joe Senior now kept even more to himself, spending most of his waking hours at work or on the golf course. Nor could he resist agonizing over the thought of what might have been. "[Joe Junior] is the boy who should have been president," he once told Manchester (New Hampshire) *Union Leader* publisher William E. Loeb. "That's the one, and he would have made a wonderful president."[48]

Not even the posthumous awarding of the Distinguished Flying Cross or the naming of a US Navy destroyer in Joe Junior's honor could lift him out of his funk. "None of that mattered to my father," Ted Kennedy wrote. "I don't think Dad ever fully recovered from the death of his eldest son." For sure, the memory of Joe Junior's sacrifice was still raw in the elder Kennedy's mind when he crossed paths with Winston Churchill at the Hialeah Race Track outside Miami in January 1946. After jocularly recalling that one of the last times they met was over dinner during a German air raid ("It didn't bother us very much, though, did it?" he remarked), Churchill suddenly grew somber. "You had a terrible time during the war; your losses were very great," he said. Kennedy thanked the aging British statesman for the kind remark but also took the opportunity to ask him whether he felt the conflict had been necessary. "After all, what did we accomplish by this war?" he asked. Caught off guard, Churchill explained at least they had their lives to be thankful for. "Not all of us," Kennedy spat back.[49]

Following his discharge from the Navy in 1945, John Kennedy briefly toyed with the idea of becoming a journalist. "He wanted to be a writer," said George Smathers. "He had prepared himself in his undergraduate days to be a writer. He wrote that book, *Why England Slept*, and he admired writers very much. I think that was one of the reasons he got along with them so well."[50] Taking advantage of his father's friendship with conservative newspaper publisher William Randolph Hearst, the twenty-six-year-old war veteran landed a special correspondent's job with the Hearst-owned *Chicago Herald American*. Though he was a cub reporter, his family connections were such that he received one of the paper's choice assignments, covering the charter conference of the United Nations in San Francisco.

While hardly Pulitzer Prize material, his UN dispatches nonetheless showed flashes of a lively intellect. "There is an impression," he wrote, "that this is the conference to end wars and introduce peace on earth and good will toward nations—excluding, of course, Germany and Japan. Well, it's not going to do that." Citing Russian fears of a "German come-back" as the main obstacle to peace, Kennedy argued that it would be naïve to think the ruling communist regime would not shore up its Euro-pean borders against another invasion. "They feel they earned this right to security," he concluded.[51]

Kennedy also traveled to Europe where he covered the Potsdam Con-ference and the British general election held that year. He came to the boldly prescient conclusion that while many Americans viewed Winston Churchill "as indomitable at the polls as he was in war," he was destined to fall out of power along with the rest of his fellow Tories. The British people "are tired after ten years of Tory government and they feel it is time for a change," he wrote.[52]

When he wasn't tapping out stories, Kennedy took the time to person-ally tour the Continent and take note of the bleak postwar conditions that predominated there. "The devastation is complete," he said of Berlin in his travel diary. "The people all have completely colorless faces—a yel-low tinge with pale blue lips. They are all carrying bundles. Where they are going, no one seems to know. I wonder whether they do." The situa-tion in France wasn't nearly as extreme, but Kennedy believed it was bad all the same. "Food is hard to get for people in the city because of lack of transportation," he observed. "This lack of transportation has contributed greatly to the difficulties all throughout Europe."[53]

Although he found newspaper work intellectually stimulating, Ken-nedy could not shake the feeling he was but a mere observer of great events. "He told me," recalled personal friend and journalist Charles Bartlett, "that the reason he decided to get out of the newspaper business was that he felt it was not effective; he wanted to be in something more active." Indeed, politics appeared to offer the kind of "effective" public involvement he was looking for. With the encouragement of his father, who privately relished the idea of his son picking up the family torch for his fallen brother Joe, Kennedy began casting about for a public office for which to run. "I wanted to run and was glad I could," he said.[54]

His opportunistic gaze eventually fell upon a US House of Represen-tatives seat in the Eleventh Congressional District of Massachusetts, a predominantly working-class Irish and Italian area that embraced Cam-bridge and portions of East Boston, Charlestown, Somerville, and Brigh-ton. What made the seat so attractive to Kennedy was the fact that his Democratic family already had a well-established political base there, thanks largely to Honey Fitz, who had represented the district in Con-gress at the turn of the century.

Nevertheless, there was one potentially troublesome obstacle in the way: James Michael Curley. As the popular incumbent congressman, the former Boston mayor was in a position to do enormous damage to Kennedy's candidacy, possibly even defeat it, were he to seek reelection. To prevent such a scenario, a way had to be found to ease Curley out of the picture. As he would at various other critical stages in his son's political career, Joseph Kennedy stepped in to provide a solution. In exchange for a pledge not to run, the elder Kennedy gave the aging Democratic leader "somewhere in the neighborhood of $100,000" to pay off long-standing personal debts. "Joe Kennedy was an ongoing factor in Massachusetts politics," then-State Representative Thomas P. "Tip" O'Neill of Cambridge recalled. "Every time a Democrat ran for governor, he would go down and see Joe, who would always send him home with a briefcase full of cash. The word was that if Joe Kennedy liked you, he'd give you $50,000. If he really liked you, he'd give you $100,000."[55]

With the Curley threat thus neutralized, John Kennedy was free to announce his candidacy for Congress on April 22. "The temper of the times," he declared in his opening campaign statement, "imposes an obligation upon every thinking citizen to work diligently in peace as he served tirelessly in war."[56] Such an appeal found resonance among returning veterans, many of whom lived in the run-down triple-decker tenement houses that so dominated the main thoroughfares of the district. They had survived one of the bloodiest conflicts in American history and were now looking for public leaders who could best represent their views and interests.

As a famous war hero, Kennedy had the distinct advantage of being able to relate to them and they with him. "You just thought this fellow would be a good representative, the kind of fellow you'd like to have in politics and you wanted to help," recalled one veteran. In what became known as the "Year of the Veteran" in American politics, the young candidate made a special point of bringing up issues that most concerned potential veteran voters: affordable housing, jobs, and a strong national defense. "We must work together," he insisted. "We must recognize that we face grave dangers. We must recognize how interdependent we are. We must have the same unity that we had during the war."[57]

He recruited veterans to go door to door on his behalf within their respective communities. "We just told them: here was an educated guy who was going to dedicate his life to do all he could for humanity and for the good of the people; and he was fearless, courageous, and had ability," remembered volunteer veteran Charles Garabedian of Charlestown.[58]

Despite Kennedy's obvious popularity among veterans' groups, many seasoned political observers did not give him much of a chance to advance beyond a crowded Democratic primary field of nine other candidates. "The first time I saw Jack Kennedy," Tip O'Neill remembered, "I couldn't believe how this skinny, pasty-looking kid was a candidate for anything." Michael J. Neville, the popular Cambridge mayor and state representative, was considered by some a "lead pipe cinch" to win the primary.[59]

But such assessments failed to take into account Kennedy's unique appeal as a politician. "He came upon the scene when people were subconsciously looking for a new type of candidate," Kennedy's Harvard classmate and Cambridge worker Anthony Galluccio contended. "And Jack fitted into this. He had the naïve appearance, he had the shock of hair that fell over his forehead. He was a multimillionaire who was very humble. Some people would say, this fellow is not the kind who would steal [as Curley did]."[60]

Curley invoked an earlier, seamier era in Boston politics, when elections were determined in smoke-filled back rooms by men dressed in pearl-gray fedoras and Chesterfield coats with black velvet collars. Kennedy eschewed these traditional outer trappings by presenting himself as a morally upright, clean-cut professional who was more in tune with the issues of the "atomic age" than with some bygone era. In other words, he was "no Irish political hack." "I would say that he was reluctant to give in to the nitty gritty of local politics," said campaign volunteer John I. Fitzgerald. "I mean he didn't want to be involved in getting contracts for getting mail out at Christmastime. He wasn't interested in patronage—he wanted a political or public life that didn't involve patronage—and that made him different from other politicians. He wanted politics, but he didn't want to be involved with what goes with it. He didn't want the 'You do this for me and I'll do this for you.'"[61]

Though he initially disliked the glad-handing that went along with traditional campaigning ("He told me the agony he suffered in going around and sticking out his hand to people he never met, never seen, and saying, 'I'm Jack Kennedy, I'm a candidate for Congress,'" Smathers recalled), he soon learned that a ready smile, a kind word, and the ability to listen could disarm even the greatest of skeptics. Joseph Kennedy was taken aback by the ease with which his son went one-on-one with voters. Standing across the street from him one day in East Boston, the ambassador voiced surprise at the sight of the Harvard-Choate product conversing with a group of "hard-boiled guys" on the corner. "I remember saying to a man who was with me," Kennedy later reminisced, "that I would have given even odds of five thousand to one that this thing we were seeing could never have happened. I never thought Jack had it in him."[62]

Logging upward to eighteen hours a day campaigning, John Kennedy simply outworked and outhustled his opponents, many of whom were not expecting such an effort. "The pros in the district thought of him as a millionaire's son," remembered Dave Powers, a popular service veteran hired by the candidate to oversee campaign activities in his native Charlestown, "and they wondered how he could get longshoremen and freight handlers and truck drivers—people who worked for a living—to vote for him. He just climbed more stairs and shook more hands and worked harder than all the rest combined. . . . He not only wanted to win, he wanted all the votes—that's what made him great."[63]

Powers knew he had something special when he witnessed the candidate address a local gathering of Gold Star Mothers one evening. "[Kennedy] started to stutter a little bit and I was getting sort of nervous [for him] and then he looked out at all these wonderful ladies and said, 'I think I know how you feel, because my mother is a Gold Star Mother too.'" What followed was a moment of sheer political magic. "He immediately was surrounded by all these [Gold Star Mothers]," Powers said, "and in the background I can hear them saying he reminds me of my own John or Joe or Pat, a loved one they had lost. Even I was overwhelmed."[64]

Still, Kennedy needed more than a good work ethic and voter empathy to put him over the top. "You know," remarked Tip O'Neill, "You can be a candidate, you can have the issues, you can have the organization, but money makes miracles and money did miracles in that campaign. Why they even had six different mailings . . . nobody had any mailings in that district."[65]

Evidence of Kennedy money was everywhere. Posters and billboards emblazoned with the campaign slogan "The New Generation Offers a Leader" blanketed the district. Pathé newsreel photographers were recruited by Joseph P. Kennedy, a former Hollywood movie producer, to shoot footage of the candidate in action, which was then "shown in theaters in the Boston area a few nights before the election." Reprints of the *Reader's Digest* version of John Hersey's PT-109 article, trumpeting the wartime heroism of the Democratic hopeful, were distributed by the thousands. Even the courageous image of Joe Junior was evoked when the candidate, in a widely publicized move before the general election, presented the Boston archdiocese with a check for $650,000 to build the Joseph P. Kennedy Jr. Memorial Hospital in Boston. "The Kennedy strategy was 'Buy you out or blast you out!'" complained Mike Neville.[66]

But the most glaring example of all concerned the financing of a "second Joe Russo" candidacy to split the vote of a popular Italian American undertaker of the same name who was also seeking the Democratic nomination. The Kennedys "must have been afraid," concluded Mark Dalton, a well-respected Cambridge attorney tapped to manage the Kennedy campaign; "with Joseph Russo on the ballot and the only Italian candidate on the ballot, there was a possibility that every Italian in the district would vote for Joe Russo."[67]

The "other Joe Russo" was, in fact, a twenty-seven-year-old custodian who lived in Boston's West End. According to this Russo, "a couple of wise guys" representing the Kennedy family approached him one day about declaring a run in return for some modest financial considerations. "They gave me favors," he later confessed to a journalist. "Whatever I wanted. I could of gone in the housing project if I wanted. If I wanted an apartment, I could have got the favor. You know."[68]

Primary day, June 18, brought more shenanigans. The Kennedys "approached a number of large families and promised them fifty dollars in cash to help out at the polls," Tip O'Neill later recalled. "They really didn't care if these people showed up to work. They were simply buying votes, a few at a time, and fifty bucks was a lot of money." Not even the transportation of voters to the polls escaped the notice of the Kennedy operation. "Every car or cab that was for hire [in the district] was taken, carrying voters for the Kennedys," Neville said. All told, a then-staggering three hundred thousand dollars was believed to have been spent on the congressional campaign. "We're going to sell Jack like soap flakes," Joseph P. Kennedy had boasted.[69]

In the end, John Kennedy may not have needed to go to such lengths to secure victory. His war hero status, boyish charm, and winning personality were probably enough to ensure success. "He had magnetism, and he seemed to float through this whole period," remembered Red Fay, a friend from his PT boat days who volunteered for the campaign. "He just attracted people. There was never any question of being ill at ease, of

Figure 1.2.   A winning smile. Kennedy celebrates his hard-earned 1946 victory with his parents and supporters. JFK Library PC 363

not getting along with almost everybody that he met during the whole of his political life." As it was, he outpolled his closest primary challenger, Neville, nearly two to one. In the general election, which was a perfunctory affair given the largely Democratic makeup for the district, Kennedy bested his Republican opponent, Lester W. Bowen of Somerville, by an even greater margin, with 79.7 percent of the vote.[70]

Initially skeptical lawmakers could not help but be impressed by this showing. "There were tough parts of that district, but Jack Kennedy showed he had what it takes to be successful in politics," O'Neill observed afterward. "Sure, he was different from a lot of voters. But he came up, shook their hands, looked them in the eye and talked about problems in the area. They respected him. . . . Eventually many of them loved him for it."[71]

Not bad for a former Mucker turned popular vote-getter.

NOTES

1. George Smathers, interview, Clay Blair Papers (hereinafter cited as CBP), University of Wyoming, American Heritage Center, Laramie, Wyoming.

2. James MacGregor Burns, *John Kennedy: A Political Profile* (New York, 1960), 22; John F. Kennedy, interview, Ralph Martin Collection (hereinafter cited as RMC), Department of Special Collections, Boston University, Boston, Massachusetts.

3. Gardner Jackson, interview, RMC; John F. Kennedy Library Introductory Film, Peter Davis Productions, 1993.

4. Norman MacDonald, interview, RMC.

5. William O. Douglas Oral History, John F. Kennedy Library (hereinafter cited as JFKL), Boston, Massachusetts; Hank Searls, *The Lost Prince: Young Joe, the Forgotten Kennedy* (New York, 1969), 60; Arthur Krock Oral History, JFKL.

6. Herbert S. Parmet, *Jack: The Struggles of John F. Kennedy* (New York, 1980), 25; Burns, *John Kennedy*, 19; George Smathers, interview, CBP.

7. Parmet, *Jack*, 22; John F. Kennedy, ed., *As We Remember Joe* (Privately published, 1945), 59; James W. Hilty, *Robert Kennedy: Brother Protector* (Philadelphia, 1997), 19; Peter Collier and David Horowitz, *The Kennedys: An American Drama* (New York, 1984), 60; Burns, *John Kennedy*, 19.

8. *Boston Herald American*, May 29, 1978; Seymour St. John and Richard Bode, "'Bad Boy' Jack Kennedy," *Good Housekeeping*, September 1985.

9. *The Kennedys: The Early Years, 1900–1961*, video documentary, WGBH-Television, September 20, 1992; Joan Myers, ed., *John Fitzgerald Kennedy As We Remember Him* (New York, 1965), 17.

10. Rip Horton Oral History, JFKL.

11. Maurice Shea Oral History, JFKL; Doris Kearns Goodwin, *The Fitzgeralds and the Kennedys: An American Saga* (New York, 1987), 488.

12. Ibid., 489; Parmet, *Jack*, 40.

13. Joseph P. Kennedy to Delmar Leighton, August 28, 1936, John F. Kennedy Personal Papers, JFKL.

14. Torbert MacDonald Oral History, JFKL.

15. John F. Kennedy, interview, RMC.

16. David Burner and Thomas R. West, *The Torch Is Passed: The Kennedy Brothers and American Liberalism* (New York, 1984), 27.

17. John F. Kennedy Library Introductory Film.

18. John F. Kennedy, "Appeasement at Munich," March 15, 1940, John F. Kennedy Personal Papers, JFKL; H. Yeomans, "Report on Thesis for Distinction." John F. Kennedy Personal Papers, JFKL.

19. Arthur Krock, interview, CBP.

20. Ronald Kessler, *The Sins of the Father: Joseph P. Kennedy and the Dynasty He Founded* (New York, 1996), 219; Burns, *John Kennedy*, 44.

21. Robert Stack with Mark Evans, *Straight Shooting* (New York, 1980), 73.

22. *The Kennedys: The Early Years, 1900–1961.*

23. *Harvard Crimson,* September 20, 1939; John F. Kennedy to Joseph P. Kennedy, n.d. (December 1940), John F. Kennedy Personal Papers, JFKL.

24. Goodwin, *The Fitzgeralds and the Kennedys,* 627.

25. Joan and Clay Blair Jr., *The Search for J.F.K.* (New York, 1976), 135; Nigel Hamilton, *J.F.K.: Reckless Youth* (New York, 1992), 684–85.

26. Goodwin, *The Fitzgeralds and the Kennedys,* 634.

27. *Boston Globe,* January 11, 1944.

28. Hamilton, *J.F.K.: Reckless Youth,* 579.

29. John Hersey, "Survival," *New Yorker,* June 17, 1944.

30. *Boston Globe,* January 11, 1944; Charles Harris, interview, CBP.

31. *Boston Globe,* June 22, 1989.

32. Robert Donovan, *PT-109: John F. Kennedy in World War II* (New York, 1960), 203.

33. *Boston Globe,* January 11, 1944.

34. Collier and Horowitz, *The Kennedys: An American Drama,* 483; Joseph P. Kennedy Jr. to John F. Kennedy, August 10, 1944, John F. Kennedy Personal Papers, JFKL.

35. Official Citation for Navy and Marine Corps Medal for Valor, May 19, 1944, John F. Kennedy Personal Papers, JFKL.

36. *New Yorker,* June 17, 1944; Parmet, *Jack,* 112.

37. Thomas Fleming, "War of Revenge," *Quarterly Journal of Military History,* Spring 2011; Richard Tregaskis, *John F. Kennedy: War Hero* (New York, 1963), 212.

38. John F. Kennedy, 26: Round-Robin Letter, August 10, 1943, in *Hostage to Fortune: The Letters of Joseph P. Kennedy* (New York, 2001), ed., Amanda Smith, 567–68.

39. Ralph G. Martin, *A Hero for Our Time: An Intimate Story of the Kennedy Years* (New York, 1963), 40.

40. Joseph P. Kennedy Jr. to John F. Kennedy, August 10, 1944, John F. Kennedy Personal Papers, JFKL.

41. Joseph P. Kennedy Jr., 29, to Rose and Joseph P. Kennedy, August 4, 1944, in *Hostage to Fortune,* 598.

42. Searls, *The Lost Prince,* 284.

43. Edward M. Kennedy, *True Compass: A Memoir* (New York, 2009), 85–86.

44. Kennedy, ed., *As We Remember Joe,* 54–55.

45. Kathleen Kennedy Hartington, 24, to Rose and Joseph P. Kennedy, September 20, 1944 in *Hostage to Fortune,* 601; Barbara Leaming, *Jack Kennedy: The Education of a Statesman* (New York, 2006), 10.

46. Goodwin, *The Fitzgeralds and the Kennedys,* 698.

47. John F. Kennedy, ed., *As We Remember Joe,* 4–5.

48. Kessler, *The Sins of the Father,* 286; Martin, *A Hero for Our Time,* 200.

49. Kennedy, *True Compass,* 86; Joseph P. Kennedy: "Memorandum of Conversation with Winston Churchill at Hialeah Race Track on January 13, 1946" in Amanda Smith, ed., *Hostage to Fortune,* 622–23.

50. George Smathers, interview, CBP.

51. *Chicago Herald American,* April 28, 1945; *New York Journal-American,* May 9, 1945.

52. *Ibid.,* June 23, 1945.

53. John F. Kennedy, *Prelude to Leadership: The European Diary of John F. Kennedy, Summer 1945* (Washington, DC, 1995), 49, 45.

54. Joan Myers, ed., *John F. Kennedy . . . As We Remember Him,* 46; Fletcher Knebel, "Pulitzer Prize Entry, John F. Kennedy" in Eric Sevareid, ed., *Candidates 1960: Behind The Headlines In the Presidential Race* (New York, 1959), 195.

55. Jack Beatty, *The Rascal King: The Life and Times of James Michael Curley* (Reading, Massachusetts, 1992), 456; Thomas P. O'Neill with William Novak, *Man of the House: the Life and Political Memoirs of Speaker Tip O'Neill* (New York, 1987), 93.

56. *Boston Post*, April 23, 1946.

57. Anthony Galluccio, Oral History, JFKL; Kenneth P. O'Donnell and David F. Powers with Joe McCarthy, *Johnny, We Hardly Knew Ye: Memories of John F. Kennedy* (Boston, 1972), 67.

58. Charles Garabedian Oral History, JFKL.

59. O'Neill with Novak, *Man of the House*, 83.

60. Anthony Galluccio Oral History, JFKL.

61. Thomas H. O'Connor, *The Boston Irish: A Political History* (Boston, 1994), 218; David Burner, *John F. Kennedy and a New Generation* (Boston, 1988), 23; Hamilton, *Reckless Youth*, 773.

62. George Smathers, interview, CBP; Meyers, ed., *John F. Kennedy . . . As We Remember Him*, 48.

63. Ibid., 49.

64. Dave Powers, interview, CBP.

65. Ralph G. Martin, *Seeds of Destruction: Joe Kennedy and His Sons* (New York, 1995), 138.

66. Collier and Horowitz, *The Kennedys*, 155; J. Anthony Lukas, *Common Ground: A Turbulent Decade in the Lives of Three American Families* (New York, 1986), 380; Hamilton, *Reckless Youth*, 755.

67. Steve Buckley, "The Other Joe Russo," *Boston Magazine*, June 1993.

68. Ibid.

69. O'Neill, *Man of the House*, 88; Mike Neville, interview, RMC; Burner, *John F. Kennedy and a New Generation*, 26.

70. Myers, ed., *John F. Kennedy . . . As We Remember Him*, 48; Commonwealth of Massachusetts, *Massachusetts Election Statistics, 1946* (Boston, 1946).

71. The Boston Globe, *J.F.K.: The Man, the President* (Boston, 1979), 27.

TWO

Beating the Best

Henry Cabot Lodge Jr. and the 1952 Massachusetts Senate Race

As a freshman congressman, John F. Kennedy struck many political observers as a "fish out of water." He was late for meetings, tardy in his paperwork, indifferent to details, and sloppy in his personal appearance. "The clothes he wore looked like they belonged to somebody else," said George Smathers, who represented Florida's Fourth Congressional District in the late 1940s. "He was totally uninterested in how he looked." Kennedy instead appeared content to fritter his time away in the pursuit of personal pleasure. Cocktail parties, one-night stands, and touch football games filled his calendar and became his raison d'être. "We had laughs in those days," admitted administrative assistant William "Billy" Sutton. "Always plenty of laughs."[1]

Accounting for this frivolous behavior was Kennedy's own awareness that he probably would not live out a normal life span. In September 1947, on a visit to England, he collapsed and was diagnosed with Addison's disease, a potentially fatal illness marked by a failure of the adrenal glands and resulting in extreme weakness, loss of weight, low blood pressure, and gastrointestinal disturbances. "That young American friend of yours, he hasn't got a year to live," a physician informed Pamela Churchill, the former British prime minister's daughter-in-law, after the latter had brought the stricken World War II veteran to the London Clinic.[2]

Such frank discussion of his poor physical condition was kept under tight wraps. Had word leaked out, questions would have been inevitably raised about his fitness to remain in public office. As it was, his congressional staff had a hard enough time explaining away his frequent absences from official duties. For example, when he was originally hospitalized in London, a cover story was released saying that Kennedy was suffering from a war-related injury and that he could be expected to be up and about in no time. "I guess the truth was it was the onset of the Addison's," *Washington Times Herald* reporter Frank Waldrop later said.[3]

Concerned that his son's responsibilities as congressman were too physically taxing given his precarious state of health, Joseph P. Kennedy gave serious thought to setting him up as a major league baseball executive. "He's got this son, John, who is brilliant in politics, but has physical problems," Brooklyn Dodgers president and general manager Branch Rickey reportedly told business associate Walter O'Malley, after the former had been approached by the ambassador about purchasing his share of the ball club. "Mr. Kennedy thinks running the Dodgers could be the greatest outlet in the world for him." A baseball career was not in the works for the former Harvard athlete, however. "It might have been Jack Kennedy, president of the Dodgers, but Joe rejected the deal when he found he'd face an unhappy minority stockholder in myself," O'Malley later claimed.[4]

A more plausible explanation is that John Kennedy no longer had the need to seek less strenuous employment. In the late 1940s the Mayo Clinic discovered that artificially produced corticosteroid hormones, or cortisone, implanted on the thigh could significantly extend the life expectancy of those afflicted with Addison's. Thus, by integrating this "miracle drug" into his daily regimen, Kennedy was able to upgrade his health dramatically as his appetite, strength, and stamina improved.[5] Though the prospect of premature death still remained a possibility, the apparent success of the cortisone treatment gave him hope that he could maintain a vigorous public and private life without serious medical consequences.

With a new lease on life, Kennedy was able to concentrate as never before on his fledgling congressional career. He took greater interest in his work, read up on the issues, and showed increased self-confidence. Acquiring the reputation of an independent thinker, he also regularly angered many of his Democratic colleagues by refusing to toe the traditional party line. Nowhere was this individualistic approach more evident than when Kennedy publicly lambasted American Legion officials in 1949 for failing to support public housing legislation. "The Leadership of the American Legion has not had a constructive thought for the benefit of this country since 1918!" he thundered. House Democrats, fearful that Kennedy's intemperate remarks about a celebrated patriotic organization would reflect unfavorably upon themselves, wasted little time in denouncing the attack. But Kennedy remained studiously unrepentant. "Jack thought for himself," noted his Washington office secretary, Mary Davis. "He stood on his own two feet."[6]

Such daring, however, had its limits. Acutely aware that his district was primarily blue collar in makeup, Kennedy tried to cast his votes in the House accordingly. He, for instance, favored an extension of social security benefits, a higher minimum wage, expanded public housing, and a national health program for the underprivileged. He also made a point of opposing efforts to eliminate rent control and to reduce the federal subsidy for school lunches. "When I first went into Congress in 1946," he later explained, "I represented a district that was very poor in Massachusetts. We had many problems, housing [for example]. Many families were in need of assistance. Therefore, my viewpoint on the necessity of social legislation came really pragmatically through just observation."[7]

In foreign affairs, Kennedy was a committed cold warrior. Agreeing with the Truman administration's assessment that the Soviet Union needed to be contained militarily, he supported military aid to Greece and Turkey, the Marshall Plan, and the establishment of the North Atlantic Treaty Organization (NATO). Where he differed from the Democratic administration was in the prosecution of the Cold War. He thought more needed to be done, especially in East Asia, to prevent the "onrushing tide" of communism from engulfing the world. To this end he was an outspoken advocate for a strong military, even going so far as to lecture his fellow legislators on not allocating enough money for national defense.[8]

Voters from the Eleventh District approved of his approach; they returned Kennedy to office by overwhelming margins in 1948 and 1950. Yet political success could not quell Kennedy's growing dissatisfaction with House life and its stifling seniority system that made him just one of 435 members. "This is not the organization which he visualized as the one [in which] he wanted to spend most of his political life," remembered one close aide.[9] Kennedy felt the time was right to make a concerted run for the US Senate in 1952.

But moving up to the next rung on the political ladder would be no easy task. For his opponent would be none other than three-term Republican senator Henry Cabot Lodge Jr., a proven vote getter with an enviable record of public service going back over two decades. "When you've beaten him," Joseph Kennedy told his son, "you've beaten the best. Why try for something less?"[10]

Henry Cabot Lodge Jr. was born on July 5, 1902, in his grandfather's home along the cold, rocky shores of Nahant, Massachusetts, which Lodge once described as sticking out "like a finger toward Europe some ten miles north of Boston."[11] The oldest of three children, he was heir to one of the most famous family names in American politics. No fewer than five family members had served in the US Senate, dating back to the early days of the republic.

His grandfather, for whom he was named, was the confidant of President Theodore Roosevelt and became chairman of the powerful Senate Foreign Relations Committee at the end of World War I. A conservative at heart, the "Old Senator," as his family and friends fondly called him, championed protective tariffs, the gold standard, and literacy tests for immigrants. In 1916 the then four-term incumbent edged Kennedy's maternal grandfather, former Boston mayor John "Honey Fitz" Fitzgerald, by thirty-three thousand votes to become the first US Senator in Massachusetts history elected by popular ballot under terms of the Seventeenth Amendment. He is best remembered for his leadership role in defeating President Woodrow Wilson's proposed League of Nations.[12]

When Lodge's father, the minor poet George Cabot Lodge, died of an apparent heart attack in 1909, Henry Cabot Lodge Sr. became his surrogate father. Apart from his mother, former Washington society belle Mathilda Elizabeth Frelinghuysen Davis, whom he credited with providing warmth, encouragement, and emotional support, Lodge's greatest influence in these formative years was his grandfather.

In the elder Lodge, Cabot, as he was known to friends and relatives, had a stern taskmaster who demanded hard work and excellence in all endeavors. When he performed poorly in geometry and Greek while prepping at the Middlesex School in Concord, Massachusetts, the grandfather offered little sympathy. "It would be a terrible disappointment for me if you should fail any of your Harvard examinations," he wrote his grandson in 1919. "You must learn to use your mind and if you apply your mind to geometry and Greek you can perfectly well master them both and pass exams in both, and I look to you to do it."[13] Chastened by the thought of earning his grandfather's displeasure, Cabot redoubled his efforts and was eventually able to pass all his entrance tests.

Aside from instruction on academics, Henry Cabot Lodge Sr. also schooled his grandson on politics. "The discussion of political topics was one of the first things I can remember," Cabot later remarked; "a haze of cigar smoke and the emphatic utterance of such words as 'caucus,' 'committee' or 'campaign'—words which were then incomprehensible to me—are vividly impressed on my mind." As a teenager, the junior Lodge spent many a late night in his grandfather's book-lined study in Washington, DC, reviewing the great issues of the day with the aging patriarch. "As you know my grandfather was pleased when I began to take an interest in public affairs," he once told a reporter. "His own sons took no interest whatsoever in politics and it was his hope that I might carry on in this field."[14]

On most political issues, Cabot not surprisingly shared the same conservative views as his grandfather. He touted the efficacy of the American free enterprise system, downplayed social reform, and cited the need for increased duties on foreign manufactures. Regarding US entry into the League of Nations, he staunchly opposed the idea. Nor was he shy about expressing these opinions. When noted Harvard English professor Charles T. Copeland publicly denounced the senior Massachusetts senator for his anti-League stand, Lodge sought out the academic for a one-on-one confrontation. "Professor Copeland, I am Senator Lodge's grandson," Cabot chastised him before a student gathering. "I think you have done him a great injustice and I want you to know I resent your unfair criticism of him."[15]

When the Old Senator passed away in November 1924, expectations were strong that Cabot would carry on in his footsteps. He did not disappoint. He won two terms to the Massachusetts state legislature and challenged the colorful and notoriously corrupt James Michael Curley for an open US Senate seat in 1936. In the campaign to follow, Curley denigrated Lodge as "Little Boy Blue," a pampered child of privilege out of his depth. Despite or perhaps because of these blistering personal attacks, Lodge emerged victorious as voters found his calm and dignified manner ("I . . . believe that this campaign is too important for the people's time to be wasted by personal abuse and mudslinging," he said) a refreshing departure from Curley's histrionics.[16] In fact, he bucked a nationwide Democratic trend that year by becoming the only Republican to win a Senate seat.

By this time Lodge was happily married to the former Emily Sears, an heir to the famed Sears shipping fortune. The two had met at a dance in Boston in 1924, and while the Ivy Leaguer impressed the young socialite with his ruggedly handsome looks and distinguished family pedigree, his intellect evidently left something to be desired. "Well, I thought him slow [intellectually]," Emily puckishly told television interviewer David Brinkley in 1960.[17] She soon revised her opinion, however, and began a courtship that lasted over two years. They married in 1926 and took up residence in Beverly, a wealthy and conservative community north of Boston. The union would eventually produce two sons, George Cabot in 1927 and Henry Sears in 1930.

As a first-term US Senator, Lodge moved away from the rigid conservatism of his grandfather as the political and economic realities of the Great Depression forced him to question the Old Senator's advocacy of a minimalist government. He became an enthusiastic supporter of such New Deal programs as the Works Progress Administration and acquired the reputation for being moderate to liberal on most domestic issues. "I decide each issue on its merits," he told a reporter upon entering office. "I have no fixed prejudices or policies. I would like [to be known] as a practical progressive. That means I take up each issue as it presents itself, or perhaps as I present it, and take a stand on it then or there. But you don't have to guess where I stand. I like to make myself clear on that and, if I'm wrong, all right. I'll admit it."[18]

On foreign policy issues, Lodge continued to toe the same isolationist line as his grandfather. He felt that the United States should not become embroiled in the affairs of countries outside the Western Hemisphere, even as German and Japanese armies were smashing their way through Europe and Asia in the late 1930s. The surprise Japanese attack on Pearl Harbor on December 7, 1941, removed him from this isolationist camp. "The time for action has come," he announced. "The time for words has passed." Years later he expressed embarrassment when reminded of his prewar views on foreign policy: "I was one hundred percent wrong in believing that we could stay out of the Second World War," he told a writer in 1952.[19]

Frustrated by his own modest contributions to the war effort and sensing that staying out of the "big show" to come in Europe would adversely affect his political future, Lodge resigned from the Senate in February 1944 for active combat duty. "The fact that the United States is entering the period of large-scale ground fighting has, after grave thought," he explained in his letter of resignation, "brought me to the definite conclusion that, given my age [he was forty-two] and military training [he had been a cavalry officer in the Army Reserve since 1924], I must henceforth serve my country as a combat soldier in the Army overseas."[20]

In so doing, Lodge became the first senator since the Civil War to give up his seat to fight for his country. None other than President Franklin Roosevelt praised him for his action. "I want you to know . . . that I would do just what you are doing, if I could," the commander in chief informed him. "I missed being with the guns in 1917–18. It's too late now. I envy you the opportunity that is yours and I congratulate you upon the decision you have made."[21]

A commissioned major with the American Sixth Army group, Lodge saw his share of action as a frontline reconnaissance officer in Italy and France. Traveling by a single-motored L-15 scout plane or by jeep, he routinely braved antiaircraft gunfire and minefields to gain an accurate understanding of the enemy's strengths and weaknesses. "He was utterly without fear," remembered one fellow officer.[22] Indeed, his commanding officer, Major General Willis D. Crittenberger, thought so highly of his displayed courage under fire that he awarded him a Bronze Star medal for bravery.

Returning home from the war, Lodge wasted little time getting back into politics. He took on the aging and scandal-plagued Democratic US Senator David I. Walsh of Fitchburg, whose name had turned up in an earlier FBI probe of a Brooklyn, New York, "house of degradation" that specialized in servicing male homosexual clients. While Walsh, a lifelong bachelor and closet homosexual, was subsequently cleared of any wrongdoing by the FBI, the political damage had been done.[23] Lodge won in a landslide.

The US Senate Lodge returned to was bursting with activity from America's newfound status as a global superpower. Momentous bills

Figure 2.1. A young Lodge in repose. Reproduction Number: LC-H25122171-A

dealing with the sending of military aid to Greece and Turkey, the Marshall Plan for the economic reconstruction of Western Europe, and the creation of NATO were debated on and passed by wide bipartisan margins. "The Senate at that time was at its best," Lodge later wrote in his autobiography.[24]

As a member of the Foreign Relations Committee, Lodge had a significant hand in shaping many of these policies and helping line up key

Democratic and Republican support. His former pronouncements about the virtues of isolationism had thus fallen away, to be replaced with new ones celebrating the merits of internationalism and cooperation. He became an outspoken advocate of the United Nations Organization and the concept of collective security. World War II had convinced him that true national security could not be achieved if the United States operated an independent foreign policy outside the family of nations. "Above all," he emphasized, "let us realize that our foreign policy exists—and our effective support of the United Nations is possible—only in proportion to the national strength behind it."[25]

On "bread and butter" issues affecting the lives of ordinary citizens, Lodge maintained his prewar liberalism. He supported better housing, a higher minimum wage, expanded social security coverage, and federal aid for education. He also opposed provisions in the National Labor Relations Act of 1947, better known as Taft-Hartley, that outlawed union shops.[26]

Figure 2.2.   Riding the rails: Freshman US Senator Henry Cabot Lodge Jr. gets down to business. Reproduction Number: LC-H22-D-477

Such liberal stands won him few friends among the "Old Guard" leadership of the Republican Party, men such as Robert A. Taft of Ohio, Kenneth Wherry of Nebraska, and William Jenner of Indiana. They saw in these positions examples of the creeping "state socialism" that had allegedly characterized the New Deal under Franklin Roosevelt. To such critics, especially Taft, who harbored presidential ambitions, Lodge offered the following rejoinder in 1950: "I don't see why we must choose between state socialism and no social progress at all. I don't see why we shouldn't use the power of the government to fill in the chinks that private enterprise can't fill for us."[27]

As chairman of the Resolutions Committee at the 1948 Republican National Convention in Philadelphia, Lodge successfully lobbied to have these liberal sentiments embedded in the party platform. Promising a newer, progressive, and forward-looking approach to governing, the platform called on the federal government to improve labor-management relations, provide better health care, promote slum clearance, end racial discrimination, and upgrade old-age benefit programs.

When the party suffered shattering election losses in November, Lodge blamed the setback on the unwillingness of party conservatives to get behind the convention platform. "The G.O.P.," he warned in a *Saturday Evening Post* article in 1949, "has been presented to the public as a rich man's club and as a haven for reactionaries. . . . To say that [the Old Guard conservatives] represent the rank and file of the Party is, in my view, a gross untruth. Certain it is, however, that the Republican Party must broaden the scope of its appeal so that there can be no doubt that it is a party for all elements of the people. . . . I have faith that we will make a liberal record, that we will try again and that the people will again use us as their servants. But we must make the decision that we want to be a popular party."[28]

Lodge supported efforts to recruit former West Point graduate and Supreme Allied Commander Dwight D. Eisenhower for the GOP nomination in 1952. In Eisenhower, Lodge felt he had the ideal candidate to defeat the Old Guard and regain the presidency for the Republican Party for the first time in twenty years. Outwardly warm, friendly, and charming, "Ike," as he was known to millions of Americans, had emerged from the Second World War as the most popular military leader since Ulysses S. Grant. The problem facing Lodge was whether he could convince Eisenhower, a closet moderate Republican, to commit to a presidential run. The task was daunting. Since 1946 several Republican as well as Democratic leaders had unsuccessfully tried to recruit the general as a standard-bearer for their parties. Each time the war hero waved them off by insisting he had no interest in the presidency.

This attitude abruptly changed on September 6, 1951, when Lodge paid Eisenhower a personal visit to his headquarters in Paris, where he was serving as the first commander of NATO. Stating that his business was to convince the general to seek the 1952 Republican nomination, the Massachusetts lawmaker presented his case. If Eisenhower did not run, Lodge argued, Taft would almost certainly become the Republican nominee and lead the GOP to another ignominious defeat in the following year's general election. "You must permit the use of your name in the upcoming primaries." [29]

Eisenhower was deeply impressed by Lodge's line of reasoning. Three years earlier, he had confided to a writer friend that Taft's nomination, given his strongly held isolationist views, would "nullify all the things I have fought for and worked for in Europe." Now it appeared that his worst fear stood a chance of becoming a reality. He thanked Lodge for his time and told him he would "think it over." Years later Eisenhower revealed in his memoirs that his conversation with the Bay State Republican was a "turning point" in his decision to seek the White House. [30]

In his 1973 autobiography, *The Storm Has Many Eyes*, Lodge claimed that his actions during this period were guided by an unselfish desire to maintain the political viability of the GOP and to preserve the two-party system. "If Senator Taft were nominated for president and defeated in 1952," he wrote, "the Republican party would either disintegrate completely or shrink into a small minority of extreme reactionaries and, in the South, a crew of patronage-hungry professionals. The great mass of rank and file Republican voters would desert it. This would destroy the two-party system and thus our ability to bring about orderly change in America, shaking the very foundations of our government." [31]

Political self-interest may have also come into play. Given the large number of registered independents in Massachusetts (about a third of the electorate in 1952) and the potential for crossover votes to the universally popular Eisenhower, Lodge could have reasonably expected to siphon off some of this support for his own Senate reelection campaign and ride to victory on the general's coattails. One local paper later conjectured that "heavy publicity" and the "immense prestige" of leading a winning presidential nomination fight were worth "endless hours of stumping in Massachusetts." [32]

Whatever the underlying motive, Lodge's intervention proved timely and decisive. On January 7, 1952, Eisenhower announced that he would allow his name to be placed on the ballot of the New Hampshire Republican primary, thus formally kicking off his presidential campaign. The person he tapped to manage his campaign was none other than Lodge. In the ensuing race for the Republican presidential nomination, Lodge won few friends among the conservative party faithful, who supported Taft without reservation and who dismissed Eisenhower's candidacy as a misguided attempt to place a moderate at the head of the ticket. Given this inclination, conservatives were understandably outraged when Lodge publicly accused the Taft forces of Texas of "stealing" delegates prior to the opening of the Republican National Convention in July. The charge stemmed from the pro-Taft Texas Republican State Executive Committee's decision not to recognize a disputed slate of Eisenhower delegates.[33]

Sensing a political opportunity, Lodge and the rest of the Eisenhower campaign brain trust made an issue of the "Texas steal" during the July convention. At the insistence of Lodge, an amendment to the convention rules was drawn up forbidding contested delegates from voting to seat themselves. On a suggestion made by Representative Hugh Scott of Pennsylvania, the name "Fair Play Amendment" was adopted to give the measure a sense of moral urgency. The hope was that a successful introduction of such an amendment at the outset of the proceedings would establish a "winning psychology" for the Eisenhower forces, who entered the convention trailing Taft in delegates.[34]

The strategy paid off as the vote on the Fair Play Amendment carried, 658-548, thus setting into motion Eisenhower's convention bandwagon. "As a result of that first victory on the floor," wrote *Boston Herald* reporter George Cabot Lodge in an unpublished account of the convention, "the Eisenhower organization won a number of wavering delegates; identified itself with a good moral cause; established the fact that they had the votes; dominated the next day's headlines; and seized the initiative."[35]

Eisenhower went on to win the GOP nomination on the first ballot. In later years, Lodge argued that any compromise on the Fair Play Amendment would have resulted in the nomination going to Taft. "The Eisenhower candidacy standing alone, could never have drawn 658 votes," he related. "Some other way had to be found to get the delegates to stand together. The 'fair play' amendment was it."[36]

Eisenhower's nomination was tremendously satisfying for Lodge. Not only had he played a prominent role in orchestrating the victory, he had more importantly secured a place of influence for moderates like himself in top GOP policy-making circles, at least for the immediate future.

Yet storm clouds were gathering over Lodge's own political horizon. One Massachusetts delegate, influential newspaper publisher Basil Brewer of New Bedford, an avid Taft supporter, became so enraged by the convention's proceedings and Lodge's part in them that he cast the sole dissenting vote against a motion that would have made the nomination unanimous for Eisenhower. "It was," noted Lodge biographer William J. Miller, "an act symbolic of further bitterness to come."[37]

Of more immediate concern was Lodge's tardiness in launching his own Senate reelection campaign. Drained by his exertions on behalf of Eisenhower, he simply failed to do the necessary organizational spadework required of an incumbent. A "senatorial contest in Massachusetts," political strategist Mason Sears once noted, "normally requires at least twelve months of campaigning. In this respect I would observe that Senator Lodge was so deeply involved in promoting General Eisenhower's candidacy for President that it was physically impossible for him to devote any time to his own candidacy until the last three months."[38]

Time did not appear to be on Lodge's side in 1952. While GOP presidential politics prevented him from spending much time in Massachusetts during the first eight months of 1952, no comparable limitations were placed on his challenger. Sensing an advantage, John Kennedy embarked on a whirlwind tour of the state, shaking as many hands, visiting as many factories, and attending as many rallies as he could. Apart from a brief and uneventful sojourn to the Democratic National Convention in the third week of July, Kennedy devoted his every waking hour to campaigning in the Bay State. "Anybody who wants to know how I beat Lodge can look into it and he'd find I beat Lodge because I hustled," Kennedy later boasted.[39] That the Democratic hopeful labored tirelessly there can be no doubt.

Subsisting on a steady diet of cheeseburgers and milkshakes that he procured from various roadside establishments, the candidate maintained a grueling campaign schedule that saw him make appearances in all 351 communities of the state. "He was on the move constantly for eight months," confirmed early Kennedy biographer Joe McCarthy, "visiting the larger cities [in the state] eight or nine times and each of the small towns at least once . . . and talking at meetings from early morning until late at night for seven days a week."[40]

Also playing a visible and active role in the campaign was his family. As one Lodge supporter lamented, "I don't worry about Jack Kennedy . . . it's that family of his . . . they're all over the state."[41] While Joseph Kennedy preferred keeping out of the public eye to avoid charges that he was manipulating his son's campaign, the rest of his family, without Ted Kennedy, who was serving a two-year hitch for the US Army in France and Germany, eagerly threw themselves into the political fight. Robert Kennedy worked behind the scenes as campaign manager while sisters Eunice, Pat, and Jean could be found delivering stump speeches, supervising the distribution of campaign literature, ringing doorbells, and generally ingratiating themselves with voters. "They were exactly like old-fashioned, burlesque pony ballet, wonderfully good looking girls, with their long legs and great manes of hair, attacking the voters sort of en masse," recalled Joseph Alsop, a nationally syndicated newspaper columnist assigned to cover the race.[42]

As impressive as these efforts were, none could equal, in terms of sheer popular enthusiasm generated, the contribution made by Rose Fitzgerald Kennedy. Simply put, she was her son's most effective goodwill ambassador, as her eloquent speech, indefatigable charm, and understated feminine beauty captured the imagination of voters statewide. "Rose wowed them everywhere," acknowledged Dave Powers. "She greeted the Italians in the North End [of Boston] with a few words of Italian and told them how she grew up in their neighborhood. In Dorchester, she talked about her days at Dorchester High School. She showed them the card index file she kept when her kids were little to keep track of vaccinations and medical treatment, and dental work. At a high-toned gathering of women, she'd talk a few minutes about Jack, and then she'd say, 'Now let me tell you about the new dresses I saw in Paris last month.' They loved her."[43]

Rose would also be crucial to the success of a series of public tea receptions held around the state that lent a much-welcomed air of refinement to the otherwise coldly efficient Kennedy political operation. "These tea parties that Kennedy is holding the length and breadth of the state appear to have many women, of all ages, quite excited about the young candidate," reported the *Haverhill Gazette*, a conservative daily published 30 miles north of Boston on October 7. "They ooh and aah when you mention him, they tell you they think he is wonderful, they give every indication of yearning to run their fingers through his tousled hair. They never mention any qualifications that he may have or may lack for service in the Senate, but this would be too much to expect."[44]

Carefully planned by Pauline "Polly" Fitzgerald, a first cousin of Rose Kennedy, and Helen Keyes, a popular gym teacher from Dorchester, the Kennedy teas were a frank play for the women's vote, which one publication at the time put at more than 52 percent of the electorate in Massachusetts. An estimated 75,000 women from diverse socioeconomic and cultural backgrounds went to these affairs.[45] Though the majority of the teas were concentrated in the Boston metropolitan area—not surprising given the traditionally strong Democratic base there—a significant number were staged in populous outlying communities like Lowell, New Bedford, Worcester, and Springfield. Always, their primary function was to attract as many potential female voters as possible.

Most of the teas were held in large rented halls or elegant hotel ballrooms such as the Hotel Sheraton in Worcester or the Hotel Kimball in Springfield. With his charismatic mother and sisters at his side, Kennedy usually began the affairs by thanking everyone in the room for coming, while expressing the hope that they would support his candidacy in November. Following these remarks, the young Democrat and his family would form a reception line and greet every person in attendance. "A few women," a veteran journalist later wrote, "got so carried away with the graciousness of the Kennedy receiving line that they concluded it by bussing the candidate on the cheek."[46]

Afterward, guests would receive in the mail a note from John Kennedy thanking them for their support, along with a reminder that they could render even greater service to the campaign by helping out on a local Kennedy-for-Senator committee.

Publicly, Lodge ridiculed the Kennedy teas. "I am told they are quite pleasant little affairs," he informed one audience, "and I'm sure they are nonfattening."[47] Privately, he was less flippant. Fearing the women's vote was slipping from him, the Republican lawmaker agreed late in the campaign to accompany his publicity-shy wife, Emily Sears, to a series of house parties organized by his supporters across the state.

In terms of issues, there was little in the way of substance separating the two candidates. "Rarely in politics have hunter and quarry so resembled each other," Kennedy biographer James MacGregor Burns has noted.[48] Both candidates favored increased spending on federal social programs, a continuation of postwar price controls, a higher minimum wage, better housing, and rent control.

But foreign policy was a different matter. "I'm going to use the same kind of stuff" that was used against Claude Pepper, Kennedy informed fellow Democrat George Smathers of Florida shortly before announcing his Senate candidacy. Smathers had registered the political upset of 1950 by accusing his Democratic primary opponent, incumbent US Senator Claude Pepper, henceforth known as the "Red Pepper," of being "an apologist" for Soviet dictator Joseph Stalin.[49] While Kennedy refrained from publicly making such outlandish statements about Lodge, he nonetheless did not shy away from portraying his opponent as being "soft" on communism.

He accused Lodge of being derelict in his duty as senator by failing to support legislation that would have "stopped" trade in war materials with Communist China or Soviet Russia. "I saw this trade actually in operation when I was out in the British port of [Hong Kong] a year and a half ago," Kennedy claimed. "Trade of that type obviously must be stopped. Mr. Lodge now agrees with me in this political year of 1952."[50]

Responding to Kennedy's charges that he had not done enough to combat communism during his tenure in the Senate, Lodge reminded voters that he had been an early supporter of the Truman Doctrine and the Marshall Plan, bipartisan measures designed to keep the Soviet Union and its allies in check. In addition, he spoke of the importance of holding the line against perceived communist aggression in Asia. "I have asserted that our corps and divisions must remain," he said of America's continued military presence on the Korean peninsula.[51]

This failure to advocate more aggressive methods, as his opponent did, made Lodge vulnerable to attacks from state conservatives within his own party who questioned his commitment to the anticommunist cause and who were looking to "punish" Lodge for his part in denying Robert Taft the GOP presidential nomination. Leading the charge from the right was influential New Bedford and Cape Cod newspaper publisher Basil Brewer, the chairman of the Taft-for-President state committee. Directing his venom at Lodge, Brewer began openly touting John Kennedy for senator over Lodge. At a September 25 press conference held at the Sheraton Plaza Hotel in Boston to explain his endorsement, Brewer minced no words. He told a throng of Boston-area newspapermen that he was supporting Kennedy because, in his opinion, Lodge had "long ago bolted his party by his votes for the Truman socialistic New Deal." That Kennedy was a Democrat made little difference. "If a real Republican was running in this race," he concluded, "I'd support that Republican against Kennedy."[52]

Brewer's efforts to "dislodge" the junior Massachusetts senator were not limited to holding press conferences. When the Lodge campaign attempted to place ads in his newspaper criticizing Kennedy's performance as a congressman, the New Bedford publisher refused to run them. The political blackout soon carried over into the paper's daily news coverage of the Republican candidate campaigning in the area. "We were told [by Brewer] not to take any pictures of [Lodge]," reporter Jeremiah Murphy recalled. "I guess [the lack of overall press coverage] is linked to the fact that Lodge didn't do too well around New Bedford."[53]

Brewer would also play a significant role in securing Kennedy the endorsement of the influential *Boston Post*. Founded in 1831, the popular daily boasted a readership of over three hundred thousand and was considered by many to be the paper of record for the city's large Irish Catholic community. Lodge, who had carried Boston by over twenty thousand votes in 1946, but who labeled the city a problem area in 1952 owing to Kennedy's unique status among Irish Catholic voters, was counting on a *Post* endorsement to negate his opponent's natural ethnic appeal. For Kennedy was regarded as an "Irish Brahmin," someone who displayed the same outward characteristics of wealth and privilege the city's ruling Brahmin class possessed minus the Protestant heritage. "I knew it would be much harder this time [to carry Boston]," Lodge later explained, "but I figured if I could get the endorsement of the *Post*, which in those days was worth forty thousand votes, I could hold my own in Boston."[54] Yet to win the *Post*'s endorsement required gaining the approval of the paper's mercurial owner and publisher, John J. Fox.

Initially, Fox had planned on supporting Lodge, with whom he had enjoyed amicable social relations for several years. But a conversation with Brewer three weeks before the election instilled doubts in Fox's mind as to the advisability of such an action. Though details remain sketchy as to what was actually said, it is clear from statements made later by Fox that Brewer had convinced him that Lodge had been "soft on the Communists" for at least the past two or three years."[55]

Interestingly enough, nowhere in this account does Fox mention that Kennedy's father had loaned him half a million dollars around this time to help offset the enormous financial losses his paper was then experiencing. Fox had already poured most of his personal fortune into the paper, but to no avail. He later insisted the loan was purely a commercial transaction with no connection whatsoever with the *Post*'s decision to endorse Kennedy. Joseph Kennedy "was merely a substitute for a bank," the Boston publisher later contended. As for Joseph Kennedy, he also denied any underlying political motives, claiming the loan was paid off on time with full interest.[56]

Nevertheless, the circumstances surrounding the *Post*'s endorsement, as Kennedy biographer Herbert Parmet has pointed out, "encouraged skepticism." Lodge, for instance, told historian Doris Kearns Goodwin years later that he "never doubted for a moment" that Joseph Kennedy and his seemingly bottomless checkbook were responsible for turning Fox around, though he imagined that the ambassador handled the situation "pretty subtly, with all sorts of veiled promises and hints, rather than an outright deal."[57]

Lodge's suspicions aside, the charge that the Kennedys "bought" the *Post*'s endorsement cannot be substantiated. No documentation has turned up, as of yet, to determine whether a quid pro quo arrangement ever existed. In fact, Fox and Kennedy consistently maintained over the years that the loan was made after the endorsement had already been finalized.

More certain is the important role television played in the campaign. Since the end of World War II, the new technology had made significant strides toward building a solid base of viewership in the Bay State, just as it was doing throughout the rest of the country. According to the "Preliminary Survey of Television Coverage for 1952 Senatorial Candidates" put out by the Radio-Television Division of the Republican National Committee in 1951, an estimated 48 percent of the state's 4.7 million population had access to 741,000 TV sets. "Alert politicians have looked forward to television for many years," reported Courtney Sheldon of the *Christian Science Monitor* at the time. "Some of them are now convinced T.V. audiences are extensive enough to take the plunge."[58]

In 1952 both Democratic and Republican candidates for US senator in Massachusetts took that plunge with varying degrees of success. John Kennedy, displaying a warm and engaging personality combined with movie star looks, was a natural for the new medium. Henry Cabot Lodge Jr., conveying a somewhat more stuffy, standoffish image, simply was not. Seeking an advantage, Kennedy's campaign purchased large blocks of advertising time from Boston-area television stations, since this was the principal broadcasting center in the state. In the three weeks leading up to the election, for example, Kennedy bought eight hours of TV advertising time, while Lodge, an apparently reluctant user of the new medium, purchased only four and a half hours. "John Kennedy knew that he was a television candidate," explained campaign aide Dave Powers.[59]

This awareness was ingrained into him by his father. As a former Hollywood movie mogul, Joseph Kennedy had a unique grasp of what it took to create a favorable image for mainstream consumption. "Mr. Kennedy was a genius about how Jack should be handled on television," recalled campaign speechwriter and the senior Kennedy's future son-in-law R. Sargent Shriver. "He knew how Jack should be dressed and how his hair should be, what his response should be and how to handle Lodge. He was really good on that. Super." [60]

Still, John Kennedy was not without initiative himself when it came to unlocking the mysteries of the new medium. A case in point was his making arrangements with CBS-TV to be a "guest student" at the network's "coaching school for political candidates" at Washington, DC, on July 1. "Mr. Kennedy has a natural approach which comes over television very well," concluded one instructor. "His good looks and strong personality lose nothing between the studio and viewer and what's more he certainly doesn't have to worry about a receding hairline which is a problem with many a politician on TV." [61]

Lodge had a more difficult time with the new technology. Though handsome and well spoken, he could not translate these qualities onto the television screen. The problem, as TV ad producer Gene Wyckoff discovered when he worked with Lodge on the latter's 1960 vice-presidential campaign, was visceral. The Republican "looked like what you would expect an American statesman to look like," Wyckoff observed. "But when he opened his mouth and he interacted with people on television, there was something not so attractive—something in his demeanor, a touch of hauteur, arrogance, aloofness, or condescension perhaps. His characterization did not ring true." [62]

This unflattering image came across when Lodge agreed to appear with Kennedy on the October 7 edition of *Keep Posted*, a national public affairs program that was broadcast live from a New York City studio and simulcast locally on WNAC-TV in Boston. Addressing the show's main topic of discussion, "Who will do more for the country, Eisenhower or Stevenson?" Lodge made a flat, uninspiring case for the general. He argued that Eisenhower's experience as NATO commander in Europe provided him the necessary managerial skills and insight to organize a "durable peace." Dressed in a dark, pin-striped suit, Lodge at times appeared distracted and bored with the proceedings. His fidgety body language seemed to tell viewers that he had better things to do than to sit around and spend time with them. This was in marked contrast to the image Kennedy projected. Alert and engaged, he gave a spirited yet lucid accounting of why he felt Stevenson was better qualified to be president. "I think his experience in bringing young, vigorous men into positions of responsibility in Illinois give[s] us hope" that he would do the same in Washington, DC, he asserted. As an indication of who actually won this televised "debate," Kennedy can be seen smiling serenely into the camera as the credits begin to roll, while Lodge can be seen scowling conspicuously. [63]

Kennedy, confirmed one newspaper, "was in complete possession of all the facts he needed to support his contention that the Democratic party is better equipped to deal with the problems facing the country than the Republican party. His manner was unrestrained, and his poise never left him."[64]

Lodge's difficulties with television did not end with this broadcast. On election eve, Dwight Eisenhower came to Boston to conclude his presidential campaign with a rousing send-off rally at the Boston Garden on Causeway Street. The general's appearance was considered a major coup because Lodge was scheduled to introduce Eisenhower, thus gaining invaluable exposure for his Senate candidacy.

Unfortunately for Lodge, such well-laid plans went for naught. The Garden's audience's initial reaction to the GOP standard-bearer reached such a "sustained pitch" and got "so out of hand" that it forced "cancellation" of Lodge's scheduled introduction out of concern for running overtime with the networks. Instead of basking in the reflected glow of the World War II hero's presidential candidacy, Lodge was left to ponder his missed opportunity. Exclaimed one exasperated Lodge supporter afterward, "We couldn't understand what happened to you, that you didn't introduce the General at the most important time . . . at the Boston Garden."[65]

It was, in many ways, a fitting epitaph for the star-crossed campaign Lodge waged against Kennedy in 1952. For the final election vote tally read: Kennedy 1,211,984 (51.5 percent), Lodge 1,141,247 (48.5 percent). Lodge initially blamed his defeat on "those fancy tea parties," which supposedly galvanized the women's vote on behalf of his Democratic opponent. He may have been on to something. Kennedy's final victory margin of seventy thousand votes closely matches the number of guests, mostly women, who attended his tea receptions statewide during the campaign. "Of course," remembered Kennedy campaign volunteer Edward C. Berube, "his theme was to hit on the women['s] vote. Of course, he indicated this to me when I met him . . . that he figured the woman was the one that was going to put him in." The strategy may well have paid off in 1952.[66]

Equally significant was the success that conservative state Republicans had under the leadership of newspaper publisher Basil Brewer in "punishing" Lodge for championing Dwight Eisenhower over Robert Taft for the GOP presidential nomination. A comparison of votes for Lodge and for the Massachusetts Republican gubernatorial candidate that year reveals, for example, that 34,708 fewer ballots were cast for the incumbent senator. "You see, Brewer could make the difference of thirty [-five] thousand votes," Lodge later claimed. "That's what he did. I was beaten by seventy thousand. If thirty[-five] thousand had gone the other way, I'd have been in the clear."[67]

Brewer had made a "difference" by using the resources at his disposal, his newspaper and his prestige as state chairman of the Taft-for-President committee, to mobilize conservative Republican opposition to

Lodge's candidacy. Moreover, he was decisive in securing Kennedy the endorsement of John Fox, the influential publisher of the *Boston Post*.

Neither, did it seem, was the Lodge family checkbook large enough to secure victory over the bulging Kennedy coffers. There were three things, Joseph Kennedy once observed, that got a person elected to public office. "The first is money and the second is money and the third is money."[68] John Kennedy obeyed this maxim to the letter in 1952, as he outspent Lodge by a substantial margin.

Then-existing campaign finance laws specified that no individual could contribute more than one thousand dollars to a candidate or committee, but Kennedy skillfully circumvented this restriction by setting up a series of paper committees, such as the Committee for Improvement of Massachusetts Textile Industry and the Committee for Improvement of Massachusetts Shoe Industry, that allowed family members and friends to make multiple thousand-dollar donations. "Thus, wrote one analyst, "the seven members of the Joseph P. Kennedy family contributed a total of $35,000 to the five main Kennedy committees; members of the George Skakel family (Kennedy in-laws) were listed as giving $25,000; and John Dowdle III and his wife (a former Skakel) gave $10,000. This brings the family total not including the candidate's personal expenditure of $15,866 to $70,000." All told, Kennedy reported expenses of $350,000 to Lodge's $59,000. As Dwight Eisenhower later observed, "Cabot was simply overwhelmed by money."[69]

Defeat was a new, unsettling experience for Lodge, who had an unbeaten campaign record dating back to 1932. His feelings on the subject were later confided to Eisenhower in a private note. "I felt rather like a man who has just been hit by a truck," he wrote. But as painful as the Senate loss was, he tried not to spend much time dwelling on it. Asked by a reporter to analyze the defeat, Lodge replied, "I don't believe in looking backwards. I have simply ended one phase of my career. Now I will embark on another."[70] Lodge was as good as his word.

Over the next decade he remained politically active as the US representative to the United Nations, a post that occupied Cabinet status in the Eisenhower administration. Ironically, the United Nations represented the same kind of global collective security organization that Lodge's grandfather had so vociferously opposed three decades earlier. Lodge, however, saw no incongruity. His grandfather had been "essentially way ahead of his time," he argued, because the United Nations Charter contained all the reservations the Old Senator had voiced over the League of Nations, including the provision that reserved member nations the right to send troops into combat.

Sensitive to the softness-on-communism charges that John Kennedy had leveled against him in 1952, Lodge gave no quarter to the Soviets or to their allies as ambassador. When Soviet delegate Semyon Tsarapkin sought recognition at a Security Council meeting, Lodge queried, "For what purpose does the gentleman from the Soviet Union take the floor?"

"I'm not a gentleman," Tsarapkin bristled, "I'm a delegate."

"I had hoped that the two were not mutually exclusive," Lodge responded to the amusement of the chamber.[71]

In 1960 Lodge ran against Kennedy again, this time as Vice President Richard Nixon's Republican running mate in that year's presidential election. Unfortunately for Lodge, the result was the same, another close loss.

The old political rivals crossed political paths one final time in 1963. Kennedy named Lodge to one of the most challenging posts in the US Foreign Service, the ambassadorship of South Vietnam. But his efforts to bring stability to the war-torn land were largely unsuccessful. "I eventually reached the conclusion that we should withdraw our troops from Vietnam as fast as could be done in an orderly way and try to negotiate a settlement," Lodge wrote in his memoirs.[72]

John Kennedy's untimely death on November 22 may have brought the curtain down on the New Frontier, but it did not end Lodge's political career. He stayed on as ambassador to South Vietnam through the spring of 1964, until events within the Republican Party forced him to resign his post and return stateside. Conservative Barry Goldwater of Arizona was in the process of winning the GOP presidential nomination, and this development greatly alarmed Lodge. To him, Goldwater represented the kind of outmoded conservative thinking that had cost the Republicans national elections in the 1930s and 1940s. Though Lodge won the New Hampshire primary by an overwhelming margin of write-in votes, he steadfastly refused to accept a draft for president. "I don't think [Lodge] would have turned [the presidency] down," remembered one close friend, "but he wasn't willing to go out and fight for it himself."[73] Lodge instead threw his support to Governor William W. Scranton of Pennsylvania, a fellow moderate who ultimately lacked the organization to compete with Goldwater.

After Lyndon Johnson's overwhelming victory over Goldwater in that fall's general election, Lodge continued to remain active in diplomatic circles. He returned to Vietnam for a second tour of ambassadorial duty from 1965 to 1967. He also held high-ranking posts as ambassador to Germany in 1968–1969, special envoy to the Vatican in 1970–1977, and chief US negotiator at the Paris Peace Talks in 1969.

When death claimed him at the age of eighty-two in 1985, condolences poured in from all parts of the country. But perhaps none were as poignant as the statement made by Senator Ted Kennedy upon hearing the news. "Henry Cabot Lodge was one of the greatest statesmen from one of the greatest families in the history of the Commonwealth," he noted. "He will be honored and remembered most for his extraordinary achievements as a senator and diplomat, but he is also remembered by all of us

JFK Library PC 473

Figure 2.3.   No hard feelings. JFK and Lodge enjoy a postelection handshake. Lodge would later be tapped by Kennedy to be his Ambassador to South Vietnam.

in the Kennedy family for the warmth and friendship that endured despite our political rivalry."[74]

John Kennedy had indeed beaten the best.

NOTES

1. George Smathers, interview, Clay Blair Papers (hereinafter cited as CBP); William Sutton, interview, Ralph Martin Collection (hereinafter cited as RMC).

2. Joan and Clay Blair Jr., *The Search for J.F.K.* (New York, 1976), 641.

3. Frank Waldrop, interview, CBP.

4. Roger Kahn, *The Boys of Summer* (New York, 1972), 427–28.

5. Pamela Churchill, interview, CBP.

6. James MacGregor Burns, *John Kennedy: A Political Profile* (New York, 1960), 75; Mary Davis, interview, RMC.

7. *Person to Person*, CBS Television Network, September 29, 1960.

8. Congressional Record, January 25, 1949; Christopher Matthews, *Kennedy and Nixon: The Rivalry That Shaped Postwar America* (New York, 1996), 75.

9. Joseph Healy, Oral History, John F. Kennedy Library (hereinafter cited as JFKL).

10. *Time*, July 11, 1960.

11. Henry Cabot Lodge, *The Storm Has Many Eyes: A Personal Narrative* (New York, 1973), 17.

12. Stephen Hess, *America's Political Dynasties* (Garden City, New York, 1966), 453–54.

13. Henry Cabot Lodge to Henry Cabot Lodge Jr., January 13, 1919, Henry Cabot Lodge Papers, MHS.

14. *Boston Globe*, January 8, 1933, July 24, 1932.

15. William J. Miller, *Henry Cabot Lodge: A Biography* (New York, 1967), 57, 49.

16. *Boston Herald*, August 2, 1960; *Boston Advertiser*, August 9, 1936.

17. Emily Sears Lodge quoted in Huntley-Brinkley Interview, September 24, 1960, *Senate Reports*, Vol. 13 (Washington, DC, 1961), 69.

18. *Boston Advertiser*, November 8, 1936.

19. *Boston Herald*, December 8, 1941; Leigh White, "He Runs the Show for Ike," *Saturday Evening Post*, May 31, 1952.

20. Henry Cabot Lodge Jr. to Hon. D. Worth Clark, February 3, 1944, Military Papers 166, Henry Cabot Lodge II Papers, MHS.

21. Franklin D. Roosevelt to Henry Cabot Lodge Jr., February 1, 1944, GC 166, Henry Cabot Lodge II Papers, MHS.

22. Miller, *Henry Cabot Lodge*, 174.

23. Dorothy G. Wayman, *David I. Walsh, Citizen-Patriot* (Milwaukee, 1952), 318; *New York Post*, May 6, 1942.

24. Lodge, *The Storm Has Many Eyes*, 61.

25. Henry Cabot Lodge Jr., "A Foreign Aid Program Which Will Aid Americans," May 14, 1947, speech copy, Essex Institute, Salem, Massachusetts.

26. Henry Cabot Lodge Jr., "Modernize the G.O.P.," *Atlantic Monthly*, March 1950.

27. *Berkshire Eagle*, February 8, 1950.

28. Henry Cabot Lodge Jr., "Think and Act Anew," *Saturday Evening Post*, January 26, 1949.

29. Dwight D. Eisenhower, *Mandate for Change: The White House Years, 1953–56* (Garden City, New York, 1963), 18.

30. Alden Hatch, *The Lodges of Massachusetts* (New York, 1973), 248; Eisenhower, *The White House Years*, 18.

31. Lodge, *The Storm Has Many Eyes*, 75–76.

32. *Haverhill Gazette*, August 8, 1952.

33. *Boston Herald-Boston Traveler*, May 12, 1952.

34. *Boston Globe*, August 16, 1976.

35. Lodge campaign memo, n.d., Ann Whitman File, Administration Series, Dwight D. Eisenhower Library, Abeline, Kansas.

36. *Boston Globe*, August 16, 1976.

37. Miller, *Henry Cabot Lodge*, 251.

38. Mason Sears to James J. Shea, December 8, 1953, Henry Cabot Lodge II Papers, MHS.

39. John F. Kennedy, interview, RMC.

40. Joe McCarthy, *The Remarkable Kennedys* (New York, 1960), 136.

41. Harold Vaughn, interview, RMC.

42. Joseph Alsop Oral History, JFKL.

43. McCarthy, *The Remarkable Kennedys*, 135.

44. *Haverhill Gazette*, October 7, 1952.

45. Congressional Quarterly News Feature, October 5, 1952, October 3, 1952, Pre-Presidential Papers, JFKL; Richard Whalen, *The Founding Father* (New York, 1964), 432.

46. *Saturday Evening Post*, September 14, 1953.

47. Cabell Phillips, "Case Study of a Senate Race," *New York Times Magazine*, October 26, 1952.

48. Burns, *John Kennedy*, 102.

49. Matthews, *Kennedy and Nixon*, 76; David Chaute, *The Great Fear* (New York, 1978), 37.

50. *New Bedford Standard-Times*, October 30, 1952, Press release, Pre-Presidential Papers, JFKL.

51. "WBZ-TV Speech," October 17, 1952, radio and television speeches, Henry Cabot Lodge II Papers, MHS.

52. "Stenographic Record of Press Conference of Basil Brewer on His Support of Mr. Kennedy," September 25, 1952, Pre-Presidential Papers, JFKL.

53. Jeremiah Murphy, interview with author.

54. PMS Analysis Poll, September 5, 1952, Senate Campaign, 1952, Henry Cabot Lodge II Papers, MHS; Doris Kearns Goodwin, *The Fitzgeralds and the Kennedys: An American Saga* (New York, 1987), 488.

55. *Boston Globe*, June 27, 1958.

56. *Christian Science Monitor*, June 27, 1958; *Boston Globe*, June 27, 1958.

57. Herbert S. Parmet, *Jack: The Struggles of John F. Kennedy* (New York, 1980), 242; Goodwin, *The Fitzgeralds and the Kennedys*, 765.

58. "Preliminary Survey of Television Coverage for 1952 Senatorial Candidates," Radio-Television Division, Republican National Committee, August 30, 1951, Henry Cabot Lodge II Papers, MHS; *Christian Science Monitor*, October 11, 1949.

59. Kennedy and Lodge television schedules, Pre-Presidential Papers, JFKL; Dave Powers, interview with author.

60. R. Sargent Shriver, interview, CBP.

61. *Boston Globe*, July 2, 1952.

62. Gene Wyckoff, *The Image Candidates: American Politics in the Age of Television* (New York, 1968), 49.

63. *Keep Posted*, CBS Television Network, October 7, 1952, Audio-Visual Archives, JFKL.

64. *Lynn Telegram-News*, October 8, 1952.

65. *New Bedford Standard-Times*, November 4, 1952; Charles Eliot Worden to Henry Cabot Lodge Jr., November 8, 1952, Henry Cabot Lodge II Papers, MHS.

66. Commonwealth of Massachusetts, *Massachusetts Election Statistics*, 1952; Goodwin, *The Fitzgeralds and the Kennedys*, 765; Edward C. Berube Oral History, JFKL.

67. Henry Cabot Lodge Oral History, JFKL.

68. Ralph G. Martin, *A Hero for Our Time: An Intimate Story of the Kennedy Years* (New York, 1963), 53.

69. Miller, *Henry Cabot Lodge*, 253.

70. Henry Cabot Lodge to Dwight D. Eisenhower, November 6, 1952; Eisenhower Correspondence, Henry Cabot Lodge II Papers, MHS; *Beverly Times*, February 28, 1985.

71. Hatch, *The Lodges of Massachusetts*, 268.

72. Lodge, *The Storm Has Many Eyes*, 206.

73. *Beverly Times*, February 28, 1985.

74. Ibid.

THREE

A Gamblin' Man

LBJ and the 1960 Democratic Nomination Fight

Although the senatorial race had required John F. Kennedy's attention for several months, he did not neglect his personal life. During the campaign he had begun dating an attractive young socialite from Southampton, New York, named Jacqueline Bouvier. Witty, accomplished, and reserved, Jacqueline possessed a joie de vivre that the new senator found appealing. Asked later by a reporter whether it was love at first sight, Kennedy demurred. "Well, I don't know," he said. "I don't know how you describe love anyway, but I was very interested."[1] The two were married at St. Mary's Church in Newport, Rhode Island, on September 12, 1953, in a lavish wedding ceremony that captured the imaginations of people nationwide. The union would eventually produce four children, Arabella in 1956, Caroline Bouvier in 1957, John Fitzgerald Jr. in 1960, and Patrick Bouvier in 1963. Arabella was a stillborn and Patrick Bouvier died less than thirty hours after entering the world. The cause of death was an inoperable lung condition.

Just a month after marrying Jacqueline Bouvier, John Kennedy appeared with his young bride on Edward R. Murrow's *Person to Person* television program. Quoting from a letter written by Alan Seeger, a famous American poet who had been killed during World War I, Kennedy told a nationwide audience that success in life to him meant "doing that thing then which nothing else seems more noble or satisfactory or remunerative. And then being ready to see it through to the end."

Whether Kennedy was ready to see a future presidential campaign through to the end had yet to be decided. He nevertheless began accepting speaking engagements around the country, just as he had in Massachusetts before his first run for the Senate in 1952. The purpose again was

47

to increase his name recognition and to set up a network of political contacts for use in a possible Kennedy-for-President campaign organization down the road. "Suddenly," fellow Bay State lawmaker Thomas P. "Tip" O'Neill observed, "he became an active person. Suddenly he became a person with a future in the Democratic Party. 'Will you go to Missouri and speak for the party?' You can't go to those places unless you have a knowledge of what is taking place in the Congress of the United States. He started to do his homework."[2]

There were some setbacks. In 1954, surgery on his spine nearly killed him. "He never said one word about what he went through at the hospital," remembered aide Dave Powers. "He was in constant pain . . . unable to sleep for more than an hour or two at a time, but he never complained about the pain, never mentioned it."[3] As he lay in bed recovering from the surgery, Kennedy was confronted with perhaps the greatest moral issue of his political career: whether to support a Senate motion to censure Joseph McCarthy for his increasingly disruptive personal behavior. Much to the dismay of liberal Democratic Party leaders such as Eleanor Roosevelt, Kennedy declined to go on the record against the red-baiting Wisconsin senator, refusing even to pair his vote with that of another absent senator in opposition to the censure.

Kennedy later claimed that poor health resulting from his back surgery prevented him from voting for the censure motion, but this falls short of the truth. "I was caught in a bad situation," Kennedy privately confessed. "My brother [Robert] was working for Joe [as a staff assistant on the Permanent Subcommittee on Investigations of the Senate Government Operations Committee]. I was against it, I didn't want him to work for Joe, but he wanted to. And how the hell could I get up there and denounce Joe McCarthy when my own brother was working for him? So it wasn't as much a political liability as it was a personal problem."[4]

Kennedy had also enjoyed close personal ties with McCarthy. According to McCarthy advisor Roy Cohn, this friendship began during World War II when the two men were stationed together in the Solomon Islands. At the time Kennedy was commanding the PT-59 (his first ship, the PT-109, had been sunk by a Japanese destroyer), and McCarthy was serving as a captain in the Marines. "On a hot, damp Sunday, Captain McCarthy got into conversation with young Lieutenant Kennedy, who took him for a ride," Cohn recounted. McCarthy appeared to have been very impressed by Kennedy. "I met this fellow Kennedy—a hell of a nice guy. His old man's the ambassador to Britain," he told Marine acquaintance Penn T. Kimball, who later became a professor of journalism at Columbia University. Kennedy reportedly let McCarthy accompany him and his crew unofficially on two night patrol missions. "Joe McCarthy did that," Kimball later confirmed. "He knew who Jack was [the son of a famous ambassador]. He probably sought him out."[5]

After the war, Kennedy and McCarthy found themselves serving together once again, this time as legislators on Capitol Hill. The two were often seen together making the rounds at various Washington, DC, cocktail parties. "I got the idea that Jack liked McCarthy," recalled George Smathers. Kennedy "thought he was a pretty good guy. . . . He was friendly all the way through."[6]

A frequent visitor to the Kennedy family's summertime retreat in Hyannis Port, McCarthy was known to participate in such time-honored family rituals as sailing, touch football, and softball, although he had to retire from the latter when he made four errors in a game. He also dated two of Kennedy's sisters. "In case there is any question in your mind," Joseph Kennedy informed a journalist in 1961, "I liked Joe McCarthy. I always liked him. I would see him when I went down to Washington and when he was visiting in Palm Beach he'd come around to my house for a drink. I invited him to Cape Cod."[7]

John Kennedy's refusal to censure McCarthy was not without political calculation. The Republican was revered by Irish Catholics in Massachusetts for his staunch anticommunism, and the idea of publicly denouncing him, however justified, risked alienating this all-important constituency group. "Hell, half my voters . . . looked on McCarthy as a hero," Kennedy told Arthur Schlesinger Jr. after the Harvard historian had lobbied him to break with the Wisconsinite.[8]

Kennedy's reluctance to take a moral stand against McCarthy belied the message he was trying to convey in his Pulitzer Prize–winning book *Profiles in Courage*, which he wrote while recuperating from the surgery in 1954. *Profiles* told the story of eight US senators—John Quincy Adams, Daniel Webster, Thomas Hart Benton, Sam Houston, Edmund G. Ross, Lucius Quintus Cincinnatus Lamar, George Norris, and Robert A. Taft—who defied the wishes of their constituents at critical periods in American history. While critics found irony in Kennedy's failure to show the courage he was writing about, the work nevertheless served the purpose of enhancing his image as a serious-minded lawmaker.

Such visibility proved useful when Kennedy made a surprisingly strong bid to attain the vice presidency at the 1956 Democratic National Convention in Chicago. Initially he had no intention of seeking the number-two spot on the ticket, but when convention delegates and television viewers nationwide saw him deliver a rousing nomination speech for the party's standard-bearer, Adlai E. Stevenson of Illinois, a Kennedy-for-Vice-President boom developed. Always seeking a political opening, Kennedy attempted to make the most of his newfound celebrity by lining up the support of northern political bosses and meeting with delegates from key western and southern states.

In the end, his effort fell short, as the prohibitive vice-presidential favorite going into the convention, Senator Estes Kefauver of Tennessee, was able to parlay his strength in the Middle West and Rocky Mountain states into a third ballot victory. Still, the near miss convinced Kennedy that he had what it took to make a successful presidential run the next time around. "If I work hard for the next four years," he confidently told aide Dave Powers after the convention, "I ought to be able to pick up all the marbles."[9]

But standing in his way of the 1960 Democratic presidential nomination was an imposing political hurdle: Lyndon Baines Johnson. The Texas power broker and Senate Majority Leader had also trained his sights on the Oval Office and had dismissed Kennedy's candidacy as quixotic. "Now I realize you're pledged to the boy," Johnson told Tip O'Neill before that year's Democratic National Convention in Los Angeles. "But you and I both know he can't win. He's just a flash in the pan, and he's got no record of substance to run on." Johnson's skepticism was not out of line. As Senator, Kennedy seemed to embody the term "lightweight." He had authored no major pieces of legislation while compiling the same glaringly spotty attendance record he had had in the House. "Very few Senators, of which Johnson was the dominant figure, thought that Kennedy would have any chance," said Horace Busby, Johnson's longtime political associate. "They felt he would be perceived by the country as they perceived him; that he was young, that he was not necessarily a serious senator, had no demonstrated ability to run something, and was a man who wanted pleasure more than he wanted to be president."[10]

As if all these factors were not discouraging enough, Kennedy's religious faith worked against him. In mainstream Protestant America, all prospective Catholic presidential candidates were operating at an electoral disadvantage due to the long-held prejudice that they could not separate their loyalty to the Roman church from their loyalty to the Constitution. Practicing Irish Catholic and Democratic nominee Al Smith discovered this political reality in 1928 when he was swamped in the general election by Republican Herbert Hoover. As the veteran journalist Fletcher Knebel wrote in 1959, "If nominated, Kennedy certainly would lose votes because he is a Catholic."[11]

Kennedy's political deficiencies aside, Johnson was determined to take the presidential prize in 1960, if for no other reason than it was there for the taking. Up to this point, his entire life and career had been about the accumulation of power and influence. The presidency would merely be the logical culmination of his soaring ambition.

The story of Lyndon Johnson begins in the rugged Hill Country of West Texas near the Gulf of Mexico. Born in 1908, he was the product of an unlikely union between a hard-drinking Texas state legislator and an aspiring novelist turned frustrated housewife. To be sure, Sam Ealy Johnson Jr. and the former Rebekah Baines were opposites in nearly every conceivable way, but when it came to Lyndon, the oldest of their five children, they seemed to be on the same page. He was the proverbial apple of their eyes, especially his mother's, who described him as "a happy, winsome child, who made friends easily, ate and slept as he should, and woke up with a laugh instead of a wail."[12]

While such comments have led many biographers to conclude that Johnson was "a momma's boy," his younger brother Sam disputed the characterization. "More often than not our mother was doing Lyndon's bidding, rather than the other way around," he said. For sure, Johnson already had the ability, even at a young age, to bend others to his will. It was a talent he would put to great use during his long and controversial political career. But before embarking on that career, he needed first to get out of West Texas. And this was no easy task given the limited financial resources available to him and his family. Young Lyndon was determined all the same, graduating at the top of his high school class in 1924 and moving on to Southwest Texas State Teachers College (now Texas State University) in San Marcos to earn a degree in education. "What you accomplish in life depends almost entirely upon what you make yourself do," he wrote in a campus newspaper editorial at the time. "If you wish strongly enough to do a thing you will be willing to go through all kinds of trials to accomplish the work you have undertaken.[13]

Before graduating in 1930, Johnson took a year off from his studies to work as a grade school teacher for an impoverished Mexican-American community called Cotulla in south Texas. While the educational resources made available to him there were meager, Johnson made the best of a bad situation. "I was determined to give [the students] what they needed to make it in this world, to help them finish their education," he later said. "Then the rest would take care of itself." By all accounts, he did a good job, insisting on a positive attitude from his students while imposing strict discipline in the classroom. "He put us to work," remembered student Manuel Sanchez. "But he was the kind of teacher you wanted to work for. You felt an obligation to him and yourself to do your work." Though he exhibited a real passion for teaching, he drifted away from the profession after graduation, citing the influence of Teachers College president Cecil Evans as the main reason. He "thought that being a public servant would be best [for me] because I'd have to meet the challenges of the time at the very moment they were happening," Johnson told his biographer Doris Kearns Goodwin.[14]

Truth be told, he did not need much of a push. Being the son of a five-term Democratic state legislator, politics had always fascinated him. Add to this the excitement that swirled around the coming to power of Franklin Delano Roosevelt and his New Deal administration in the early 1930s and Johnson was irretrievably hooked. In 1937, he won a special election for a congressional seat representing the Tenth Texas District, an area that encompassed Austin and his old stomping grounds in the Hill Country.

Running as an avid New Dealer, Johnson hit the campaign trail with an almost boundless enthusiasm. "He was energetic; had long legs; he covered lots of territory," remembered a supporter. "He went all over every town, every community, and every hamlet, shaking hands. 'I'm Lyndon Johnson. I want to be your congressman.' He'd look them in the eye. He liked to 'press the flesh,' as he said, and 'look them in the eye.' This was the reason for his tremendous success."[15]

Adding to Johnson's appeal was his comely young wife, the former Claudia Taylor of East Texas, whom he married in 1934. The Johnsons had two daughters, Lynda in 1944 and Luci in 1947. The couple's courtship had lasted only a few weeks, as Johnson had been immediately smitten. It was easy to see why. As the holder of two bachelor of arts degrees from the University of Texas, "Lady Bird" had the perfect qualifications to be a politician's wife. She was smart, well-mannered, steadfastly loyal, and came from money, a reported $10,000 of which found its way into Johnson's congressional campaign coffers. Upon first meeting Johnson, her father was impressed. "Daughter," he said, "you've been bringing home a lot of boys. But this is the first time you've brought home a man."[16]

As a Congressman, Johnson emerged as a political and personal favorite of President Franklin Delano Roosevelt. "I want you to work with that young Congressman from Texas, Lyndon Johnson," FDR instructed a White House staffer. "He's a comer, and he's a real liberal." Roosevelt invited Johnson over for dinner on several occasions, once making him privy to a politically sensitive phone conversation with then Ambassador to Great Britain Joseph P. Kennedy. "I'm going to fire the sonofabitch," he confided to his young protégé. For his part, Johnson was appreciative of the special attention and access, likening Roosevelt to a second father who was unafraid to follow his own convictions. "He always talked to me just that way," he said. "Whatever you talked to him about, whatever you asked him for, like projects for your district, there was just one way to figure it with him. I know some of them called it demagoguery; they can call it anything they want, but you can be damn sure that the only test he had was this: was it good for the folks."[17]

In terms of federal largesse, there was no doubt Johnson was good for his constituents back home in the Tenth District. Thanks to his close ties to Roosevelt, he was able to secure funding for rural electrification, emergency farm loans, dam construction, and various other public works projects. "Johnson could get things done, and that is what impressed Roosevelt," remembered New Deal "brain truster" Tommy "The Cork" Corcoran. "He was never much impressed with theory or theoreticians. He always wanted to know what you could do and had you done it and was there someone else who could have done it better. Roosevelt, contrary to some, was a very down-to-earth politician, and so was Lyndon, and that's why they got along."[18]

With Roosevelt's blessing, Johnson announced his candidacy for an open US Senate seat in 1941, but came up short up when his opponent, Texas governor and former flour merchant Wilbert Lee "Pappy"

O'Daniel, surged late in the polls. He delivered Johnson his one and only defeat in a campaign for elected office. Charges of voter fraud were leveled at the O'Daniel campaign, but Johnson refused to contest the results because, he told supporters, "even if you win the contest, you go into office under a cloud, and you haven't won anything."[19] These words would come back to haunt Johnson seven years later when he prevailed in an even more controversial Texas Senate race. But that was all in the distant future.

In the interim, Johnson took the 1941 loss hard, briefly entertaining thoughts of leaving politics altogether. However, the idea of removing himself from Washington's cozy inner sanctums of power made him shudder, especially since he had been able to retain his House seat. "Besides," he later said, "with all those war clouds hanging over Europe, I felt that someone with all my training and preparedness was bound to be an important figure."[20]

Johnson surmised right. With America's entry into World War II following the surprise Japanese attack on Pearl Harbor on December 7, "Roosevelt's boy" did become an extremely influential figure on Capitol Hill, chairing a House subcommittee that investigated several pressing manpower and procurement issues associated with the naval war effort.

As vital as this task was, however, it did not garner Johnson the kind of widespread notice he received when he volunteered to serve in uniform along with seven other congressional colleagues. For while his tour of duty with the US Navy was mostly desk-bound and limited to seven months due to a 1942 presidential edict (Roosevelt ruled that no member of Congress could be both a soldier and legislator), Johnson still managed to see action. He was an observer on board a B-26 bomber when it came under heavy enemy attack over New Guinea in the South Pacific. "Boy," he told one of the crew members as Japanese bullets raked the plane, "it's rough up here, isn't it?" Impressed by Johnson's composure under fire and no doubt seeking a political favor down the line, General Douglas MacArthur, the Supreme Allied Commander for the region, awarded him a Silver Star for "gallant action." Johnson could not have been more pleased and subsequently embellished his brush with combat for political gain. He portrayed himself to his constituents back home as a courageous fighting man straight out of the pages of an Ernest Hemingway novel. "Sometimes you could hardly restrain yourself from shouting: Oh, bullshit, Lyndon," remembered one bemused political observer.[21]

Capitalizing further on his "war hero" status, Johnson made a second run for the US Senate in 1948 and came away the winner. The victory was not without its share of complications. Although he easily managed to bury his Republican opponent in the general election, Johnson barely survived a Democratic primary runoff with former Texas governor turned rancher Coke Robert Stevenson. His final margin of victory was eighty-seven votes, and that was attained only after the contents of a disputed ballot box in south Texas were allowed to stand by state and federal authorities. Stevenson, who believed to the day he died that he had won the election, cried foul but to no avail. "Everybody knew what had happened," maintained a Texas journalist who later investigated the matter thoroughly. "This was no mystery to anybody that the election was crooked." Just the same, "Landslide Lyndon" did not seem all that concerned over how he won the race, only that he had won. "I just could not bear the thought of losing everything," he later explained.[22]

In the Senate, it did not take long for Johnson to master all the intricate rules and procedures associated with being a member of that venerable institution. In fact, he seemed to thrive politically as never before. This was not surprising. Johnson had always been at his best in small, intimate gatherings. His exuberant personality, ribald humor, and outsized physical presence could dominate a room. What's more, he wasn't shy about seeking out the advice of others. Bobby Baker, then a precocious twenty-year-old Senate page, could testify to this fact. Johnson "solicited opinions of, and thumbnail sketches of, senators little known to him; he peppered me with keen questions for a solid two hours," wrote Baker of their first meeting in 1948. "I was impressed. No senator had ever approached me with such a display of determination to learn, to achieve, to attain, to belong, to get ahead. He was coming into the Senate with his neck bowed, running full tilt, impatient to reach some distant goal I then could not even imagine. It was, as I came to know, wholly characteristic of Lyndon Johnson and close to a typical performance. Politics simply consumed the man."[23]

Johnson rose rapidly through the leadership ranks, becoming minority leader in 1953 and then majority leader in 1955. In the process, he honed his already considerable skill at getting people to do his political bidding. "Nobody could match him," said Senate colleague J. William Fulbright of Arkansas. "He knew every personal interest of every member of the Senate just like he knew the palm of his hand. He knew how to bring people together, because he could appeal to their different interests. If he asked Harry Byrd [of Virginia] to do something, he always knew what Harry wanted in return."[24]

At the same time, Johnson was not averse to using less genteel methods in getting his way. He would employ what became known as "The Treatment," a drawn-out process of persuasion whereby Johnson would physically and psychologically wear down would-be opponents. "It ran the gamut of emotions," nationally syndicated newspaper columnists Rowland Evans and Robert Novak said. "Its velocity was breathtaking, and it was all in one direction. Interjections from the target were rare. Johnson anticipated them before they could be spoken. He moved in close, his face a scant millimeter from his target, his eyes widening and narrowing, his eyebrows rising and falling. From his pockets poured clippings, memos, statistics. Mimicry, humor, and the genius of analogy made The Treatment an almost hypnotic experience and rendered the target stunned and helpless."[25]

With this strong-armed approach, Johnson was able to steer through the Senate a number of problematic bills that had no chance under a weaker leader. A case in point was the Civil Rights Act of 1957, an Eisenhower administration initiative aimed at the Jim Crow South that called on the federal government to strengthen its efforts in upholding the constitutional voting rights of African Americans. Facing a wall of opposition from white southern Democrats who wished to continue their region's tradition of effectively excluding black voters from the polls, Johnson cobbled together a bipartisan coalition of Northern liberals and Midwestern moderates to win passage of the bill.

Though the bill was later criticized for lacking a means of enforcement, it still represented the first major civil rights legislation to come out of Congress since Reconstruction. And Johnson had been the principal driving force behind it. While he claimed at the time to be acting out of concern for social justice ("A man without a vote is a man without protection," he said), an equally valid explanation is that he was looking to his own political future. Realizing that neither he nor his party could continue toeing the segregationist line and expect to remain in power given the more progressive racial attitudes taking hold in postwar American society, Johnson believed it was prudent to make a decisive break with the past. As he freely admitted, "One real slip and we're done for."[26]

It also stood to reason that such a reformist stance would aid Johnson as he moved inexorably toward a presidential run in 1960. Party liberals had grown disenchanted with Johnson in the late 1940s and 1950s, as he seemingly abandoned the New Deal activism of his youth and took a more conservative approach that was in line with the rightward trend in Texas politics. He, for example, became a strong backer of the antiunion Taft-Hartley bill and repeatedly sided with his state's powerful oil and natural gas lobby against increased federal regulation. While this stratagem had allowed Johnson to secure reelection to the Senate in 1954, it did not win him any friends among northern intellectuals or organized labor, key liberal constituency groups whose support he needed if he wished to become the Democratic nominee. Viewed in this light, his championing of the Civil Rights Act, a measure these groups admittedly held dear, can be interpreted as Johnson's earnest if belated attempt at making political amends.

Not that it did him any good. As the fight for the 1960 Democratic presidential nomination got under way, Johnson saw such prominent liberals as historian Arthur Schlesinger Jr., economist John Kenneth Galbraith, and future Supreme Court Justice Arthur Goldberg flock to the candidacy of John Kennedy. Since there existed no major differences of domestic or foreign policy between Kennedy and Johnson, their choice largely boiled down to one of preferred style. Whereas Johnson could

often come across as loud, crude, profane, and overbearing, Kennedy
was the direct opposite. He appeared a living testament to youth, charm,
intellect, and coolness under pressure. "Unlike most politicians," former
Truman White House Counsel Clark Clifford related, "[Kennedy] did not
respond well to the excessive and empty flattery that is such a large part
of normal political intercourse, and he looked for deft ways to deflate or
deflect it. His wit, much of it highly sardonic, was justly celebrated." [27]

Even former First Lady Eleanor Roosevelt, an initial skeptic of Kennedy's candidacy due to his previous close ties to Joseph McCarthy, eventually came around to an endorsement as she saw qualities of her late
husband in the Massachusetts Democrat. "Franklin would sometimes begin a campaign weary and apathetic, but in the course of the campaign he
would draw strength and vitality from the audiences, and would end in
better shape than he started," she said. "I feel Senator Kennedy is much
the same—that his intelligence and courage elicit emotions from his
crowds which flow back to him, and sustain and strengthen him." [28]

As welcomed as these liberal endorsements were, Kennedy was
shrewd enough to realize that his success or failure as a candidate did not
depend on them. Rather his road to the Democratic nomination would be
predicated on how well he fared in a series of preconvention primaries,
the most important being in West Virginia on May 10. For the political
conventional wisdom of the day held that if he scored a decisive victory
in this overwhelmingly Protestant state, many of the reservations about
his Catholicism would disappear. As Kennedy explained, "I have no
right to go before the Democratic convention and claim to be a candidate
if I can only win in primaries in states with twenty-five percent or more
Catholics. I must go in there. And I am going in." [29]

Things did not get off to an auspicious start in the Mountain State.
When Kennedy's campaign manager, younger brother Robert, addressed
a packed gathering of local Democratic operatives in Charleston and
asked what their chief concerns were, he got an earful. "There's only one
problem," he was told. "He's a Catholic. That's our God-damned problem!" [30] Nor did it help matters that Kennedy's main primary opponent,
Senator Hubert H. Humphrey of Minnesota, was a practicing Congrega-
tionalist with a solid record of legislative accomplishment on Capitol
Hill.

Thus having their work cut out for them, the Kennedy campaign
pulled out all the stops, blanketing the state with television ads, organizing mass rallies, going door-to-door in key communities, and not insig-
nificantly, spending boatloads of cash. The historian David Burner has
written that the campaign paid agreeable local sheriffs $1,000 apiece to do
their part for the cause, while poll workers, county bosses, and sundry
other politically connected individuals were also said to have received
significant compensation. Watching all of this unfold with increasing
alarm, a woefully underfinanced Humphrey lamented that he could not

"afford to run around this state with a little black bag and a check-book."[31]

Kennedy insiders like speechwriter and close political advisor Theodore Sorensen always disputed the notion that his boss tried to purchase the election. "Kennedy didn't buy any votes, he sold himself to the people of West Virginia," he said. Irrespective of the money spent, there is no question that the notoriously corrupt and impoverished mining state, which Kennedy won with a resounding 61 percent of the vote on Election Day, had a profound effect on him. "It was the first time that he came into direct contact with poverty," remembered campaign aide Pierre Salinger. "Prior to that he knew what had happened because of the technological changes in coal mining, but in West Virginia he saw the human face of poverty up close—actual people, hundreds of them, sitting around with absolutely nothing to do, just sitting there letting grains of coal run through their hands."[32]

While Kennedy was having his eyes opened both as a candidate and as a person, Lyndon Johnson found himself stuck in a political trap of his own making. Due to his heavy responsibilities as majority leader, he had always planned on sitting out the primaries and, according to one biographer, using Humphrey "as a stalking horse to stop the Kennedy juggernaut." Then, with that political deed accomplished and presumably no other Democratic challenger strong enough to command a majority of delegates, he would bargain his way to the nomination at the scheduled July party convention in Los Angeles. It all seemed so simple. But Humphrey, while a good candidate, proved to be no match for Kennedy or his wallet. He officially dropped out of the race after West Virginia, guaranteeing Kennedy a clean sweep of the seven primaries he entered. Thus, Johnson's well-laid strategy of preemptively knocking off "the boy" never panned out, leaving the Texan to reflect on his reduced political circumstances. "Jack was out kissing babies while I was out passing bills," he complained. "Someone had to tend to the store. There I was looking for the burglar coming in the front door, and little did I know that the fox was coming through the fence in back. When I woke up the chickens were gone."[33]

Still, Johnson had enough fight left in him to formally announce his candidacy on July 5, just six days prior to the opening of the nominating convention. And he wasted no time painting Kennedy as a shallow, inexperienced politician, whose poor Senate attendance record indicated he could not be trusted to take on the awesome burdens of office. The next President, he admonished, "should be a working President." But these remarks were relatively minor in comparison to the fierce line of personal attack he unleashed upon Kennedy at the start of the convention. Using campaign manager John Connolly as a surrogate, he had the trusted longtime aide circulate derogatory stories about Kennedy's health, specifically his hidden fight with Addison's disease. "That's part of cam-

Figure 3.1.   LBJ in a rare moment of inaction as Senate Majority Leader. Reproduction Number: LC-DIG-ppmsca-03141

paign life," said Johnson supporter Jack Valenti, the future president of the Motion Picture Association of America.[34] "I've never seen a campaign yet that was conducted under Marquis of the Queensbury Rules. They just never are."

Nor were members of Kennedy's family spared. Johnson went out of his way to point out that Joseph P. Kennedy had been pro-appeasement and therefore a "Chamberlain-umbrella policy man" leading up to the Second World War. The not-so-subtle implication was that his Democratic front-running son could be counted on to do more of the same, this time with the Soviets if he became president. In both cases, no serious political damage was done. The Kennedy campaign released a phony medical report that pronounced the candidate physically fit and all but ignored the appeasement by association smear, though Robert Kennedy privately stewed over the propriety of Johnson's tactics. "I knew he hated Jack, but I didn't think he hated him that much," he said.[35]

Ever the political gambler, Johnson still had one final card to play. Taking advantage of a standing offer from Kennedy's camp to meet with all convention delegates, Johnson used the invitation as an excuse to get his fellow Democrat to appear before a nationally televised seating of the Texas and Massachusetts delegations and debate him on the issues. The showdown proved anticlimactic. Johnson lamely tried to generate fireworks by contrasting Kennedy's relative inexperience and privileged background with his own seasoned leadership and modest roots. "Whatever I have and whatever I hope to get will be because of whatever energy and talent I have," he thundered.[36]

Kennedy refused to take the bait, insisting to the amusement of the audience that he had nothing but high regard and affection for Johnson . . . as Senate Majority Leader. He also pointed out that no "great issues" divided them and that it was their party's responsibility "to help build in this country a society which serves our people and serves as an attraction to those who determine which road they shall take." At debate's end, a clearly humbled Johnson could do nothing but politely shake his opponent's hand and ponder the shambles his campaign had become. "Kennedy did a tremendous job," noted an impressed Johnson strategist. "He made a talk that was really very persuasive and nice and complimented Johnson. . . . You couldn't argue with a man who was treating you so good, and really it didn't come off as we had expected it to."[37]

"That's when I became a great fan of John Kennedy," said Valenti. "Because he was so masterful. And I yield to no man my love and affection for Johnson, but he was handled with such skill by Kennedy who was like some great toreador handling one of the great Andalusian bulls. Kennedy just massacred him. It wasn't even close."[38]

Johnson fared no better once the official delegate counting began. With his campaign organization working at peak efficiency, Kennedy easily carried the proceedings, securing well in excess of the 761 votes needed to win the nomination on the first ballot. By contrast, Johnson finished a distant second with 409 votes. "We had the votes," boasted Kenneth O'Donnell. "We had the votes on the second ballot, the third ballot, or the tenth ballot. Didn't matter—we had the votes!"[39]

To say Johnson felt mortified by these results would be an understatement. He had no one blame but himself. He had badly underestimated Kennedy and waited too long to announce his candidacy. Indeed, Johnson had spent most of his time holed in his office in Washington "expecting somehow to make the right deals with the right people." While that smoky back room approach had served him well in the clubby Senate when it came to passing legislation, it failed him completely during the nomination fight. Owing to the growth of mass media, the decline of big city machines outside of Mayor Richard Daley's Chicago, and changing political and cultural attitudes, presidential candidates were now expected to be out on the hustings, actively seeking votes and wooing delegates. As Doris Kearns Goodwin notes, "Johnson's experiences in the Senate might have been considerably more relevant in 1952 or even in 1956, when conventions were still the vast bargaining areas they had been since Andrew Jackson's time."[40] Kennedy intuitively grasped the change taking place; Johnson did not.

With victory in hand, Kennedy turned his attention to the task of selecting a running mate. And the more he thought about it, the more Johnson stood out as a preferred option. As a southerner and a Texan in particular, Johnson could shore up Kennedy's support below the Mason-Dixon Line, which had become shaky due to the Republican inroads made during the Eisenhower years. In point of fact, the Eisenhower-Nixon ticket had carried Louisiana, Florida, and electoral-rich Texas during the 1956 presidential election, thus breaking up the "Solid South" voting bloc the Democrats had enjoyed for almost a century. "If Texas did not go for the Democrats, they could not win the presidency," maintained Connecticut Democrat and future Kennedy cabinet member Abraham Ribicoff. "Johnson was the only one who could bring him something."[41]

The question left was whether Johnson actually wanted the number-two spot. The vice presidency as then constituted had all the makings of a political step down for the Texas lawmaker, in terms of the immense institutional power he was used to wielding as Senate Majority Leader. The position had no real authority and existed mainly for the purpose of having someone available to replace the president should he die or be removed from office. Former occupants like John Adams had famously called the post "the most insignificant office that ever the invention of man contrived," while John Nance Garner had denounced it as "a no man's land somewhere between the legislative and executive branch."[42] Though it may have seemed like a long shot at the time, Kennedy felt compelled out of pragmatic political considerations to make the offer anyway. In the unlikelihood that Johnson accepted, Kennedy would have a formidable running mate who strengthened him politically where he was at his weakest. If not, Kennedy could at least then be comforted with the knowledge that he had paid the proper respect due to one of the party's most influential figures.

Johnson did accept Kennedy's offer but not without considerable controversy. Organized labor and party liberals led by United Auto Workers president Walter Reuther and Americans for Democratic Action founder Joseph Rauh objected violently to Kennedy's choice. From their perspective, Johnson was too conservative and tied to "the old hack machine politicians" that Kennedy's candidacy implicitly seemed to be rejecting. Even close campaign advisors like Kenneth O'Donnell could not help but feel a little outraged. "This is the worst mistake you could have made," he told Kennedy. "You came here to this convention like a knight on a white charger, this clean-cut young Ivy League college guy. . . . And now in your first move after you get the nomination you go against all the people who supported you."[43]

Taken aback by this strong reaction, Kennedy tried to come up with a graceful way of backing out of his offer to Johnson. "We were afraid there would be a floor fight to prevent Johnson's nomination [as vice president]," Robert Kennedy said. "We didn't know whether he'd be willing to go through . . . all the acrimony again." Consistent with his role as the campaign's troubleshooter, Robert was given the unpleasant task of communicating to Johnson's camp his brother's change of heart. Things did not go well. Johnson became understandably hurt and confused over the news, especially since the message had been conveyed not by the nominee himself but by that "little shitass, Bobby."[44] More importantly, Johnson refused to give any indication that he was willing to step aside gracefully.

As to why Johnson was so insistent on this latter point, an appreciation of his underlying personal and political motives must be considered. Having served as Senate Majority Leader for close to a decade, Johnson had exhausted nearly all of his political capital. "Johnson felt he had lost control of the Senate," said journalist Eliot Janeway. "He had lost emotional control of the Senate. And he was very bitter against a good third of the Democratic caucus." The vice presidency then must have seemed like a welcomed soft landing, a place where Johnson could depart the Senate on his own terms without having to deal with the inevitable decline of his political authority. Besides, if the Democratic ticket won, he would be a heartbeat away from the presidency. As he confided to former congresswoman and ambassador Clare Booth Luce, "I looked it up: One out of every four presidents has died in office. I'm a gamblin' man, darlin,' and this is the only chance I got."[45]

The only problem was that Kennedy was not a gambling man, and he now was of the mind to drop Johnson from the ticket for being more political trouble than he was worth. For this reason, Robert Kennedy paid yet another visit to Johnson to try to convince him to make way for another less controversial VP choice, someone like Senator Stuart Symington of Missouri or Senator Henry "Scoop" Jackson of Washington. But shortly after Robert had made his unwelcomed pitch, his brother received a call from *Washington Post* publisher Phil Graham, who as "Lyndon's go-between man" wanted to know if the Democratic nominee really intended to drop Johnson. "Bobby's been out of touch and doesn't know what's going on," Kennedy tersely informed him. In other words, the vice presidency was still Johnson's if he so desired it. And he did, much to the chagrin of Robert Kennedy, who feared liberal and labor defections. "Today is my worst day," he said.[46]

So what happened? "The whole story will never be known," John Kennedy told press aide Pierre Salinger afterward. "And it's just as well that it won't be." What Kennedy meant by this mysterious comment is not entirely clear. But it is probable that in such a highly fluid situation, Kennedy came to a last-minute determination that he needed Johnson as a running mate, particularly if he had any hope of carrying Texas that November. Unfortunately, Robert Kennedy became the last to know of the switch, forever earning Johnson's enmity for supposedly being "the agent of an effort to destroy his political career." Not that Robert cared all that much what Johnson or anyone else associated with the campaign felt. "I'm not running a popularity contest," he explained. "It doesn't matter if people like me or not."[47]

With the vice presidency at last secured, Johnson flung himself into the general election campaign against the Republican presidential tandem of Richard Nixon and Henry Cabot Lodge Jr. with all his trademark energy and drive. Focusing on the south, where his political appeal was naturally considered the greatest, Johnson made a point of downplaying all his earlier criticisms of the Democratic nominee whom he had dismissed as an "inexperienced boy." "The primary thing was not selling himself but selling Jack Kennedy," said campaign supporter James Blundell. "His entire theme through the South was that you don't make an issue out of a man's religion. And he would always tell the story of Jack Kennedy's brother, Joe Junior, going down in that airplane with a copilot from New Braufels, Texas, and he said, 'I'm sure that they didn't ask each other what church they went to. They both died for their country.' He made a lot of points with that story."[48]

Johnson was also effective in rallying the support of wavering Democrats in the Senate who felt their party's presidential ticket was doomed with a Catholic receiving top billing. "I don't want you to feel sorry for me and Mr. Kennedy," LBJ told them. "If we [lose] the election in November, we surely aren't going to be out of work. But, gentlemen, how do you think you are going to get your favorite bills through the Senate, if Mr. Kennedy and I are sitting there solely because you didn't produce the votes that should have elected us?" Still, there were moments, such as on the triumphant eve of their historic victory, when Johnson's contained bitterness over his earlier convention loss bubbled over. "I hear you're losing Ohio, but *we're* doing fine in Pennsylvania," he informed Kennedy during an awkward phone conversation.[49]

As vice president, Johnson was about as content as a grizzly bear at a cotillion. He was utterly miserable. "I cannot stand Johnson's damn long face," Kennedy complained. "He just comes in, sits at the Cabinet meetings with his face all screwed up, never says anything. He looks so sad." Johnson could not help himself. As Senate Majority Leader he had made his political presence felt throughout the entire legislative process. But now in an era before powerful vice presidents like Dick Cheney in the 2000s, he found himself in a subordinate position where he was expected to keep his own counsel and leave all the tough decision making to the Commander in Chief. "One got the very clear impression of a man who was quite unhappy with his lot," said state department official George Ball. "Here is a man who was an activist, who was used to being at the center of power . . . who suddenly found himself with no power whatsoever." It was almost too much for Johnson's enormous ego to bear,

Figure 3.2.   Going for the big prize: LBJ campaigning with his wife Lady Bird at the Democratic National Convention in Los Angeles in 1960. Reproduction Number: LC-DIG-ppmsca-03127

especially since Kennedy had been a back-bencher in the Senate and therefore his political supplicant. "I spent years of my life when I could not get consideration for a bill until I went around and begged Johnson to let it go ahead," Kennedy acknowledged.[50]

To his credit, Johnson played the role of the good soldier, going out of his way not to bad-mouth the President to the press or to undermine his authority within administration circles, although he did once privately complain that the White House didn't know "any more about Capitol Hill than an old maid does about fuckin.'" All the same, it must have taken a supreme effort on his part to reign in his feelings of frustration and unhappiness. "Johnson showed great self-discipline and strength," said Secretary of State Dean Rusk. "I think it was a major effort of self-control to fit into that role—with all that volcanic force that was part of his very being."[51]

Those closest to Kennedy within the administration did not reciprocate. They treated Johnson with haughty disregard in spite of Kennedy's insistence that the flamboyant Texan be accorded full courtesy and respect for performing "the worst fucking job I can imagine." Indeed, to the Kenneth O'Donnells, John Kenneth Galbraiths, Arthur Schlesingers, and Robert McNamaras of the "inner circle," Johnson was "Uncle Cornpone," a crude, cartoonish figure with a thick southern drawl who was better left sight unseen and unheard in the sophisticated salons of Camelot. "They actually took pride in snubbing him," related Tip O'Neill. "No question about it," said Jack Valenti of the petty slights. "And I think that rankled [Johnson], it certainly hurt him, he was humiliated by it. Here he was the second most powerful man in the nation, and now he was treated like a school boy by school boys."[52]

Robert Kennedy was among the worst offenders, having never quite gotten over Johnson's nasty personal attacks on his brother and father during the nomination fight. He had no qualms about savagely reproaching the vice president behind his back. For in his accusatory frame of mind, Johnson was "mean, bitter, vicious—an animal in many ways." Unsurprisingly, Johnson took an equally antagonistic view of the president's brother, privately referring to him as "the little son-of-a-bitch." Yet Johnson was painfully aware to whom John Kennedy most deferred when push came to shove. "Every time they have a conference, don't kid anybody about who is the top adviser," he complained. "It isn't [Defense Secretary] McNamara, the chiefs of staff, or anybody else like that. Bobby is first in, last out. And Bobby is the boy he listens to."[53]

"[Johnson] was not happy about his treatment by Bobby," said Valenti, "because he thought Bobby put the word out to cut him out of [White House] meetings. And several times he got word back that meetings were held and he wasn't invited."[54]

In 1963 Johnson began to have serious doubts about whether he would remain on the Democratic ticket the following year. That's because his past close ties to the Secretary to the Senate Majority Leader Bobby Baker had suddenly become a major political liability. Baker, who also held the post of Secretary-Treasurer to the Democratic Senatorial Campaign Committee, had become ensnared in an unsavory influence-peddling scandal. "I was the man to whom people came when they wanted to cut a big deal, and I was the man who went to my powerful superiors to relay the offers," Baker later explained.[55] The South Carolinian eventually ended up serving time in a federal prison for his unethical behavior, but from the beginning Johnson sought to muddy the political waters by ludicrously insisting that he and his former top legislative aide were slight acquaintances.

Nobody in Washington's notoriously cynical corridors of power bought this explanation. "Bobby Baker was Lyndon's bluntest instrument in running the show the way he wanted it," claimed one Capitol Hill insider. Kennedy was thus put in a difficult spot. What if his credibility-stretching vice president was more directly involved in the Baker scandal than he was publicly letting on? Would this not sully the administration's otherwise solid reputation for probity among voters? Already details were about to emerge showing that Johnson had had some questionable business dealings with a known Baker associate over the years, suggesting a "petty payola" arrangement. If ever there was a more opportune time to dump Johnson, it was now. But Kennedy held back, reasoning that his ouster would be highly problematic for the Democratic ticket's reelection chances in 1964. "Why would I do a thing like that?" Kennedy asked his friend and journalist Charles Bartlett. "That would be absolutely crazy. It would tear up the relationship and hurt me in Texas."[56]

Ironically, Texas, more specifically Dallas's Dealey Plaza, was where Kennedy met his mortal end on November 22. The president had made the journey largely at the insistence of Johnson, who was trying at the time to referee an ugly political battle over federal patronage between rival state Democratic factions led by liberal US Senator Ralph Yarborough and conservative Governor John Connally. "The trip [was designed to] be a joint effort to conciliate the two factions," confirm Johnson biographers Irwin and Debi Unger. But an unforeseeable and violent chain of events made Johnson the 36th President of the United States. To say that he was prepared for this shockingly rapid transition of power would be giving Johnson too much credit. He had certainly wanted to be President but not under such tragic and emotionally draining circumstances. It took him some time to find his bearings. "I took the oath," Johnson later said. "I became president. But for millions of Americans I was still illegitimate, a naked man with no presidential covering, a pretender to the throne, an illegal usurper."[57]

For the balance of what would have been Kennedy's remaining term and the next four years following his landslide victory over Republican Barry Goldwater in the presidential election of 1964, Johnson did his best to erase this perceived "accidental president" image. He did so by pushing through Congress most of Kennedy's languishing New Frontier initiatives like tax reform and civil rights. "I think he felt sort of a personal responsibility to Kennedy to get his program through," said George Ball. "I think he deeply felt this, and he did it superbly. He did it much better than Kennedy could ever have done it." Encouraged by this legislative success, Johnson next unveiled the most ambitious domestic reform program since the New Deal: the Great Society. Designed to eliminate poverty, end racism, and create greater social and economic opportunity for all Americans, the Great Society was launched with considerable high hopes. "I saw it as a program of action to clear up an agenda of social reform as old as this century and to begin the urgent work of preparing the agenda of tomorrow," Johnson later said.[58]

While the Great Society achieved a number of noteworthy legislative milestones, including Medicare, Head Start, Medicaid, the Voting Rights Act, and federal loans to college students, the overall social and political thrust of the program eventually petered out due to rising financial costs, dogged conservative opposition, festering societal racial tensions, and the Vietnam War. Indeed, it was particularly on this last issue that Johnson found himself increasingly at odds with his predecessor's political heir apparent: Robert Kennedy. Although he had been an early supporter and architect of the war in his brother's administration, the now junior Senator from New York denounced the American-led fight as immoral and unwinnable by 1968. "We have sought to resolve by military might a conflict whose issue depends upon the will and conviction of the South Vietnamese people," Kennedy said. "It's like sending a lion to halt an epidemic of jungle rot."[59]

As the ultimate expression of his unhappiness with the war's direction, Kennedy announced that spring his intention to challenge Johnson for the Democratic nomination. For Johnson, who had just earlier come within a whisker of losing the New Hampshire primary to antiwar challenger Senator Eugene McCarthy of Minnesota, the decision represented a perfect political storm of sorts: the charismatic "Bobby" making his bid "to reclaim the [presidential] throne in the memory of his brother." Worn down by poor health and the burdens of office, Johnson soon after determined that he did not have either the heart, energy, or desire to continue on as president. "Accordingly," he told the nation in a terse television address on March 31, "I shall not seek, and will not accept, the nomination of my party for another term as your president." Kennedy, like everybody else, expressed surprise over the announcement. "I wonder if he would have done it if I hadn't come in," he mused.[60]

The answer to this question, of course, is unknowable, just as it is unknowable whether Kennedy would have been elected president in 1968. He was assassinated in Los Angeles on June 6, after winning the California Democratic primary. His death left Johnson with a torrid mix of emotions. As he later said, "It would have been hard on me to watch Bobby march to 'Hail to the Chief,' but I almost wish he had become President so the country could finally see a flesh-and-blood Kennedy grappling with the daily work of the Presidency and all the inevitable disappointments, instead of the storybook image of great heroes who, because they were dead, could make anything anyone wanted happen."[61]

Like most former presidents, Johnson used his final years trying to burnish the accomplishments of his administration. But he could never quite escape the long political shadow cast by John Kennedy. For thanks to the historic bond he had forged with his one-time political foe out of the white-hot crucible that was the 1960 Democratic nominating convention, Johnson was forever linked to Kennedy in public memory. Johnson eventually came around to accepting this fact when he told Robert Kennedy in their final White House meeting together on April 3 that he regarded his presidency as "carrying out the Kennedy-Johnson partnership."[62] To this statement, not even that "little shitass" could offer disagreement.

NOTES

1. John F. Kennedy Library Introductory Film.

2. *The Kennedys: The Early Years, 1900–1961*, video documentary, WGBH-Television, September 20, 1992.

3. Kenneth P. O'Donnell, and David F. Powers with Joe McCarthy, *Johnny, We Hardly Knew Ye: Memories of John F. Kennedy* (Boston, 1972) 100.

4. John F. Kennedy, interview, Ralph Martin Collection (hereinafter cited as RMC).

5. Roy Cohn, *McCarthy* (New York, 1968), 16; Penn T. Kimball, interview, Clay Blair Papers (hereinafter cited as CBP).

6. George Smathers Oral History, John F. Kennedy Library (hereinafter cited as JFKL).

7. *New York Post*, January 9, 1961.

8. Arthur Schlesinger Jr., *A Thousand Days: John F. Kennedy in the White House* (Boston, 1965), 12.

9. O'Donnell and Powers with McCarthy, *Johnny, We Hardly Knew Ye*, 128.

10. Thomas P. O'Neill with William Novak, *Man of the House: The Life and Political Memoirs of Speaker Thomas P. Tip O'Neill* (New York, 1987), 181; Horace Busby Oral History, Lyndon B. Johnson Library (hereinafter cited as LBJL), Austin, Texas.

11. Fletcher Knebel, "Pulitzer Prize Entry: John F. Kennedy," in *Candidates 1960: Behind the Headlines in the Presidential Race*, ed. Eric Sevareid (New York, 1959), 210.

12. Irwin Unger and Debi Unger, *LBJ: A Life* (New York, 1999), 7.

13. Merle Miller, *Lyndon: An Oral Biography* (New York, 1980), 11; Richard Harwood and Haynes Johnson, *Lyndon* (New York, 1973), 28.

14. Robert Dallek, *Lone Star Rising: Lyndon Johnson and His Times, 1908-1960* (New York, 1991), 78; Robert Caro, *The Path to Power: The Years of Lyndon Johnson* (New York, 1982), 169; Doris Kearns Goodwin, *Lyndon Johnson and the American Dream* (New York, 1991), 68.

15. Miller, *Lyndon: An Oral Biography*, 61.

16. Harwood and Johnson, *Lyndon*, 30; Goodwin, *Lyndon Johnson and the American Dream*, 82.

17. Robert Caro, *The Path to Power: The Years of Lyndon Johnson* (New York, 1982), 668; Horace Busby Oral History, JFKL; Harwood and Johnson, *Lyndon*, 36.

18. Miller, *Lyndon: An Oral Biography*, 78.

19. Ibid., 87.

20. Goodwin, *Lyndon Johnson and the American Dream*, 94.

21. Robert Caro, *Means of Ascent: The Years of Lyndon Johnson* (New York, 1990), 43; Unger and Unger, *LBJ: A Life*, 112; Caro, *Means of Ascent*, 49.

22. Kelly Shannon, "LBJ's 1948 Election Still Generates Interest," Associated Press, July 21, 2008; Goodwin, *Lyndon Johnson and the American Dream*, 100.

23. Bobby Baker with Larry King, *Wheeling and Dealing: Confessions of a Capitol Hill Operator* (New York, 1978), 40.

24. Miller, *Lyndon: An Oral Biography*, 171.

25. Rowland Evans and Robert Novak, *Lyndon Johnson: The Exercise of Power* (New York, 1966), 104.

26. Randell B. Woods, *LBJ: Architect of American Ambition* (New York, 2006), 330; Goodwin, *Lyndon Johnson and the American Dream*, 147.

27. Clark Clifford with Richard Holbrooke, *Counsel to the President: A Memoir* (New York, 1991), 304.

28. Ralph G. Martin, *A Hero for Our Time: An Intimate Story of the Kennedy Years* (New York, 1963) 205.

29. Geoffrey Perret, *Jack: A Life Like No Other* (New York, 2002), 248.

30. O'Donnell and Powers with McCarthy, *Johnny, We Hardly Knew Ye*, 160.

31. David Burner, *John F. Kennedy and a New Generation* (Boston, 1988), 48; Evan Thomas, *Robert Kennedy: His Life* (New York, 2000), 95; Michael O'Brien, *John F. Kennedy: A Biography* (New York, 2005), 453.

32. *Charleston Gazette*, May 10, 2010; Pierre Salinger, *P.S.: A Memoir* (New York, 1995), 76-77.

33. Woods, *LBJ: Architect of American Ambition*, 353; Martin, *A Hero for Our Time*, 155.

34. *New York Times*, July 6, 1960; Jack Valenti Oral History, JFKL.

35. Thomas, *Robert Kennedy: His Life*, 97; Peter Lisagnor Oral History, JFKL.

36. Martin, *A Hero for Our Time*, 158.

37. *New York Times*, July 13, 1969; Miller, *Lyndon: An Oral Biography*, 249.

38. Jack Valenti Oral History, JFKL.

39. Helen O'Donnell, *A Common Good: The Friendship of Robert F. Kennedy and Kenneth P. O'Donnell* (New York, 1998), 207.

40. Goodwin, *Lyndon Johnson and the American Dream*, 161.

41. Gerald S. Strober and Deborah H. Strober, *"Let Us Begin Anew": An Oral History of the Kennedy Presidency* (New York, 1993), 20.

42. Jack Shepherd, *The Adams Chronicles: Four Generations of Greatness* (Boston, 1975), 157; Patrick Cox, "John Nance Garner on the Vice Presidency-In Search of the Proverbial Bucket," The Center for American History, The University of Texas at Austin (www.cah.utexas.edu).

43. O'Donnell and Powers with McCarthy, *Johnny, We Hardly Knew Ye*, 192.

44. Dick Schaap, *R.F.K.* (New York, 1968), 84; James W. Hilty, *Robert Kennedy: Brother Protector* (Philadelphia, 1997), 162.

45. Dallek, *Lone Star Rising*, 577; Sally Bedell Smith, *Grace and Power: The Private World of the Kennedy White House* (New York, 2004), 15.

46. O'Donnell and Powers with McCarthy, *Johnny, We Hardly Knew Ye*, 196; Katherine Graham, *Personal History* (New York, 1998), 266; Thomas, *Robert Kennedy: His Life*, 98.

47. Salinger, *P.S.: A Memoir*, 81; Goodwin, *Lyndon Johnson and the American Dream*, 200; Schaap, *R.F.K.*, 85.

48. Woods, *LBJ: Architect of American Ambition*, 355; Miller, *Lyndon: An Oral Biography*, 267.

49. *Look*, May 9, 1961; *The Kennedy Wit: The Humor and Wisdom of John F. Kennedy* (New York, 1967), ed. Bill Adler, 84.

50. Unger and Unger, *LBJ*, 257; George Ball Oral History, LBJL; Schlesinger, *A Thousand Days*, 703–4.

51. Baker with King, *Wheeling and Dealing*, 133–34; Miller, *Lyndon: An Oral Biography*, 279.

52. Baker with King, *Wheeling and Dealing*, 116, 147; O'Neill with Novak, *Man of the House*, 183; Jack Valenti Oral History, JFKL.

53. *Robert Kennedy in His Own Words: The Unpublished Recollections of the Kennedy Years* (New York, 1988), ed. Edwin O. Guthman and Jeffrey Schulman, 417; Baker with King, *Wheeling and Dealing*, 136; Collier and Horowitz, *The Kennedys*, 289.

54. Jack Valenti Oral History, JFKL.

55. Baker with King, *Wheeling and Dealing*, 115.

56. *Life*, November 22, 1963; Unger and Unger, *LBJ*, 275; Martin, *A Hero for Our Time*, 527.

57. Unger and Unger, *LBJ*, 275; Goodwin, *Lyndon Johnson and the American Dream*, 170; Lyndon B. Johnson, *The Vantage Point: Perspectives of the Presidency, 1963-69* (New York, 1971), 104.

58. George Ball Oral History LBJL; Jules Witcover, *Party of the People: A History of the Democrats* (New York, 2003), 518.

59. Jeff Shesol, *Mutual Contempt: Lyndon Johnson, Robert Kennedy, and the Feud That Defined a Decade* (New York, 1997), 414.

60. Goodwin, *Lyndon Johnson and the American Dream*, 343; *New York Times*, April 1, 1968; Shesol, *Mutual Contempt*, 436.

61. Goodwin, *Lyndon Johnson and the American Dream*, 350.

62. Ted Sorensen, *Counselor: A Life at the Edge of History* (New York, 2009), 462.

FOUR

Looking like a Loser

Richard Nixon and the 1960 Presidential Campaign

On the November night John F. Kennedy beat Henry Cabot Lodge Jr. for the US Senate in 1952, the forty-three-year-old Democrat became distracted by something he had seen on the television set at his campaign headquarters. The jowl-faced Richard M. Nixon, the California grocer's son now turned vice-president-elect, flickered on the screen. "Imagine— he and I came into the Congress together and now he's Vice President of the United States," marveled Kennedy.[1]

He wasn't jealous. Rather, Kennedy respected and admired his contemporary's rapid ascent in political office. Indeed, the two Navy veterans had established a rapport if not a friendship since first arriving together as freshmen congressmen in Washington back in 1947. They both served on the House Education and Labor Committee and had to endure the vicissitudes of Congress's ancient seniority system. "Kennedy drew the shortest straw among the Democrats, and I drew the shortest straw among the Republicans," Nixon later explained. "As a result, he and I shared the dubious distinction of sitting at the opposite ends of the committee table, like a pair of unmatched bookends."[2]

On April 21, 1947, the two were tapped to present their parties' respective positions on the Taft-Hartley labor bill at a public meeting in McKeesport, Pennsylvania. Historians and writers would later dub this occasion the first Kennedy-Nixon debate, but real-time observers were struck by the "genuine friendliness" both participants displayed toward one another. "Neither could be called a stuffed shirt," the debate's moderator said. On the long overnight train ride back to Washington aboard the *Capital Limited*, Kennedy and Nixon drew lots to determine who would get the lower berth (Nixon won) and otherwise spent the time exchanging views on foreign policy. Kennedy would later think well enough of Nixon to invite him to his wedding in 1953, while Nixon similarly held Kennedy in such high stead that he could barely hold back tears when he learned his onetime bunkmate hovered near death following back surgery in 1954. "In those early years we saw ourselves as political opponents but not political rivals," Nixon wrote.[3]

The events of 1960 would change all that.

Heading into that year's presidential election, Nixon seemingly had everything going his way. Unlike Kennedy, Nixon did not have to fight through a series of bruising primaries to secure his party's nomination. His one major political challenger, Governor Nelson Rockefeller of New York, had agreed to step aside before the GOP National Convention in July after Nixon paid lip service to supporting a pair of issues near and dear to the liberal Republican's heart: higher spending on national defense and greater civil rights for African Americans. In addition to this, Nixon greatly benefited from having been in the national spotlight the previous eight years as Dwight Eisenhower's vice president. He had, in fact, earned universal praise for effectively subbing for Eisenhower in

Figure 4.1. Ring of champions. The Vice President and junior Massachusetts Senator meet heavyweight boxing legend Rocky Marciano years before their own epic political fight. JFK Library PC 807

Cabinet and National Security Council meetings when the president became temporarily incapacitated during a string of serious health scares, including a heart attack in 1955. According to White House speechwriter Emmet John Hughes, Nixon's "poised and restrained" handling of this difficult period easily ranked as "his finest official hour."[4]

Still, not everything was as rosy as it appeared. The nation's economy had plunged into a deep recession during Eisenhower's second term, and although there were signs of a recovery, the overall picture remained murky at best—hardly a selling point for someone representing the party in power. Even in the realm of foreign affairs, long considered a strong suit for the internationally minded Republican administration, things turned sour. A highly anticipated peace summit between the United States and the Soviet Union collapsed that spring in Paris when an American U-2 spy plane was shot down from the skies of central Russia during a routine military surveillance mission. The pilot, a CIA employee named Gary Francis Powers, publicly confessed and apologized for his role in the embarrassing affair shortly after his capture and interrogation by Soviet authorities.

As politically damaging as these events were, Nixon himself was confident in his ability to overcome them in the upcoming race against Kennedy. When he saw Kennedy deliver a less-than-rousing televised acceptance speech to delegates at the Democratic National Convention in Los Angeles on July 15, he could barely contain his glee. Nixon "decided that Jack Kennedy could be bested," Kennedy biographer Christopher Matthews concluded.[5]

He had not always possessed such driving confidence. The product of a religiously devout and poor Quaker family from Whittier, California, Nixon grew up insecure and unhappy in the late 1910s and 1920s. Along with his brothers Harold, Donald, Arthur, and Edward, he had to contend with economic hardship and a dysfunctional home life. His father, Frank Nixon, was an argumentative, quick-tempered man who owned a local "mom and pop" grocery and service station. He fought a daily battle for survival during the Great Depression. "The whole family worked the store," recounted Nixon, adding that he lived in constant dread of his father's frequent outbursts of verbal abuse and physical violence. His mother, the former Hannah Milhous, was by all accounts a kindly, thoughtful, and selfless woman who produced a calming effect on her volcanic husband. Of the two, however, Frank exerted the most lasting influence on his son, passing on what Nixon later characterized as "the will to keep fighting no matter what the odds."[6] A less generous interpretation is that he stressed the importance of winning at all costs.

Despite these rough beginnings and the tragic premature deaths of Arthur and Harold, who both succumbed to tuberculosis at the ages of seven and twenty-four, respectively, Nixon was able to excel in his studies as a teenager and become an accomplished debater. "He liked to argue about anything," confirmed a friend. "No matter what was discussed, he would take the opposite side just for the sake of argument. I remember once we went on a picnic in the mountains. We argued all the way back about which would be more useful to take with you into the wilds—a goat or a mule. Dick said a goat, and then argued in favor of a mule."[7]

With this ability, Nixon entertained hopes of attending an eastern college after high school, perhaps even Harvard or Yale. But his family's precarious financial situation foreclosed that possibility. "I had no choice but to live at home, and that meant that I would have to attend Whittier College," Nixon explained.[8] While lacking the prestige of an Ivy League school, the small, Quaker-run institution nevertheless offered a solid liberal arts education with small classes and a dedicated faculty. Nixon excelled in this intellectually challenging environment and earned a reputation for being an earnest scholar.

Yet he left his most lasting impression on his contemporaries in organizing the Orthogonians, a social club made up of scholarship boys like Nixon who resented being looked down upon by a "highbrow" rival student group known as the Franklins. "Franklins always wore black ties to school functions and when posing for photographers," noted Nixon biographer Earl Mazo. "The Orthogonians, most of whom couldn't afford evening clothes, adopted slouch sweaters and open, tieless collars as their trademark." Not unexpectedly, the laid-back Orthogonians became more popular than the straitlaced Franklins on campus and provided the basis of support for Nixon's eventual election as student body president. In the decades to follow, Nixon would time and again utilize this "Orthogonian resentment" to win public office.[9]

Upon graduation in 1934, Nixon moved on to Duke University Law School in Durham, North Carolina, where he made Law Review and lived up to his nickname "Gloomy Gus." "He never expected anything good to happen to him, or to anyone close to him, unless it was earned," said classmate Lyman Brownfield. "Any time someone started blowing rosy bubbles, you could count on Dick to burst them with a pin prick of reality."[10] Reality had its own cruel surprise in store for Nixon after he picked up his diploma. Confident that his high academic ranking would garner him a job at a top Wall Street firm, he was crushed to discover he had no offers.

At loose ends, he made the long trek home to Whittier, where he passed the California bar exam and joined a local law firm named Wingert and Bewley. There he worked on divorce and estate cases and began courting Pat Ryan, a prim and attractive high school teacher whom he married in 1940, and subsequently had two daughters, Tricia in 1946 and Julie in 1948. "Our life was happy and full of promise," Nixon recalled. But World War II soon shattered their domestic idyll as Nixon enlisted for naval duty and was assigned to the South Pacific in a noncombat role as a supply officer. Though he was popular with the men under his command, who affectionately called him Nick, he found the experience tedious and spent a considerable amount of his spare time playing poker, which he described as "an irresistible diversion." "It was a lonely war for most of the men . . . filled with seemingly interminable periods of waiting while the action unfolded thousands of miles away," he wrote.[11]

Following the service in 1946, Nixon returned to California, where he brushed aside thoughts of resuming his old Whittier law practice, opting instead for a career in politics. The decision did not come out of the blue. He had long relished the rough-and-tumble of the political arena, as evidenced by his spirited involvement with the Orthogonians as an undergraduate. He had even seriously entertained thoughts of running for the state assembly before the war. But he failed to act on this impulse for elected office until a unique opportunity arose in 1946, courtesy of a group of local Republican leaders calling themselves the Committee of 100. The committee's purpose was to recruit a challenger who could take on popular Democratic incumbent Jerry Voorhis in the 12th Congressional District, which was composed of Whittier and a sizable chunk of Los Angeles Valley.

Nixon, with his fine war record and strong local ties, appeared a good fit politically. The only question was whether he was indeed a Republican. On this particular score, Nixon was rather coy. "I guess I'm a Republican," he said when asked by one of the committeemen.[12] His lack of partisan zeal was understandable. Even though Nixon had voted for GOP presidential nominees Wendell Willkie and Thomas Dewey in 1940 and 1944, respectively, he had admired aspects of Franklin Roosevelt's New Deal domestic reform program in the 1930s. No matter. The committee identified him as the best man available to beat Voorhis. Their confidence in Nixon would not go unrewarded, as the newly minted Republican proceeded to bury Voorhis in the general election with 56 percent of the vote.

Nixon was able to pull off the victory by tapping into the Red Scare that had already begun to take hold throughout California and the rest of postwar America. He smeared his opponent, calling him a communist stooge, someone whose New Deal voting record was "more Socialistic and Communistic than Democratic." A pipe-smoking Yale graduate who lacked the stomach for such hardball politics, the mild-mannered Voorhis was simply no match for his younger, more aggressive opponent. And Nixon knew it. On the eve of the election, he arranged for campaign workers to anonymously call up voters in the district and tell them that "Jerry Voorhis is a communist." "I had been the Congressman 10 years," Voorhis recounted. "I'd done the best I could. And I really felt if the voters wanted to throw me out, by golly, okay. I'm afraid this was on my mind the whole time, to some extent. I hated a fight like that, especially because of its effect on my family."[13]

None of this angst registered with Nixon because he was too caught up in his own victory. "I had to win," he said afterward to a Voorhis supporter. "That's the thing you don't understand. The important thing is to win." [14] The hard life lessons of Frank Nixon had sunk in.

In Congress, Nixon quickly established himself as a gifted, driven legislator, supporting such Republican pet causes as restrictive labor legislation, tax cuts for the wealthy, elimination of rent control, and anticommunist loyalty probes of federal employees. Unlike John Kennedy, who kept irregular hours and often showed up for votes on the House floor in sneakers, Nixon exhibited a far more serious mien. He was meticulous, hardworking, demanding of his staff, and always focused on the task at hand. "He pushed himself hard, as all who worked for him were supposed to do," confirmed his office manager Bill Arnold.

Such grit and determination came in handy in 1948 when as a member of the House Un-American Activities Committee, Nixon faced what he later termed "the first major crisis of my political life." [15] At issue was an investigation he led of a former senior State Department official named Alger Hiss, who stood accused of passing classified government documents to the Soviets in the 1930s. The charge originated from Whittaker Chambers, a disheveled-looking *Time* magazine editor who claimed to have once been a courier in a domestic spy ring. Hiss, a former law clerk to Supreme Court Justice Oliver Wendell Holmes and president of the Carnegie Foundation for International Peace, denied the allegations under oath before a federal grand jury. But corroborating evidence produced by Chambers discredited Hiss's testimony, as Nixon was shown microfilm copies of confidential government documents taken from a hollowed-out pumpkin on Chambers' Maryland farm. Chambers explained that the "Pumpkin Papers" had been given to him by Hiss in the late 1930s to forward to Soviet agents. Unable to refute these allegations, Hiss was convicted of perjury, the statute of limitations having run out for an espionage charge, and sentenced to five years in prison. "By going forward with the investigation, I risked everything," Nixon asserted. "Failing would deal a severe setback to a promising political career." [16]

The Hiss case transformed the formerly obscure freshman congressman into a national celebrity. His picture, especially one in which he was shown using a Sherlock Holmes–style magnifying glass to examine a reel of microfilm from the Pumpkin Papers, was featured prominently in newspapers around the country. "But there was a downside," Nixon conceded. Since many media members had been initially skeptical of Hiss's guilt, Nixon claimed they did not appreciate his investigation proving them wrong. There is no question that Nixon began to feel he was being unfairly treated by the press. These feelings of persecution only intensified in the years ahead, when syndicated political cartoonist Herbert Block, aka Herblock, portrayed Nixon crawling out of a sewer like a rat. "Look what the press did to me—the Herblock cartoons and whatnot," raged Nixon to a friendly biographer near the end of his life.[17]

Nonetheless, not even Herblock could stop the forward momentum of Nixon's political career after the Hiss case. In 1950 he soundly trounced congresswoman and former Hollywood actress Helen Gahagan Douglas for a California US Senate seat. As in the earlier Voorhis race, Nixon unfairly questioned his opponent's commitment to democratic values, claiming she was a "pink lady." And while he later privately expressed regret for having portrayed the liberal-voting Douglas as a communist sympathizer, he publicly remained unrepentant about his ethically questionable tactics. "Helen Douglas lost the election because the voters of California in 1950 were not prepared to elect as their senator anyone they perceived as being soft on or naïve about communism," he wrote in his memoirs.[18] Douglas did achieve a moral victory of sorts. During the course of the campaign she began referring to Nixon as "Tricky Dick," a moniker that would dog him the rest of his career.

In 1952 Dwight Eisenhower tapped Nixon to be his vice presidential running mate in an effort to bolster his support among conservative Old Guard elements within the GOP. As the man who brought Hiss to justice, Nixon seemed the perfect choice for the former Supreme Allied Commander, whose candidacy for the White House had been opposed by many Republican Old Guarders as being too liberal. Ike described Nixon as a leader "who has a special talent and ability to ferret out any kind of subversive influence wherever it may be found and the strength and persistence to get rid of it." At least one of Nixon's congressional colleagues could not help gushing over his good fortune. "I was always convinced that you would move ahead to the top—but I never thought it would come this quickly," wrote John Kennedy in a warm letter of congratulation. "You were an ideal selection and will bring to the ticket a great deal of strength."[19]

Nixon had helped grease the skids for his own selection by sabotaging the dark-horse presidential candidacy of California governor Earl Warren. Pretending to be a loyal member of Warren's delegation at the Republican nominating convention in Chicago, Nixon obligingly fed the Eisenhower campaign political intelligence about the future Supreme Court Chief Justice's overall strategy. "Nixon's machinations revealed him to be a shrewd politician who maximized his opportunity to achieve high national office at a young age," notes the historian Lewis L. Gould. But "[t]he scars that he left among the California Republicans loyal to Warren would soon lead to the major crisis of the 1952 Republican presidential race."[20]

These same disgruntled Warren supporters tipped off the media that Nixon had engaged in an alleged personal impropriety involving an eighteen-thousand-dollar expense fund drawn from political supporters. Eisenhower, who was making a big campaign issue out of the number of high-profile corruption scandals during the Truman administration, was mortified by the news. He even gave serious thought to dumping Nixon, claiming his younger understudy had to be "as clean as a hound's tooth."[21] The pressure built on Nixon to pull a proverbial rabbit out of his hat to save his floundering vice presidential candidacy. Amazingly, he did it.

Addressing the charge that he accepted illegal cash contributions, Nixon told a national television audience that he was innocent of any wrongdoing. In fact, he said, the only unsolicited gift he received was a little cocker spaniel dog his six-year-old daughter Tricia named Checkers. "And you know the kids, like all kids, love the dog and I just want to say this right now, that regardless of what they say about it, we're gonna keep it." Public response to the so-called Checkers speech was overwhelmingly positive, thus preserving the Republican's place on the ticket. Observed the *Christian Science Monitor*, "No other medium could have registered, pictured, relayed, and implanted the drama of Senator Richard M. Nixon's appeal and self-defense as television did."[22]

With the former Orthogonian securely on board, the Eisenhower-Nixon presidential express easily steamrolled to victory over the Democratic ticket of Illinois Governor Adlai Stevenson and Alabama Senator John Sparkman that November. Now vice president, Nixon would earn the dubious distinction of being Ike's hatchet man, the one administration figure always counted on to make a fiery partisan speech or to do the political dirty work. While the role was something he initially relished, especially when he got to attack Democratic stalwarts like Harry Truman and Dean Acheson, whom he once claimed to be "primarily responsible for the unimpeded growth of the Communist conspiracy within the United States," he grew weary of it as time went on. "I'm tired, bone tired," he said. "My heart's not in it."[23]

Making the situation even more complicated was the fact that Eisenhower had an uneasy personal relationship with his second in command. "They were never pals; they were of such different ages and backgrounds," said former Republican attorney general Herbert Brownell. "Eisenhower was quite formal in all his relationships with political associates." Nevertheless, Nixon did not appreciate the perceived offhand manner in which he was being treated, once complaining, "Do you know he's never asked me into that house yet?" Nixon would be given even greater reason to be upset as the 1956 election approached. Coming to the conclusion that Nixon was not "Presidential timber," Eisenhower sought to dump him from the ticket and put him in a Cabinet post. "He said it was too bad that my popularity had not grown more during the last three years," Nixon remembered bitterly. But Nixon surprised his boss by holding his ground and refusing to go quietly. If Ike wanted to get rid of him, he signaled, then there would be political ramifications for the president within the GOP, especially among Old Guard conservatives. Unwilling to run the risk of splitting the party in a reelection year, Eisenhower backed down.[24]

Ever the political survivor, Nixon had dodged yet another bullet. But his luck would run out four years later when he squared off against John Kennedy for the presidency. Never before and never again would he face such a formidable opponent. "I considered Kennedy's biggest assets to be his wealth and the appeal of his personal style," Nixon assessed. "Some Republican strategists thought that these would weigh against him, but I felt in the new decade of the sixties, after eight years of Eisenhower's rather grandfatherly manner, people might be ready for an entirely new style of presidential leadership."[25]

Nixon did not do himself any favors coming out of the gate by selecting Henry Cabot Lodge Jr. as his running mate. While he had instant name recognition among voters, owing to his lengthy years of service as US Senator and UN ambassador, Lodge could not realistically be expected to deliver a key swing state like his Democratic vice-presidential counterpart. That's because Lyndon Johnson could make the difference in his native Texas, whereas Lodge could not hope to do the same in Massachusetts with Kennedy's record level of popularity there. But Nixon had his reasons for going this curious route.

Seeking someone who could draw attention to international issues, a perceived GOP strength, the Republican nominee believed Lodge made an exceptionally fine choice. "If you ever let [the Democrats] campaign only on domestic issues, they'll beat us—our only hope is to keep it on foreign policy," he said. Forgotten was the disappointment of Lodge's 1952 Senate defeat. "People's minds are short and all that they recall about Cabot is that for eight years he has been on television speaking out against the likes of [Soviet foreign minister Andrei] Gromyko, etc.," Nixon explained. For Lodge's part, he left no doubt as to whom he owed this new honor. "If I hadn't lost to Jack [Kennedy]," he said, "I never would have had eight years in the U.N., and I might not be running for Vice President."[26]

Regardless of whom Nixon chose as his running mate, Kennedy was determined to be on the offensive throughout the campaign. Taking a page from his 1952 playbook, he accused Nixon and by extension the Eisenhower administration of lying down before the onslaught of international communism. "In the election of 1860," he thundered, "Abraham Lincoln said the question is whether this nation could exist half slave or half free. In the election of 1960, and with the world around us, the question is whether the world can exist half slave or half free, whether it will move in the direction we are taking, or whether it will move in the direction of slavery."[27]

If this wasn't bad enough, he said, the Republican administration had acquiesced to the Soviets by letting them set up a puppet communist regime in Cuba, just ninety miles south of Florida. Yet there was more at

stake than mere strategic advantage. "This is not a struggle for supremacy of arms alone," Kennedy pointed out. "It is also a struggle for supremacy between two conflicting ideologies: freedom under God versus
ruthless, godless tyranny."[28]

Nixon was completely thrown off balance by this line of attack, as it
was precisely the kind of hardline anticommunism he had used so effectively against his political opponents in the past. The difference this time
around was that he was playing the thankless role of the "pink lady." He
never really recovered. "I don't mean to suggest that I was not perfectly
willing to defend the record of the Administration of which I had been a
part," Nixon later groused. "But I knew from long experience that in
debate, the man who can attack has a built-in advantage that is very hard
to overcome. Almost automatically, he has the initiative and is the ag-
gressor."[29]

As they had throughout the primaries and into the Democratic nominating convention, the Kennedy family played a prominent role in the
campaign. Robert Kennedy continued to man the controls as campaign
manager, while Joseph P. Kennedy worked behind the scenes paying the
bills, hiring consultants, and lining up the support of Democratic bosses
in key states. The rest of the clan, including the radiant Jacqueline Bouvier Kennedy, who was nearing the end of her third pregnancy, did their
part by attending rallies, delivering speeches, holding teas, shaking
hands, and making themselves available for television and newspaper
interviews. As campaign organizer and best-selling novelist James A.
Michener put it, "They were potent campaigners and lent our whole
operation a class it would not otherwise have attained. People wanted to
see them, hoping, I suspect, that they would prove to be harpies whom
they could dislike, but when they found them to be normal, good-looking
young American married women, the audiences took them to their
hearts. The girls were amazing workers, appearing at three to six meetings each day, dispensing charm and warmth each time." Nixon, by comparison, with his smaller and less glamorous family could not compete.
Years later when he was leaving the White House in disgrace on the heels
of the Watergate scandal, Nixon made a bitter reference to this fact. Rose
Kennedy had just come out with a highly anticipated personal memoir of
her years as matriarch of the most famous political clan in America. "Nobody will ever write a book, probably, about my mother," Nixon said.[30]

The turning point in the campaign, however, came during the first of
four televised debates before a nationwide audience of seventy million
on the night of September 26. Against the advice of Eisenhower, who saw
no tangible political benefit for his vice president to be debating the less-
er-known but telegenic Massachusetts Senator, Nixon had warily agreed
to take on Kennedy. "I knew the debates would benefit Kennedy more
than me by giving his views national exposure, which he needed more
than I did," Nixon later confessed. "But there was no way I could refuse

to debate without having Kennedy and the media turn my refusal into a central campaign issue." Top Eisenhower aide Emmet John Hughes detected another motive behind Nixon's decision. The previous year, Nixon had traveled to Moscow, where he scored a major public relations victory over Soviet dictator Nikita Khrushchev during their famed "kitchen debate" at the American Exhibition. Nixon had stood firm then and lectured a clearly perturbed Khrushchev on putting aside his demonstrated bellicosity against the West in favor of peaceful coexistence. "Such success encouraged him confidently to leave a large part of his political fate to a like encounter on the more familiar soil of the United States," Hughes wrote. "And so a most incongruous fate was reserved for the man whose political fame rested upon his passionate combat with all whom he viewed as agents of Soviet Communism: to triumph in Moscow—and to blanch in Chicago."[31]

And blanch he did in that first debate. Looking tan, fit, and robust, Kennedy simply outperformed Nixon, who was still showing the effects of a painful infection that had caused him to be hospitalized several days prior with a 102-degree temperature. "My God! They've embalmed him before he even died," exclaimed Chicago Mayor Richard Daley, who was in the studio control room to monitor the proceedings. "It didn't really come down to the better man," television producer and debate coordinator Don Hewitt later concluded. "It came down to the better performer. The matinee idol won."[32] People listening to the debate over the radio felt that Nixon had clearly bested his Democratic challenger in terms of the substantive points he made on issues ranging from US-Soviet relations to the reduction of the federal debt.

Yet the unforgiving glare of the "electric mirror" was not interested in substance, only style. And in this all-important category Kennedy excelled, as his inviting smile, handsome face, and smooth delivery made him appear the more presidential of the two candidates. "He spoke with rapidity and force," Michener wrote. "Along with seventy million other Americans, I sat up." Nixon, by comparison, looked like a grotesque caricature of a backroom politician with his heavy jowls, five o'clock shadow, shifty eyes, and sweaty upper lip. "He seemed like a ghost," Michener observed. "I doubt if any other viewer in the nation was as astonished by the complete collapse of a public figure as I was." Watching his running mate's disastrous showing on television with increasing irritation, Henry Cabot Lodge exclaimed, "That son of a bitch just lost the election."[33]

In truth, Lodge's own lackluster efforts did nothing to endear voters to the GOP ticket, which only served to further bring into question Nixon's judgment in selecting him as his running mate in the first place. Refusing to campaign around the clock as Kennedy and Nixon did, Lodge instead opted for an hour of sleep after lunch each day. This laid-back approach did not sit well with anxious local campaign chairmen.

"We didn't mind him having a nap in the afternoon," complained one hardened Republican veteran, "but why did he have to put on his pajamas?" In his own defense, Lodge argued that he needed the rest to maintain his energy level for the demanding campaign schedule he kept. "There are really two essential things in campaigning," he explained. "First, you must be in good humor. If you're going to be irascible, you ought to stay home. Second, you ought to make sense in your speeches. These are two things you must do. Unless you're a saint, you can't be in good humor when you're exhausted."[34]

Fear of personal fatigue was not the only concern facing Lodge during these hectic days. In early October he told a Harlem rally that the GOP ticket was committed to placing "a Negro in the Cabinet." The only problem was that he had failed to clear his remarks in advance with his running mate or any official at the Republican National Committee. "It hurt us in the South unquestionably," Nixon later claimed. "And it did us no good in the North. To Negroes as well as other voters it appeared to be a crude attempt to woo the support of Negroes without regard to the qualifications an individual might have for high office—something that Lodge had never remotely intended to suggest."[35]

Nixon did not exactly acquit himself well with black voters either. In late October, Kennedy had been persuaded by his liberal advisors Sargent Shriver and Harris Wofford to make a spur-of-the-moment phone call to Coretta Scott King and offer his sympathy when her high-profile husband, civil rights leader Dr. Martin Luther King Jr., was thrown into a Georgia prison cell on trumped-up charges. "I want to express to you my concern about your husband," he said. "I know it must be very hard for you . . . and I just want you to know that I was thinking about you and Dr. King." "It showed he had compassion," Shriver later said. "It showed he had feeling. It showed he had heart. Nowadays that's nothing to say, but in those days that meant a lot because for black people, if you show you had heart, that was a huge difference." Robert Kennedy followed up his brother's phone call by personally contacting the presiding judge in the case and securing King's release on bond. "It grilled me," Kennedy told campaign aide John Seigenthaler afterward. "The more I thought about the injustice of it, the more I thought what a son of a bitch the judge was."[36]

In contrast, Nixon remained conspicuously silent throughout the entire affair, having his press secretary Herb Klein issue an official "no comment" to reporters. Nixon later claimed that he felt every bit as morally outraged by King's arrest as his opponent but that it would have been "completely improper of me or any other lawyer to call the judge [as Robert Kennedy did]." Nixon did privately approach Attorney General William Rogers about the possibility of using federal action to free King, but the White House rejected the idea, leaving the candidate to ponder the political might-have-beens. "The ironic part . . . is that well-informed

Washington observers knew that I had been one of the most consistent and effective proponents of civil rights legislation in the [Eisenhower] Administration," Nixon lamented.[37]

Nixon had been a strong backer of the landmark Civil Rights Act of 1957 that strengthened voting rights for blacks and could count among his loyal political supporters such a pioneering integrationist as former Brooklyn Dodgers baseball star Jackie Robinson. He had also hit it off personally with King when they first met in his vice-presidential office in 1957. "[Nixon] has one of the most magnetic personalities that I have ever confronted," King said afterward. But all that was forgotten now in the wake of Kennedy's dramatic gesture. Remembered King, "I always felt that Nixon lost a real opportunity to express . . . support of something much larger than the individual, because this expressed support of the movement for civil rights in a way. And I had known Nixon longer [than Kennedy]. He had been supposedly close to me, and he would call me frequently about things, getting, seeking advice. And yet, when this moment came, it was like he had never heard of me, you see. So this is why I really considered him a moral coward and one who was really unwilling to make a courageous step and take a risk."[38]

All of these political missteps notwithstanding, Nixon still appeared to have two unmistakable advantages entering the critical final stages of the campaign: Kennedy's religion and Eisenhower's popularity. Many Protestant voters were continuing to voice the concern that a Catholic president might be unduly influenced by the pope or other high church officials. "The religion issue permeated every meeting I conducted," said James Michener, who was chairman of a Kennedy for President committee in Bucks County, Pennsylvania. "It influenced Republicans and Democrats alike. Ministers preached politics publicly and churches distributed the most vicious electioneering materials."[39] Truth be told, Nixon went out of his way to promote this kind of intolerant attitude by quietly working behind the scenes with the country's most admired and popular Protestant preacher: the Reverend Billy Graham.

A longtime personal friend and supporter of Nixon, Graham had no desire to see a Catholic sitting in the White House, much less Kennedy, for whom he did not hold an especially high personal regard. But realizing, as Nixon did, that to state such a view in public would invite charges of bigotry, Graham chose to launch his religious-based attacks from the shadows. He helped recruit "an all-star roster of clergy to plan, fund, and execute a strategy to raise the religion issue across the country on Nixon's behalf without directly endorsing Nixon," noted the historian Shaun A. Casey in his groundbreaking study of the campaign.[40]

When these clandestine efforts failed to produce the kind of anti-Kennedy fervor he had initially hoped for, Graham decided to up the political ante and release a glowing testament to Nixon's religious character in the pages of *Life* magazine just two weeks prior to Election Day. The article would have been nothing short of a formal political endorsement of Nixon by the charismatic evangelical had it gone forward. But Kennedy had been tipped off by *Life* publisher Henry Luce beforehand, and he persuaded the conservative opinion maker to kill the piece at press time. His father's close personal friendship with Luce over the years had no doubt played a decisive role here. What eventually ran in the article's place was a relatively bland Graham write-up urging Christians of all political stripes to get out to vote for the candidates of their choice. "I believe both the Old and the New Testament Scriptures plainly teach that we have a responsibility as citizens to participate in good government," Graham wrote.[41]

Still, the not-so-impartial shepherd could not resist getting in one final dig, warning the electorate against choosing someone solely on the basis of their good looks or charming personality. The intended personal reference to Kennedy was obvious, but the candidate never appeared to give such attacks any serious mind. "The Kennedy attitude was that you take that stuff in stride; you assume that it is going to happen; you get mad if you see real evidence of it; but you have to live with it," aide Ralph Dungan noted. "He was extremely pragmatic in things like that."[42]

This brand of steely pragmatism had already led Kennedy to confront on September 12 the popular fears engendered by his religious faith when he addressed the Greater Houston Ministerial Association, an influential Protestant group that had been openly hostile to the idea of a Catholic president. "I believe in an America," he told the clergymen, "where the separation of church and state is absolute—where no Catholic prelate would tell the President, should he be a Catholic, how to act, and no Protestant minister would tell his parishioners for whom to vote." He added that this was the kind of America he went off to fight for in the South Pacific during World War II and the one his brother gave up his life for in Europe. A virtuoso performance, Kennedy's talk appeared on the surface to allay Protestant concerns about where his true loyalties lay. "Martin Luther himself would have welcomed Senator Kennedy and cheered him," assessed a Lutheran minister in attendance. "By God, look at him—and listen to him!" exclaimed elderly Texas power broker Sam Rayburn as he watched the event on television. "He's eating 'em blood raw! This young feller will be a great President."[43]

Not everyone in the Kennedy camp came away as optimistic. "He made an excellent presentation, one that would have impressed any fair-minded person, but I suspected the majority of the people who were upset about the religious issue were not fair-minded and were not going to be swayed by even the most rational statement by the candidate," Kennedy campaign strategist Larry O'Brien later wrote. Robert Kennedy concurred with this sentiment—up to a point. "I think the speech in Houston . . . was an extremely important event," he said. "It didn't destroy the problem we were having, but it did dilute a good deal of the

Figure 4.2.   Nixon mixes it up with Soviet leader Nikita Khrushchev during their famed "Kitchen Debate" in 1959.

opposition. Although ultimately the fact that he was a Catholic certainly cost him a great number of votes for him, the meeting with the ministers in Houston was very important." [44]

As for Eisenhower's continued high standing among American voters, Nixon did his best to exploit the situation. He presented himself as Ike's deserving heir who would lead the country into another decade of peace and prosperity. "Experience Counts," proclaimed his campaign posters. Yet Nixon managed to garble his own message during the first televised debate with Kennedy by appearing to question the wisdom of the president's policies. "The things that Senator Kennedy has said many of us can agree with," conceded Nixon after his opponent spent most of his opening remarks excoriating the Eisenhower administration for not doing enough to keep up with the Soviet Union economically or militarily. Eisenhower, who contemptuously viewed Kennedy as "the young whipper snapper," found it difficult to mask his disappointment afterward. He admonished Nixon to "not appear to be quite so glib, to ponder and appear to think about something before answering a question." [45]

Privately, Eisenhower still harbored strong doubts about Nixon's suitability for the Oval Office, but given how the 1960 election had shaped up to be a referendum on his own presidency, he was willing and eager for the opportunity to strike back at Kennedy's attacks. Unfortunately, he had earlier hurt his side's cause when he told a reporter during a televised press conference that he could not recall any "big decision" Nixon had participated in during his administration. "If you give me a week, I might think of one," he commented. "I don't remember." "Eisenhower had meant, 'Ask me at next week's conference'—but he immediately knew that it had come out wrong, and he called that afternoon to express his regret," Nixon later wrote. "The Democrats leaped on Eisenhower's slip to undercut my emphasis on experience and to imply that Eisenhower was less than enthusiastic about my candidacy." The Kennedy campaign ran television attack ads replaying Eisenhower's now-famous remarks along with this devastating voiceover tag line: "President Eisenhower could not remember, but the voters will remember. For real leadership in the sixties, help elect Senator John F. Kennedy president."[46]

To make up for this embarrassing gaffe, Eisenhower offered to barnstorm around the country on Nixon's behalf during the crucial stretch drive of the campaign. But Nixon could not accept his offer. His wife Pat had received an emotional phone call from First Lady Mamie Eisenhower asking that Nixon drop any stepped-up plans he had to use Eisenhower on the campaign trail. "She reminded Pat that Ike was 70 years old," recalled Nixon's daughter Julie Nixon Eisenhower, who married Eisenhower's grandson David in 1968. "He was not well . . . and his blood pressure simply could not withstand the pressure of campaigning." Mamie told Pat she did not want Ike to ever learn she had called.[47]

Honoring her request, Nixon tried to break the news to Eisenhower without revealing the real reason behind the move. It did not go well. "He was confused—to put it mildly—when I opened the discussion with half a dozen rather lame reasons for his not carrying out the expanded itinerary," Nixon remembered nearly two decades later. "At first he was hurt and then he was angry. But I stood my ground and insisted that he should limit himself to the original schedule and to the election eve telecast with Lodge and me."[48] Eisenhower reluctantly agreed with this line of reasoning, but their relationship, never exactly warm and fuzzy to begin with, would never be the same.

But Nixon had an even greater problem to contend with as Election Day approached. Thanks to the investigative reporting of syndicated newspaper columnist Drew Pearson, Nixon was forced to publicly admit that his younger brother Donald had received a $205,000 loan from billionaire industrialist Howard Hughes back in 1956 after the former's struggling restaurant business had run him into severe financial difficulty. Hughes, who had a well-earned reputation for purchasing influence in high circles, had been only too willing to provide a helping hand. "I want the Nixons to have the money," he reportedly said upon granting the loan. And who could blame him. Shortly after bailing out Donald, Hughes received favorable federal action on a defense contract he had been seeking, in addition to securing long-sought-after tax-exempt status for the Howard Hughes Medical Institute in Chevy Chase, Maryland, which reportedly netted him millions.[49]

The appearance of impropriety could not have been greater, although no direct proof ever surfaced of a formal quid pro quo. Even so, the political damage had been done. Eight years after the messy Checkers affair, Nixon once again found himself fending off charges he had abused his public office. The Kennedy campaign could not have been more delighted. Robert Kennedy even let slip publicly afterward that he felt the Hughes revelation damaged Nixon's candidacy. Whether his older brother shared these sentiments is unknown, but it is clear that John Kennedy's opinion of his old congressional colleague had fallen precipitously since the start of the race. "When I first began this campaign," he confided to campaign advisor and noted Harvard economist John Kenneth Galbraith, "I just wanted to beat Nixon. Now I want to save the country from him."[50]

It was Nixon who needed saving—from himself. Unwilling to delegate authority when it came to the day-to-day running of his campaign, the control-obsessed candidate tried to do everything himself. The results were neither impressive nor pretty. Disorganized and nearly spent physically, Nixon did not so much sprint to the finish line as stagger. He wasted a good portion of a day campaigning in Alaska the weekend before Election Day, an electoral-poor state that was projected to be firmly in the Kennedy column anyway. But he felt he had no choice, given he had earlier promised to campaign in all fifty states. "I was determined to keep my commitment," Nixon explained. While he surprised nearly everyone by carrying Alaska, he would have been better off using the time to seal the deal in places like Illinois and Texas, key battleground states that ultimately decided the contest. Typically, Eisenhower was spot-on in his analysis of Nixon during these final hectic days. "Goddammit, he looks like a loser," he said.[51]

Kennedy, meanwhile, projected the image of a confident winner, and it showed on election night when he went to bed at his Hyannis Port, Massachusetts, home before learning the outcome of what was the closest presidential race of the twentieth century. When old friend Dave Powers inquired how he could possibly go to sleep with so much still in doubt, Kennedy coolly replied, "Because it's too late to change a vote." Powers need not have worried. Kennedy managed to eke out a victory over Nixon by less than 1 percent of the popular vote. While his electoral college margin was more impressive, 303-219, it was also deceptive. If Kennedy had lost Illinois and Texas, states he carried by the slimmest of margins, Nixon would have emerged as the winner. As it was, there was considerable doubt whether he in fact won those states, especially Illinois, where Chicago mayor Richard Daley's Cook County political machine was operating in high gear. Charges of voting fraud were rampant. "Nixon had to decide whether to contest the results," Herbert Klein said.

"We talked about it, and Nixon decided that it would disrupt the country too much were he to contest, and that it would take a long time, and leave the country in turmoil." On top of that, Nixon fretted that he would be seen as a "sore loser," and that appellation "would follow me through history and remove the possibility of a further political career."[52]

So Nixon conceded, thereby bringing the curtain down on the worst defeat of his political life. As for the belief that Mayor Daley, who cryptically called Kennedy on election night to reassure him "with a little bit of luck and the help of a few close friends, you're going to carry Illinois," had stolen the election, such speculation overlooks the fact that even with the Prairie State in his pocket, Nixon would still have needed Texas to secure the needed electoral majority to win.[53] All things considered, Nixon lost because he was unable to convince voters that he would be the man best suited to stand up to Khrushchev. Indeed, from his hard-hitting attacks on the Eisenhower administration's alleged mishandling of the international communist threat to his sterling televised debate performance, Kennedy better demonstrated that he possessed the strength, clarity of mind, and vision to prevail in the Cold War. Add to this his obvious appeal to Catholic voters (he captured 80 percent of their vote) and his outreach to Dr. Martin Luther King Jr., which helped him secure the overwhelming support of African Americans in important swing states he carried like Illinois, South Carolina, Michigan, and New Jersey, Kennedy undeniably had the winning hand, albeit barely.

In spite of the crushing loss, Nixon was not finished with politics. In 1962 he decided to take on popular incumbent Democrat Edmund G. "Pat" Brown for the governorship of California. It was a bid to keep his name alive on the national political scene, and it was a huge mistake. Having spent most of the previous decade in Washington concentrating on pressing domestic and international issues, the now-former Vice President appeared ill-suited for the more mundane task of state governance. He vowed to "clean up the mess in Sacramento," but this charge rang hollow as Brown ran a relatively competent and scandal-free administration.[54]

If this wasn't bad enough, Nixon was hamstrung by his continued insistence on doing everything himself. "The man didn't take advice very well," remembered *Sacramento Bee* editor Richard Bergholz. "I knew someone who was in the campaign who told me of the time Nixon was in a cab and this fellow said, 'Why don't you go by the McClatchy newspaper and talk to them?' Nixon said, 'I wouldn't give them the sweat off my balls.' This is a local paper, so instead of Nixon asking him: What should I tell them? [H]e says this."[55]

Taking advantage of his old foe's political stumbling, Kennedy made a point of personally stumping for Brown in California. He also had operatives like the notorious political gamesman Dick Tuck remind voters of the controversial Hughes loan that Nixon still had difficulty addressing. "I have made mistakes," the candidate conceded, "but I am an honest man." Honest or not, Nixon could do nothing about the impact the Cuban Missile Crisis had on the final days of the campaign. Kennedy's successful resolution of this turning point in the Cold War between the US and the Soviet Union gave a big boost to Democratic candidates around the country, including Brown. "We lost the election," a dejected Nixon told his aide Bob Haldeman. The final electoral tally confirmed Nixon's worst fears as he went down to defeat in a landslide.[56]

Humiliated by the outcome, Nixon initially tried to be philosophical about the loss. "Losing California after losing the Presidency—well, it's like being bitten by a mosquito after being bitten by a rattlesnake," he told his closest staffers. But this even-tempered approach evaporated when Nixon met with reporters for an election postmortem. Years of pent-up anger and bitterness over how he felt he had been mistreated by the press at last boiled over. "You won't have Nixon to kick around anymore, because, gentlemen, this is my last press conference and it will be one in which I have welcomed the opportunity to test wits with you," he snarled.[57]

Kennedy could not help but be amused by this wantonly self-destructive behavior. "I must remember to smile when I get defeated," he told *Washington Star* reporter Mary McGrory afterward. Others were less glib. *New York Times* columnist James Reston declared Nixon politically dead while speculating that his public legacy would be "left to the historians and psychological novelists." A victorious Brown was even less judicious, privately characterizing Nixon to Kennedy as "a very peculiar fellow." "I really think that he is a psycho. He's an able man, but he's nuts!"[58]

Nixon remained unrepentant. "I received thousands of letters and wires from friends and supporters across the country who said they were glad that someone finally had the guts to tell the press off," he later claimed.[59] With the political wounds from his most recent defeat still fresh, he decided to relocate his family to New York City, where he thrived for several years as a corporate attorney.

It was on the streets of Manhattan that Nixon first learned that Kennedy had been gunned down in Dallas on November 22, 1963. "While the hand of fate made Jack and me political opponents," he wrote Jacqueline Kennedy in a moving letter of condolence on November 23, "I always cherished the fact that we were personal friends from the time we came to the Congress together in 1947." In reply, the emotionally shattered widow took the time to thank Nixon for his thoughtfulness and to wish him well if he chose to pursue "the greatest prize" again. "Just one thing I would say to you—if it does not work out for you as you hoped for so long—please by consoled by what you already have—your life and your family."[60]

Nixon did attain the presidency in 1968 after another close, nail-biter of a campaign. But this time around he had the far less formidable Hubert H. Humphrey as an opponent. Still, not even the ultimate victory could erase the scars left over from 1960. Nixon was determined never to be outdone again by what he later called "the most ruthless group of political operators ever mobilized for a presidential campaign." He established a clandestine political surveillance and espionage unit within the White House known as the "Plumbers," which targeted Nixon's domestic political enemies, most especially his likely Democratic opponent for his successful reelection bid in 1972. The operation culminated in the Watergate scandal, which forced Nixon to resign from office in disgrace on August 8, 1974. "It's so sad. It's so sad," his wife said as they departed from Washington via the Marine One presidential helicopter.[61]

In retirement, Nixon spent the remainder of his days trying to rehabilitate his tarnished image, writing a number of well-received books on international affairs, and reliving past political battles. Always his thoughts returned to 1960 and the man who beat him. "Jack was not nearly as upstanding or honorable as his supporters would have you believe," he maintained.[62]

Neither was Nixon.

NOTES

1. Joseph Healy Oral History, John F. Kennedy Library (hereinafter cited as JFKL).

2. Richard Nixon, *RN: The Memoirs of Richard Nixon* (New York, 1978), 42.

3. Christopher Matthews, *Kennedy and Nixon: The Rivalry That Shaped Postwar America* (New York, 1996), 52; Nixon, *RN*, 43.

4. Emmet John Hughes, *The Ordeal of Power: A Political Memoir of the Eisenhower Years* (New York, 1963), 317.

5. Matthews, *Kennedy and Nixon*, 135.

6. Ibid.; *RN*, 4–5, 12–13.

7. Bela Kornitzer, *The Real Nixon: An Intimate Biography* (New York, 1960), 52.

8. Nixon, *RN*, 15.

9. Earl Mazo, *Richard Nixon: A Political and Personal Portrait* (New York, 1959), 21; Matthews, *Kennedy and Nixon*, 25.

10. Kornitzer, *The Real Nixon*, 119.

11. Nixon, *RN*, 25, 29.

12. Frank Holeman, "The Curious Quaker: Richard M. Nixon" in *Candidates 1960*, 131.

13. Greg Mitchell, *Tricky Dick and the Pink Lady: Richard Nixon vs. Helen Gahagan Douglas—Sexual Politics and the Red Scare, 1950* (New York, 1998), 43; Mazo, *Richard Nixon*, 49.

14. Mitchell, *Tricky Dick and the Pink Lady*, 43.

15. Richard Nixon, *Six Crises* (New York, 1990), 1.

16. Richard Nixon, *In the Arena: A Memoir of Victory, Defeat, and Renewal* (New York, 1990), 191.

17. Ibid.; Monica Crowley, *Nixon Off the Record: His Candid Commentary on People and Politics* (New York, 1996), 82.

18. Nixon, *RN*, 78.

19. *New York Times*, July 15, 1952; Nixon, *RN*, 91.

20. Lewis L. Gould, *Grand Old Party: A History of the Republicans* (New York, 2003), 331.

21. Eric F. Goldman, *The Crucial Decade—and After, America, 1945-1960* (New York, 1960), 227.

22. *Christian Science Monitor*, October 11, 1952.

23. Kornitzer, *The Real Nixon*, 230; Stephen Ambrose, *Nixon: The Education of a Politician, 1913-1962* (New York, 1988), 347.

24. Gerald S. Strober and Deborah H. Strober, *Nixon: An Oral History of His Presidency* (New York, 1994), 8; Anthony Summers, *The Arrogance of Power: The Secret World of Richard Nixon* (New York, 2000), 147; Hughes, *The Ordeal of Power*, 173; Nixon, *RN*, 167.

25. Nixon, *RN*, 214.

26. Ambrose, *Nixon*, 191, 553–54; *Newsweek*, August 8, 1960.

27. Matthews, *Kennedy and Nixon*, 150.

28. Michael Beschloss, *The Crisis Years: Kennedy and Khrushchev, 1960-1963* (New York, 1991), 25.

29. Nixon, *Six Crises*, 323.

30. James Michener, "Inside Kennedy's Election," *Look*, May 9, 1961; Nixon, *RN*, 1088.

31. Ibid., 217; Hughes, *The Ordeal of Power*, 323.

32. Gerald S. Strober and Deborah H. Strober, *"Let Us Begin Anew": An Oral History of the Kennedy Presidency* (New York, 1993), 31; David Hochman, "Kennedy Out-Glams Nixon," *Entertainment Weekly*, September 27, 1996.

33. Michener, "Inside Kennedy's Election"; Fawn M. Brodie, *Richard Nixon: The Shaping of His Character* (New York, 1981), 427.

34. *Washington Post*, April 15, 1964; *Time*, September 26, 1960.

35. *New York Times*, September 26, 1960; Nixon, *Six Crises*, 351.

36. Michael O'Brien, *John F. Kennedy: A Biography* (New York, 2005), 485; The President's Call to King Oral History, JFKL, 190; Harris Wofford, *Of Kennedy and Kings: Making Sense of the Sixties* (New York, 1980), 21.

37. Nixon, *Six Crises*, 362.

38. Jeffrey Frank, *Ike and Dick: Portrait of a Strange Political Marriage* (New York, 2013), 152; Martin Luther King Jr. Oral History JFKL.

39. *Look*, May 9, 1961.

40. Shaun A. Casey, *The Making of a Catholic President: Kennedy vs. Nixon 1960* (Oxford, 2009), 126.

41. Billy Graham, "We Are Electing a President of the World, *Life*, November 7, 1960; Nancy Gibbs and Michael Duffy, *The Preacher and the Presidents: Billy Graham in the White House* (New York, 2007), 102.

42. Ibid.; Strober and Strober, *"Let Us Begin Anew,"* 38.

43. *Time*, September 26, 1960; Kenneth P. O'Donnell, and David F. Powers with Joe McCarthy, *Johnny, We Hardly Knew Ye: Memories of John F. Kennedy* (Boston, 1972), 210.

44. Lawrence F. O'Brien, *No Final Victories: A Life in Politics From John F. Kennedy to Watergate* (Garden City, New Jersey, 1974), 94; Joan Myers, ed., *John Fitzgerald Kennedy As We Remember Him* (New York, 1965), 96.

45. *New York Times*, September 27, 1960; Tom Wicker, *One of Us: Richard Nixon and the American Dream* (New York, 1995), 242; Ambrose, *Nixon*, 575.

46. *New York Times*, August 25, 1960; Nixon, *RN*, 219; "Experience," 1960 Kennedy Campaign Commercial, Audio-Visual Archives, JFKL.

47. Julie Nixon Eisenhower, *Pat Nixon: The Untold Story* (New York, 1986), 194.

48. Nixon, *RN*, 222.

49. Mark Feldstein, *Poisoning the Press: Richard Nixon, Jack Anderson, and the Rise of Washington's Scandal Culture* (New York, 2010), 62.

50. Ibid., 73; Ralph G. Martin, *A Hero for Our Time: An Intimate Story of the Kennedy Years* (New York, 1963), 208–9.

51. Nixon, *Six Crises*, 371; Matthews, *Kennedy and Nixon*, 174.

52. Martin, *A Hero for Our Time*, 219; Strober and Strober, *Nixon*, 9; Nixon, *RN*, 224.

53. Benjamin C. Bradlee, *Conversations with Kennedy* (New York, 1975), 33.

54. Ambrose, *Nixon*, 647.

55. Strober and Strober, *Nixon*, 7.

56. Matthews, *Kennedy and Nixon*, 215; Nixon, *RN*, 243; *San Francisco Examiner*, December 6, 1998.

57. Ambrose, *Nixon*, 669; Nixon, *RN*, 245.

58. Richard Reeves, *President Kennedy, Profile in Power* (New York, 1993), 435; *New York Times*, November 9, 1962; *San Francisco Examiner*, December 6, 1998.

59. Nixon, *RN*, 246.

60. Ibid., 253–55.

61. Ibid., 225, 1090.

62. Crowley, *Nixon Off the Record*, 32.

FIVE

The Perfect Failure

Fidel Castro and the 1961 Bay of Pigs Invasion

Not even bone-chilling temperatures or a blanket of freshly fallen snow could prevent John F. Kennedy from getting his administration off to a rousing start on January 20, 1961. After taking the oath of office at the east front of Washington, DC's Capitol Building, the youngest man ever elected president proceeded to deliver one of the greatest Inaugural Addresses in modern memory.

"We observe today not a victory of party but a celebration of freedom—symbolizing an end as well as a beginning—signifying renewal as well as change," he began from a 1,364-word text he had spent weeks laboring over with longtime speechwriter and close aide Theodore Sorensen. "The world is very different now. For man holds in his mortal hands the power to abolish all forms of human poverty and all forms of human life. And yet the same revolutionary beliefs for which our forebears fought are still at issue around the globe—the belief that the rights of man come not from the generosity of the state but from the hand of God."[1]

He stressed that his elevation to the Oval Office was no ordinary transfer of power, as he represented a rising new generation of Americans who had come of age on the battlefields of Europe, North Africa, and the Pacific during the Second World War and had been disciplined by the "hard and bitter peace" of the Cold War that followed. They wanted to live in a safer and more economically prosperous society while staying true to the precepts of individual liberty that refused "to witness or permit the slow undoing of those human rights to which this nation has always been committed at home and around the world."[2]

Interestingly, Kennedy made scant reference to domestic affairs in his just under fourteen-minute address. Instead he made a conscious effort to allude to what he believed was the greatest threat facing the United States and democracy in general: Soviet Communism. "In the long history of the world, only a few generations have been granted the role of defending freedom in its hour of maximum danger," he maintained. "I do not shrink from this responsibility—I welcome it. I do not believe that any of us would exchange places with any other people or any other generation."[3]

Although he did not rule out using diplomacy as a means to meeting the challenge ("Let us never negotiate out of fear. But let us never fear to negotiate."), he implied that this approach alone would be inadequate in dealing with such a formidable foe. "We dare not tempt them with weakness," he warned. "For only when our arms are sufficient, can we be certain beyond doubt that they will never be employed." In closing, Kennedy expressed confidence that "[t]he energy, the faith, the devotion" his countrymen demonstrated to the anticommunist cause would turn the tide in favor of freedom-loving peoples everywhere. "And so, my fellow Americans: ask not what your country can do for you—ask what you can do for your country."[4]

The speech was universally praised for its eloquent language and soaring sense of optimism. "We find it hard to believe, that an Athenian or Roman citizen could have listened to it unmoved, or that Cicero, however jealous of his own reputation, would have found reason to object to it," the *New Yorker* gushed. The *Washington Star* did not disagree, arguing that the speech's activist tone spoke well of Kennedy's leadership qualities. "No problems were solved, no cold wars were won," the newspaper said. "But as a general statement of aims and purposes (which is all one should expect in an inaugural address), this 'trumpet summons,' we thought, was a magnificent performance." Indeed, so inspiring were Kennedy's words that the normally hard-boiled Sam Rayburn of Texas was moved to hyperbole. "That speech he made out there was better than anything Franklin Roosevelt said at his best—it was better than Lincoln," the Democratic Speaker of the House exclaimed. "I think—really think—that he is a man of destiny."[5]

Kennedy's first months in office seemed to bear out this attitude. He and his advisors were determined to make the new administration the most proactive since the heady days of the New Deal back in the 1930s. Gone was the cumbersome Eisenhower committee system, whereby presidential decisions were arrived at consensually after a lengthy process of bureaucratic review by designated staff heads. Kennedy favored instead a more streamlined, ad hoc approach that put the onus of decision making on himself and a few close aides. "Kennedy really changed the nature of how the White House staff functioned," said administration member William Smith. "Until then staff had been primarily involved in organizing things for discussion by the president, as formulated in the departments. Under Kennedy the White House staff began to take a much larger role in initiating action, so they became the center for a lot of ideas, and for asking other agencies to do things, rather than being responsive. This allowed them to get into a lot more things than some less competent people would have wanted to do or could have done."[6]

Kennedy scoured the halls of academia and the boardrooms of corporate America to fill the top posts of his administration. Later dubbed the "best and brightest" by journalist David Halberstam, these men came from elite educational and social backgrounds and could count in their ranks such high achievers as McNamara, who boasted degrees from Berkeley and Harvard and had served a short but highly successful stint as head of the Ford Motor Company. Such was his confidence that when he interviewed for the defense post, he told Kennedy that he could easily handle the responsibility, as he had already consulted with outgoing Republican secretary Tom Gates. "I talked over the presidency with Eisenhower, and after hearing what it's all about, I'm convinced I can handle it," Kennedy quipped back. "JFK regarded [the California native] as the star of his team," remembered Theodore Sorensen, "calling upon him for advice on a wide range of issues beyond national security, including business and economic matters. He liked McNamara and his crisp, authoritative no-nonsense style."[7]

Other administration standouts included National Security Affairs Advisor McGeorge Bundy and Secretary of State Dean Rusk. Bundy was the product of a proud old Boston Brahmin family, graduating from the Groton School and Yale before becoming the youngest dean of the faculty in Harvard's history at the age of thirty-four. Known for his dry wit and formidable debating skills, Bundy had assisted former FDR Secretary of War and longtime Washington establishment icon Henry Stimson in writing his memoirs. He "could grasp an idea and produce an answer as fast as a computer," noted one flattering account. Bundy also wasn't afraid to speak his mind. He once scolded Kennedy for allowing a comely young secretary to rub stylizing gel in his hair. "I said I didn't think this kind of thing was sufficiently dignified for the Oval Office," he recalled.[8]

Rusk came from a humbler rural Georgia background and possessed an equally facile intellect, befitting someone who had been a Rhodes Scholar and who had served with distinction as an Assistant Secretary of State for Far Eastern Affairs and president of the Rockefeller Foundation. "Rusk is the best explainer of things I know," praised an early admirer. Reticent by nature, the former Cherokee County schoolboy basketball star was reluctant to share his views, often to the consternation of those who worked closest with him. "Rusk would just keep quiet [at meetings], and you never knew whether he would slip into the president's office afterward," complained former state department official Roger Hilsman. Still, no one came more highly recommended. "I thought [Rusk] had been strong and loyal and good in every way," former Secretary of State Dean Acheson told Kennedy of his onetime protégé.[9]

Such plaudits were not extended to Robert Kennedy. The new Attorney General had been a problematic choice from the very beginning. Egged on by his father, who insisted that his son needed someone of unquestioned loyalty beside him in the executive branch, John Kennedy had announced his younger brother's appointment the previous December. "Let's grab our balls and go," he said.[10] The news was greeted with a collective gasp of anger and disbelief by political opponents who immediately condemned the move as an act of nepotism. Robert, after all, had never so much as set foot in a courtroom; now he was the country's chief law enforcement officer. It didn't matter.

As John argued, "An Attorney General is supposed to run a department of some 30,000 people, and it needs a hell of a manager, and my brother is the best manager I've ever had and the best one that I know of—and that's why he's going to be the Attorney General." To his credit, Robert tried to make light of the controversy. He said that prior to the official word coming down, the president-elect had ordered him to fix the unruly locks on his head for photographers. "It was the first time the president had ever told the attorney general to comb his hair before they made an announcement," he joked.[11]

Despite the glittering array of intellectual talent at his disposal, it seems almost inconceivable that John Kennedy would stumble into a major foreign policy debacle so soon after assuming the presidency. But that is precisely what happened when he approved of a covert action plan originally conceived by the Eisenhower administration to overthrow the regime of Cuban dictator Fidel Castro in April 1961.

Codenamed Zapata, in honor of the early twentieth-century Mexican revolutionary Emiliano Zapata, the plan entailed using a military strike force of 1,500 anti-Castro Cuban exiles that had been trained and equipped by the CIA at a secret base in Guatemala. The force, known officially as Brigade 2506, was expected to board a flotilla of transport ships and invade the island at the Bay of Pigs, a small inlet along the southern coast that was accessible to the Caribbean Sea. It was believed that the "shock and awe" generated from this surprise amphibious assault would sow enough panic and disorder in Castro's ranks as to bring about his government's downfall. "It all sounded easy, almost too easy to be true; and it was," Theodore Sorensen later reflected.[12]

For what Kennedy and his "best and brightest" advisors had failed to take into account when embarking upon this high-stakes venture was the utterly ruthless and indomitable character of Fidel Castro. The son of a prosperous sugar planter, Castro grew up as a "child of privilege" in a remote hilly region of eastern Cuba called the Oriente. "That's like Texas for Americans," he told a journalist in 1959. "It is the biggest province in Cuba. We do the most work, we make the most rum and sugar, we make the most money too." His father, Angel Castro, had served with the Spanish army during the second Cuban War for Independence in the 1890s before opting for permanent residency on the island in 1905. After his first marriage ended in divorce, Angel married Lina Ruz Gonzalez, an illiterate domestic maid in his employ, in a union that would produce seven children, including Fidel in 1926."He was a man of great will, great determination," Castro remembered. "He taught himself to read and write, with great effort. Without question he was a very active man—he moved around a lot, he was a go-get-'em kind of person, and he had a natural talent for organization." He also possessed a violent temper that young Fidel ran afoul of when he misbehaved, which was often in these formative years. "I didn't like authority, because at that time there was also a lot of corporal punishment, a slap on the head or a belt taken to you—[my siblings and I] always ran that risk, although we gradually learned to defend ourselves against it," he said.[13]

This inclination for rebellion continued well into his early school years. "I remember that whenever I disagreed with something the teacher said to me, or whenever I got mad, I would swear at her, and immediately leave school, as fast as I could," he said. On one occasion this exit strategy backfired when he leaped on a board holding a wooden box with a nail protruding precariously from its contents. "As I fell, the nail stuck in my tongue," Castro recalled. "When I got back home, my mother said to me: 'God punished you for swearing at the teacher.' I didn't have the slightest doubt that it was really true."[14]

When he wasn't getting into trouble, Castro excelled on the baseball diamond. A standout left-handed pitcher with a wicked fastball, he eventually garnered the attention of the Washington Senators, who reportedly tried him out on two separate occasions. Alas, he was unable to make the grade as a big-league pitching prospect. "Let's just say he [Castro] was the equivalent of a good collegiate player," noted one longtime US-Cuban sports organizer. Castro did, however, earn a measure of hardball glory in 1950 when he "bolted from the stands" as a spectator and boldly inserted himself into a professional ball game.[15]

"During this demonstration," *Washington Post* writer Vance Garnett recounted, Castro "commandeered the pitcher's mound and began hurling fastballs across the plate [before local police removed him]." The recipient of those fastballs was Don Houk, a future major leaguer and a key contributor to the 1960 pennant-winning Pittsburgh Pirates. Accounts differ on whether Houk struck out or even bothered to swing at a pitch. But one matter was beyond dispute: Castro could really bring the heat. "Actually, Fidel was a good athlete," says Peter C. Bjarkman, a noted historian of the Cuban baseball scene.[16]

In 1945 Castro entered the University of Havana and took up the study of law. But being an attorney did not appeal to his restless personality. He found campus politics more to his liking and became a prominent student leader. "At the time, I loved Fidel Castro," an acquaintance from this period recalled. "He was like me—a political agitator. Besides, he was very intelligent. A megalomaniac with a sense of grandiosity! He never could be a democratic president, but he was a man who was personally very attractive and charming. When you were with him, you liked to be with him or liked yourself more."[17]

A lackluster student before his university days, he now experienced a major intellectual awakening. He began reading Marx and Engels and blamed the endemic corruption, inequality, and privation that traditionally plagued his nation on the larger economic forces of capitalism. "I felt that I had been conquered, so to speak, by that literature," he later said. "Marxism taught me what society was. I was like a blindfolded man in a forest, who doesn't even know where north or south is. If you don't eventually come to truly understand the history of the class struggle, or at least have a clear idea that society is divided between the rich and the poor, and that some people subjugate and exploit other people, you're lost in a forest, not knowing anything."[18]

Emboldened by these ideas, Castro organized a rebellion against Fulgencio Batista in 1953. The former elected president of Cuba, Batista had decided to ditch all trappings of democracy and declare himself military dictator with the blessings of the US government and his country's upper classes. "I believed everyone would come together to wipe out Batista's tyranny," Castro said. "It was clear to me that Batista had to be overthrown by arms and that constitutional government had to be restored." Only it didn't happen that way. His insurrection, which involved the storming of an army barracks in eastern Cuba, proved to be an unmitigated disaster. His small, underequipped rebel force, which was culled from the island's teeming working classes and included in its ranks Castro's younger brother Raul, was no match for the superior firepower of Batista's trained soldiers. They were easily routed, and Castro was placed under arrest. "I know that for me imprisonment will be harder than it ever was for anyone," he told the courtroom at his trial, "but I do not fear it, as I do not fear the fury of the miserable tyrant who killed my brothers. Condemn me! It does not matter! History will absolve me!"[19]

After serving almost two years of a fifteen-year jail sentence, Castro was granted a general amnesty in 1954 when, according to the biographer Peter G. Bourne, Batista succumbed to the argument that his regime "could have legitimacy only if he freed all of the political prisoners."[20] It proved to be a catastrophic error. More determined than ever to topple Batista, Castro decided to launch another rebellion, this time from the impenetrable forests of the Sierra Maestra mountain range in the Oriente. "I am fighting for a democratic Cuba and an end to dictatorship," he said.[21]

Assisted by newcomer Ernesto "Che" Guevara, a charismatic Argentine physician turned Marxist revolutionary whom he had met through Raul, Castro was able to create an effective guerrilla fighting force. "We studied the terrain as we fought," he recalled. "Batista was carrying on a fierce repressive campaign, and there were many burned houses, and many murdered peasants. We dealt with the peasants in a very different manner from the Batista soldiers, and we slowly gained the support of the rural population—until that support became absolute. Our soldiers came from that rural population."[22]

All the while, the future "Maximum Leader" stumbled upon a popular emblem that would be forever associated with his daring leadership and those who followed him: beards. "We didn't have any razor blades, or straight razors," he explained. "When we found ourselves in the middle of the wilderness, up in the Sierra, everybody just let their beards and hair grow, and that turned out into a kind of badge of identity." Sporting whiskers also had the added benefit of making it exceedingly difficult for Batista's intelligence agents to gain access to his tight-knit band of rebels. "[I]n order for a spy to infiltrate us," Castro said, "he had to start preparing months ahead of time—he'd have had to have a six-months' growth of beard you see. So the beards served as a badge of identification, and as protection, until it finally became a symbol of the guerrilla fighter."[23]

By January 1959, these guerrilla fighters had clearly gained the upper hand. Following a string of impressive military victories, Castro's forces came streaming down from the Sierra Maestra and seized Havana, effectively ending Batista's dictatorial reign. "This war was won by the people!" Castro announced. But in magnanimously declaring victory, Castro demonstrated he was not above settling a few personal scores. Special "revolutionary tribunals" were set up to prosecute the alleged "war crimes" of former Batista regime members. Thousands were executed, some on live Cuban television, leading many previous Castro admirers in the United States and overseas to shake their heads in disgust. The "savior of Cuba" was unapologetic, however. "We don't regret having done it," he later claimed, "although I do feel pity when I remember how bitter it must have been for (the accused) to experience the hatred that the people quite rightly felt for them because of their repugnant crimes."[24]

Castro's actions, along with his increasingly open embrace of Marxist-Leninist ideology, which called for the end of private property and the need for strong, centralized state control, drew the attention of an apprehensive Eisenhower administration. As early as 1958, CIA Director Allen Dulles had reported to Ike that "Communists and other extreme radicals" had penetrated the Castro movement. "If Castro takes over, they will probably participate in the government," he warned.[25]

Now with Castro firmly in charge, the situation only seemed to worsen, especially when his government announced in February 1960 that it had reached a lucrative trade agreement with the Soviet Union and intended to scrap plans for a national election. "The Castro regime is moving toward a complete dictatorship," Dulles said.[26]

Richard Nixon arrived at a similar conclusion in April when he had a private three-hour meeting with the Cuban leader in his office on Capitol

Hill. Castro was visiting Washington at the invitation of the American Society of Newspaper Editors, and the Vice President was eager to gain insight into his political views. Castro did not disappoint. "In every instance he justified his departure from democratic principles on the ground that he was following the will of the people," Nixon said in a confidential memorandum to Eisenhower afterward. "He is either incredibly naïve about communism or under Communist discipline—my guess is the former." For his part, Castro appeared nonplussed by such concerns. "You Americans are always so afraid—afraid of Communism, afraid of everything," he lectured Nixon. "You should be talking more about your own strengths and the reasons why your system is superior to Communism or any other kind of dictatorship."[27]

Eisenhower thought he had heard and seen enough. Fearing a Soviet beachhead was about to be established on America's doorstep, he broke off all official diplomatic ties with the former US ally and approved of a CIA proposal to train a group of Cuban exiles in Guatemala for the purpose of overthrowing Castro's regime. In reaching this decision, Eisenhower was aware of the diplomatic and political risks involved, principally those having to do with the United States' relationship with its sister republics in the Western Hemisphere. He acknowledged that "precipitate, unilateral action" might undermine efforts to rally effective popular resistance against Soviet expansionism in the region. "Fidel Castro was a hero to the masses in many Latin American nations," he later explained. "They saw him as a champion of the downtrodden and the enemy of the privileged who, in most of their countries, controlled both wealth and governments. His crimes and wrongdoings that so repelled the more informed peoples of the continent had little effect on the young, the peons, the underprivileged, and all the others who wanted to see the example of revolution followed in their own nations."[28]

Still, the risks were worth taking, according to Eisenhower. Castro represented a dire threat to the region and therefore had to go. The only problem with this line of reasoning was that the Cuban exile force would not be combat ready until well after Ike left office. He would thus need to rely on his successor to carry through on the invasion plan.

This was something John F. Kennedy was more than happy to do, as he had repeatedly railed against the "loss" of Cuba on the presidential campaign trail. In fact, he falsely accused Nixon of being part of an administration that had failed "to strengthen the non-Batista Democratic anti-Castro forces in exile." Understandably, Nixon became upset with Kennedy for putting him in such an awkward political position, particularly when the Democrat had already been briefed by the CIA about the pending invasion operation. "In order to protect the secrecy of the planning and the safety of the thousands of men and women involved in the operation," Nixon later wrote, "I had no choice but to take a completely opposite stand and attack Kennedy's advocacy of open intervention in

Cuba." Consequently, Kennedy came across to voters as "tougher on Castro and communism than [Nixon] was."[29]

This bit of political gamesmanship aside, Kennedy was sincere about seeking Castro's ouster. Befitting the prevailing Cold War attitudes of the day, he believed in the domino theory. If Castro's regime was allowed to survive, this argument went, then his brand of revolutionary Marxism would engulf all of Latin America. Kennedy said as much in his first State of the Union Address on January 31, 1961. "Communist agents seeking to exploit that region's peaceful revolution of hope have established a base on Cuba, only 90 miles from our shores," he maintained. "We are pledged . . . to free the Americas of all such foreign domination and all tyranny, working toward the goal of a free hemisphere of free governments, extending from Cape Horn to the Arctic Circle."[30]

Despite these fears of a rising Red tide, there was significant opposition to the Cuban invasion plan within administration circles. Undersecretary of State Chester Bowles, who had served as Ambassador to India under Truman, believed the operation was ill-conceived and would violate existing treaty obligations the United States had with other friendly Latin American governments. These obligations included a bar against the use of armed force or other coercive means that violated the territorial integrity of another state. "To act deliberately in defiance of these obligations would deal a blow to the Inter-American System from which I doubt it would soon recover," Bowles wrote his superior, Secretary of State Dean Rusk.[31]

Presidential aide Arthur Schlesinger Jr. seconded these reservations, arguing that however "well disguised" the American hand would be in the operation, responsibility would ultimately be "ascribed to the United States." "At one stroke," he wrote Kennedy in a confidential memorandum, "[the invasion] would dissipate all the extraordinary good will which has been rising toward the new Administration through the world. It would fix a malevolent image of the new Administration in the minds of millions."[32]

Veteran Cold War diplomat Dean Acheson, a frequent visitor to the Kennedy White House during these hectic early days, expressed his misgivings along more pragmatic lines. "I remember saying [to Kennedy] that I did not think it was necessary to call in Price Waterhouse to discover that 1,500 Cubans weren't as good as 25,000 Cubans [the believed number of troops Castro could put up in opposition]," he said. "It seemed to me that this was a disastrous idea. . . . I really dismissed it from my mind because it seemed like such a wild idea."[33]

Longtime Kennedy friend and former Senate Foreign Relations Committee colleague J. William Fulbright, whom Acheson once derisively dismissed as "half-bright" for his alleged intellectual failings, also found the underlying rationale for the invasion hard to swallow. "To give this activity even covert support is of a piece with the hypocrisy and cynicism for which the United States is constantly denouncing the Soviet Union in the United Nations and elsewhere," the Arkansas lawmaker declared. "This point will not be lost on the rest of the world, nor on our own consciences."[34]

These reservations notwithstanding, Kennedy refused to back down. Persuaded by the confident assurances of CIA Director Dulles and his Deputy Director of Plans Richard M. Bissell, who viewed the project as having a high likelihood for success, Kennedy gave the go-ahead for Brigade 2506 to invade. Yet he insisted that the "noise level" of the operation be lowered, meaning that he wanted to be able to claim afterward the United States had no direct military involvement. "The minute I land one Marine, we're in this thing up to our necks," he explained. "I can't get the United States into a war and then lose it, no matter what it takes. I'm not going to risk an American Hungary. And that's what it could be, a fucking slaughter."[35]

In accordance with these presidential guidelines, the CIA scrapped the idea of providing US air cover, leaving that up to the exiles themselves, who would be flying a squadron of aging B-26 bombers from Nicaragua for that purpose. But the question remains more than five decades later, did the CIA sincerely believe Kennedy would not intervene with American firepower under any circumstances? According to the late McGeorge Bundy, the answer is no. "They believed if [Kennedy] once got as far in as the initial enterprise would put him, and then it was about to fail, he would change his mind and see the light from their point of view and put American forces in," the National Security Affairs Advisor said. "They were simply wrong on that. That difference of approach between the people in charge of the operation and what they had heard but didn't really believe from the president is at the center of the problem, I think."[36]

The agency also moved the initial proposed invasion landing site from the southern Cuban coastal city of Trinidad to the more secluded Bay of Pigs region a hundred miles away. "[It] was selected because its distance from a major population center eased the president's concern about noise and attracting undue attention," Bissell wrote. This latter move was of particular significance because in the original draft invasion plan even if the exile force were defeated, they could still melt away to the nearby Escambray Mountains and become guerrillas. But switching to the Bay of Pigs eliminated that option, as the area was surrounded by swampy, inhospitable terrain. Incredibly, Kennedy and top administration officials were kept in the dark about this until well after the fact. As Bissell later noted, "The concept that had been appropriate for a Trinidad landing was retained even though it was inapplicable to a Bay of Pigs landing."[37]

The invasion commenced in the wee morning hours of April 15 and almost immediately things went awry. Castro's air force, which was supposed to have been destroyed in an opening brigade air assault, experi-

Figure 5.1. Fidel Castro addresses the media during his 1959 visit to the United States. Reproduction Number: LC-DIG-ppmsc-03256

enced significant but not overwhelming damage. Left to fight another day, the surviving Cuban pilots and their intact planes proceeded to regroup and deliver a devastating counterstrike against the invaders, knocking out two ships and leaving the surrounding beachhead area littered with corpses. "We were told the invasion was a lost cause," remembered brigade member Jose Flores.[38]

If this wasn't devastating enough, Castro's ground forces, which had been alerted to an impending invasion beforehand by leaked reports in various US and Latin American media outlets ("Castro does not need agents over here," Kennedy fumed. "All he has to do is read our newspapers!"), moved in for the kill, encircling the beachhead with tanks and twenty thousand troops. "The shit has hit the fan," Robert Kennedy said. "The thing has turned sour in a way you wouldn't believe." Running low on ammunition and morale, many brigade members either surrendered or attempted to escape through the nearby swamplands. "We had nothing to shoot at them with," complained one survivor. With defeat looking more and more a certainty, pressure built on Kennedy to reverse his ban on the direct use of American force. But he steadfastly refused.[39]

"Burke," he pointedly told Admiral Arleigh Burke of the Joint Chiefs of Staff, "I don't want the United States involved in this." An incredulous Burke shot back, "Hell, Mr. President, but we *are* involved." "There was no good option once he started the damn thing," Undersecretary of State George Ball said. "[Kennedy] couldn't pull back, and, if we had committed our own forces, then it would have been a big, imperialistic war against a little country. This was the last thing in the world he wanted to be involved in." Additionally, Kennedy worried that any overt demonstration of US military strength might provoke a similar show of force by the Soviet Union in some other vitally strategic area around the globe. "This means that there is a good chance that, if we move on Cuba, [the Russians] will move on Berlin," he said. "I just don't think we can take that risk."[40]

Kennedy did exhibit some flexibility near the end of the crisis. He authorized six unmarked US jets to escort a B-26 attack group flown by Cuban exile pilots against Castro's forces. The move turned out to be too little, too late. By April 19 Castro's forces had overrun the beachhead and taken 1,189 prisoners. Over a hundred brigade members already lay dead. "It was a grim and sad two days," Arthur Schlesinger Jr. wrote in his diary. "Many fine men have been killed or lost; one cannot resist the belief that this was an ill-considered and mistaken expedition." The invasion had indeed become what one historian termed "the perfect failure."[41]

Bathing in the afterglow of the victory, a jubilant Castro could not resist thumbing his nose at the man he once derided as "a rich illiterate." He gloated in a televised speech that Kennedy's government had egregiously erred when it came to understanding the support most Cubans had for the Marxist regime. "Imperialist mentality is the reverse of the revolutionary mentality," he explained. "The imperialist looks at the geography, analyzes the number of cannons, of planes, of tanks, the positions; the revolutionary goes to the social population and asks, 'Who are these people?' To the imperialist, it doesn't matter at all what the population thinks or feels, this is outside of his concern; the revolutionary thinks first of the people, and the people of the [Bay of Pigs] were entirely ours."[42]

Back in Washington, the mood was considerably more downcast. "This is the worst day of my life!" exclaimed Allen Dulles. The CIA director was not alone. United Nations Ambassador Adlai Stevenson,

Figure 5.2.   Making international waves: Castro visits the UN in 1960. Reproduction Number: LC-USZ62-13450

whom Kennedy dismissed as weak and ineffectual, had been deliberately kept out of the loop with regard to details of the final invasion plan. As a result, he was unaware that two of the planes used in the brigade's initial air attack had been piloted by US-trained Cuban exiles and not defectors from Castro's air force as news reports originally claimed. "They took off from Castro's own fields," he had assured the UN. When he subsequently learned this explanation was merely an elaborate CIA cover story, the former Illinois governor and two-time Democratic presidential nominee grew outraged. "I took this job at the President's request on the understanding that I would be consulted and kept fully informed of everything," he angrily told a friend. "I spoke in the United Nations in good faith on that understanding. Now my credibility has been compromised, and therefore my usefulness." Stevenson gave serious thought to resigning from his post, but decided against it. "The young President and the country are in enough trouble," he said.[43]

Although he had played only a marginal role in the decision-making process leading up to the invasion, Robert Kennedy also felt personally betrayed. "We've got to do something," he lashed out at his brother's advisors at one point. "All you bright fellows have gotten the President into this and if you don't do something now, my brother will be regarded as a paper tiger by the Russians." Maintaining a professional yet avuncular tone, Deputy Assistant for National Security Affairs W. W. Rostow told him that in a fight, "the most dangerous thing" to do was to get up swinging after being knocked down. "That's constructive," Robert responded. From here on in, John Kennedy would accord his younger brother principal advisory status in all major foreign policy decisions. "I made a major mistake in putting Bobby in the Justice Department," the president later admitted. "He is wasted there. Bobby should be in the CIA."[44]

The full impact of the Bay of Pigs defeat did not hit John Kennedy until he had a chance to quietly sit down with his wife Jacqueline and unburden himself. "It was in the morning and he came back over to the White House to his bedroom and he started to cry, just with me," the First Lady told Arthur Schlesinger Jr. in a 1964 oral history interview. He "just put his head in his hands and sort of wept. And I've only seen him cry about three times." Tormenting his mind were thoughts of the "poor men" he had abandoned on the beaches who had sacrificed everything to free their country from Castro. He had "sent them off with all their hopes high and promises that we'd back them and they were, shot down like dogs or going to die in jail," Jacqueline said. "He cared so much about them."[45]

Such concern was not reciprocated. Captured brigade commander Jose Perez "Pepe" San Roman grew embittered at Kennedy and his administration for failing to take the necessary military steps to retrieve the situation. "I was discouraged with everything," he said. "I hated the

United States, and I felt that I had been betrayed. Every day it became worse and then I was getting madder and madder and I wanted to get a rifle and come and fight against the U.S. Sometimes the feeling came very strong to me that they had thrown us there knowing that they were not going to help us."[46]

After receiving prison sentences of thirty years at hard labor, San Roman and the rest of his seized comrades were freed on Christmas Eve 1962 when Castro agreed to ransom them for fifty-three million dollars in cash and medicine. Robert Kennedy had been the driving force behind the deal as he insisted the United States had a moral obligation to secure their release. "It was a question of doing it that way or not getting the money—and letting those men be shot," he said. "I haven't any regrets about it and I'd do it again." San Roman experienced difficulty adjusting to his newly won freedom. In the years ahead he could never get over the hurt and humiliation he experienced at the Bay of Pigs. Unable to cope, he eventually took his own life.[47]

Although Kennedy publicly assumed full credit for the debacle ("I am the responsible officer of the government," he said), this did not inoculate him from strong criticism in the national media. "The invasion fiasco . . . probably has greatly strengthened the Communists in the Cuban regime," wrote William Ryan of the *Associated Press*. "From now on . . . Fidel Castro will a better and more willing tool than ever before for the Communists. And the abortive invasion has given the regime whatever excuses it may have needed for relentlessly rooting out and eliminating its enemies on the island." *Life* magazine dismissed the operation as being "prematurely timed, inadequately mounted, strategically doomed and based upon woefully inept intelligence or wildly wishful thinking—or both." *Newsweek* didn't pull any punches either, claiming that Kennedy had suffered a setback "as great as any that befell President Eisenhower" during his tenure in the Oval Office. "At best, the U.S. appears before the world as a meddler; at worst as a nation which pretends to virtue, yet seems to have committed open aggression against a tiny country," the magazine said.[48]

Politicians from both sides of the aisle also got in their licks. Democratic Senator Wayne Morse of Oregon, who later gained fame for his opposition to the Vietnam War, characterized the entire affair as "a colossal mistake" that could not be justified under international law or any principles of sound foreign policy. "Cuba is not a dagger at our hearts, but a thorn in our flesh, irritating and painful," he said. Republican Governor Nelson Rockefeller of New York reserved his most withering comments on what he felt were the big strategic consequences. "There's a new element in the Western Hemisphere and it is a very serious one," he said. "We don't want to kid ourselves. We aren't just talking about some agrarian leaders in Cuba, we are talking about a highly organized, well-equipped Communist-dominated effort." He added that Cuba was not a problem confined merely to the Cuban people. "Cuba today is a problem of international Communism," he argued.[49]

Kennedy did receive support from an unlikely source: Richard Nixon. His 1960 presidential opponent had journeyed to the White House at Kennedy's request on April 20 to confer with him on the crisis. "Everything had been going so well for him; a few days earlier he stood high in the polls, and his press was overwhelmingly favorable," Nixon noted. But that was before the Bay of Pigs. The Commander in Chief who presently stood before him appeared distracted and upset, nervously pacing around the Oval Office in a state of agitated bewilderment. "His anger and frustration poured out in a profane barrage," Nixon revealed. "Over and over he cursed everyone who had advised him: the CIA, the Chairman of the Joint Chiefs of Staff, members of his White House staff." After letting him vent some more, Nixon assured his old rival that he would publicly support him "to the hilt" on Cuba. This gesture of selfless bipartisanship seemed to genuinely touch Kennedy. "It really is true that foreign affairs is the only important issue for a President to handle, isn't it?," he confessed to Nixon as he escorted him through the Rose Garden to a waiting car. "I mean, who gives a shit if the minimum wage is $1.15 or $1.25, in comparison to something like this?"[50]

To restore badly needed confidence in his administration, Kennedy asked for and received the resignations of Dulles and Bissell. None of this must have come as any great surprise to either man. Although still highly respected in the intelligence community, both were holdovers from the previous Republican administration and therefore convenient political scapegoats. "If this were the British government," Kennedy confided to Bissell, "I would resign, and you, being a senior civil servant, would remain. But it isn't. In our government, you and Allen have to go, and I have to remain."[51]

Not that this explanation provided much solace. Dulles, in particular, never forgave Kennedy for what he considered was a critical failure of nerve. "Great actions require great determination," he later fulminated. "In these difficult types of operations, so many of which I have been associated with over the years, one never succeeds unless there is a determination to succeed, a willingness to risk some unpleasant political repercussions, and a willingness to provide the basic military necessities. At the decisive moment of the Bay of Pigs operation, all three of these were lacking."[52]

The Bay of Pigs did not end Kennedy's efforts to eliminate Castro's regime. If anything, the defeat intensified them as the president authorized the CIA to come up with a more effective covert action plan. That plan became known as "Operation Mongoose," and it relied on a combination of anticommunist propaganda, sabotage, and hit-and-run guerrilla raids to stir up anti-Castro opposition on the island. "No time, money, effort or manpower is to be spared," read an official CIA memorandum on the subject. So determined was Kennedy to see the operation succeed that he tasked his brother Robert with overseeing things. This the attorney general did with great relish as he sought to avenge the stinging humiliation that Castro had brought down upon the administration. "Bobby was his brother's wire-brush man," noted future CIA Director Richard Helms. "And he was as tough as nails on Cuba."[53]

Such toughness apparently did not rule out assassination. Under the aegis of the operation, several attempts on Castro's life were made with the help of organized crime figures including Sam Giancana of Chicago, who were eager to remove the leader who had shut down their lucrative gambling and prostitution businesses throughout the island. Thanks to an impressive domestic and foreign intelligence network, Castro was able to sniff out most of these plots and stop them before they could be brought to fruition. But this wasn't always the case. "Chance sometimes intervened against them," Castro recalled. "There was an agent who had a cyanide pill and was about to put it into a chocolate milkshake in this place I often went to, a coffee shop in the hotel Havana Libre. Fortunately, the ampoule [sic] froze, and just as he was about to throw it in, he realized that it was stuck to the ice in the freezer he'd put it in."[54]

US-Cuban relations would reach their nadir in October 1962, when Castro prevailed upon his Russian allies to install offensive nuclear missile sites on the island to prevent a reprise of the Bay of Pigs invasion. "Throughout our revolutionary history, any time that we have smelled danger, we've taken the necessary steps," he said. "And we would rather make the mistake of taking excessive precautions than be taken by surprise because of carelessness."[55] But it was Castro and the Soviets who were caught off-guard when the uncompleted missile sites were discovered by American U-2 spy planes.

Under tremendous military and diplomatic pressure from Kennedy, Khrushchev removed the missiles rather than risk the outbreak of World War III. This did not sit well with Castro. He thought the Russian leader had acted in a cowardly way and should have launched a preemptive nuclear attack against the United States. Khrushchev scoffed at such talk as madness. As he later told Castro, "If the war had begun we would somehow have survived, but Cuba no doubt would have ceased to exist. It would have been crushed into powder. Yet you suggested a nuclear strike."[56]

After the Cuban Missile Crisis, Kennedy kept the pressure on Castro by allowing Operation Mongoose to continue. "There is a good deal of unfinished business in Cuba," he explained. "We have not been successful in removing Mr. Castro. He still remains a major danger to the United States." Yet in pursuing this cloak-and-dagger approach, Kennedy did not rule out diplomacy as an option. He made a major push to open a secret dialogue with Castro when a diplomatic source suggested the dictator had become "unhappy with Cuba's satellite status [to the USSR] and looking for a way out."[57]

Using such figures as United Nations official William Attwood and French journalist Jean Daniel as go-betweens, the president discreetly tried to assure Castro that normalization of relations between their two rival nations was still possible. In fact, Kennedy publicly signaled the terms for such a rapprochement on November 19, 1963, when he told a Miami Beach gathering of the Inter-American Press Association that Cuba had been unwittingly made "a weapon" by "external powers" to subvert other American republics in the Western Hemisphere.[58]

"This, and this alone, divides us," he said. "As long as this is true, nothing is possible. Without it, everything is possible. Once this barrier is removed, we will be ready and anxious to work with the Cuban people in pursuit of those progressive goals which a few short years ago stirred their hopes and the sympathy of many people throughout the hemisphere."[59] For his part, Castro seemed open to such entreaties. Kennedy, he said, "has all the possibilities of being in the eyes of history, the greatest President of the U.S.—the one who might at last understand that there can be co-existence among capitalists and socialists, even in the American zone. He would then be a President superior to Lincoln." Any chance for a major diplomatic breakthrough, however, collapsed when Kennedy was gunned down in Dallas, Texas, on November 22. "Everything is going to change," a downcast Castro said upon hearing the news. "Kennedy was an enemy to whom we had become accustomed. This a very grave matter, very grave."[60]

Castro was being needlessly pessimistic. Kennedy's successor, Lyndon Johnson, viewed Operation Mongoose and its embrace of political assassination as akin to running "a damn Murder, Inc. in the Caribbean."[61] He shut it down, thereby removing a dark cloud over Castro's head. In the near term, the hero of Sierra Maestra could feel reasonably assured that he would be able to carry out his duties as Cuba's head of state without the fear of additional CIA plots on his life.

Nevertheless, Johnson was hostile to the notion of restoring full diplomatic relations. He felt that any official move in this direction had to be predicated on Cuba leaving the Russian fold, a highly unlikely prospect. As one frustrated state department official commented, "How could Castro break ties with the Soviet Union *before* reaching an accommodation with us? How could he renounce Soviet military assistance when he still faced a hostile United States? How could he renounce Moscow's economic aid without being certain of finding a benefactor? Obviously, he couldn't."[62]

Johnson's intractable stance may have also been influenced by his belief that Castro had had a hand in the assassination of his predecessor. "Kennedy tried to get Castro, but Fidel Castro got Kennedy first," Johnson once remarked. Castro certainly had motive. Kennedy *did* seek his elimination, and Castro had gone out his way to publicly warn the president of the consequences of pursuing such a goal. "United States leaders should think that if they assist in terrorist plans to eliminate Cuban leaders, they themselves will not be safe," he ominously informed an Associated Press reporter two months prior to Kennedy's death. Still, there exists no conclusive proof to link Castro or any member of his government to the murder.[63]

True, Lee Harvey Oswald, Kennedy's assassin, was a Castro admirer and a member of the Fair Play for Cuba Committee, a US-based group dedicated to raising popular support for the Communist regime. But to suggest that he was taking direct orders from Castro is unsupportable. Castro threw cold water on the idea in the immediate wake of the assassination. "If they had proof," he said in reference to a radio report on the subject, "they would have said [Oswald] was an agent, an accomplice, a hired killer. In saying simply that he is an admirer [of the Cuban leader], this is just to try and make an association in people's minds between the name of Castro and the emotion awakened by the assassination."[64]

Castro would stay in power for another four decades, until old age, sickness, and increasing infirmity forced him to step down in favor of his brother Raul in 2008. "It would betray my conscience to take up a responsibility that requires mobility and total devotion, that I am not in a physical condition to offer," he said. Despite his fragile state of health, Castro remained active politically in his retirement. Calling himself "a soldier of ideas," he published several essays and commented regularly on a number of timely regional and international topics. But as the 50th anniversary of the Bay of Pigs rolled around in 2011, he could not help but take a wistful look back in time. He revealed a special pride in the role he had played in bringing about the "first defeat of imperialism in the Americas."[65]

Castro's victory belied the heady optimism that permeated the early days of the Kennedy administration. Then anything seemed possible, as the charismatic young president promised to "pay any price, bear any burden, meet any hardship, support any friend, oppose any foe to assure the survival and the success of liberty."[66]

The Bay of Pigs cruelly shattered that illusion.

NOTES

1. John F. Kennedy, "Inaugural Address (January 20, 1961)," *Public Papers of the Presidents: John F. Kennedy 1961*, 1.

2. Ibid.

3. Ibid., 2–3.

4. Ibid., 3.

5. *New Yorker*, February 4, 1961; *Washington Star*, January 21, 1961; Ralph G. Martin, *A Hero for Our Time: An Intimate Story of the Kennedy Years* (New York, 1963), 10.

6. Gerald S. Strober and Deborah H. Strober, *"Let Us Begin Anew": An Oral History of the Kennedy Presidency* (New York, 1993), 138.

7. *Time*, April 28, 1961; Ted Sorensen, *Counselor: A Life at the Edge of History* (New York, 2009), 232.

8. Martin, *A Hero for Our Time*, 238; Sally Bedell Smith, *Grace and Power: The Private World of the Kennedy White House* (New York, 2004), 149.

9. Walter Isaacson and Evan Thomas, *The Wise Men: Six Friends and the World They Made* (New York, 1986), 596; Strober and Strober, *"Let Us Begin Anew,"* 167; Dean Acheson Oral History, John F. Kennedy Library (hereinafter cited as JFKL).

10. James W. Hilty, *Robert Kennedy: Brother Protector* (Philadelphia, 1997), 190.

11. Jean Stein and George Plimpton, ed., *American Journey: The Times of Robert Kennedy* (New York, 1970), 75; Richard D. Mahoney, *The Kennedy Brothers: The Rise and Fall of Jack and Bobby* (New York, 2011), 86.

12. Sorensen, *Counselor*, 315.

13. David Halberstam, *The Fifties* (New York, 1993), 717; *Time*, January 26, 1959; Fidel Castro, *Fidel Castro: My Life* (New York, 2009), 24.

14. Tad Szulc, *Fidel: A Critical Portrait* (New York, 1986), 109.

15. *Arizona Republic*, September 5, 2006; Jim Reisler, *The Best Game Ever, Pirates vs. Yankees: October 13, 1960* (New York, 2007).

16. *Washington Post*, April 19, 1998; *Arizona Republic*, September 5, 2006.

17. Georgie Anne Geyer, *Guerrilla Prince: The Untold Story of Fidel Castro* (Boston, 1991), 50.

18. Castro, *Fidel Castro*, 100.

19. Ibid., 91; *Newsweek*, June 12, 1959.

20. Peter G. Bourne, *Fidel: A Biography of Fidel Castro* (New York, 1986), 104.

21. *Newsweek*, June 12, 1959.

22. Szulc, *Fidel*, 402.

23. Castro, *Fidel Castro*, 195.

24. Szulc, *Fidel*, 459; Castro, *Fidel Castro*, 220.

25. Dwight D. Eisenhower, *Waging Peace: The White House Years 1956-1961* (Garden City, New York, 1965), 521.

26. Ibid., 523.

27. Richard Nixon, *RN: The Memoirs of Richard Nixon* (New York, 1978), 202; Geyer, *Guerrilla Prince*, 234.

28. Eisenhower, *Waging Peace*, 525.

29. Richard J. Walton, *Cold War and Counterrevolution: The Foreign Policy of John F. Kennedy* (New York, 1972), 38; Nixon, *RN*, 220–21.

30. Kennedy, "Annual Message to the Congress on the State of the Union (January 30, 1961)," *Public Papers of the Presidents 1961, John F. Kennedy*, 23.

31. Chester Bowles, "Memorandum from Under Secretary of State Chester Bowles to Secretary of State Dean Rusk," March 31, 1961, in Mark White, ed., *The Kennedys and Cuba: A Declassified Documentary History* (Chicago, 2001), 23.

32. Jim Rasenberger, *The Brilliant Disaster: JFK, Castro, and America's Doomed Invasion of Cuba's Bay of Pigs* (New York, 2011), 129.

33. Dean Acheson Oral History, JFKL.

34. Peter Wyden, *Bay of Pigs: The Untold Story* (New York, 1979), 122–23.

35. Michael Beschloss, *The Crisis Years: Kennedy and Khrushchev, 1960-1963* (New York, 1991), 114.

36. Strober and Strober, *"Let Us Begin Anew,"* 344.

37. Richard M. Bissell Jr. with Jonathan E. Lewis and Frances T. Pudlo, *Reflections of a Cold Warrior: From Yalta to the Bay of Pigs* (New Haven, Connecticut, 1996), 170, 172.

38. Victor Andres Triay, *Bay of Pigs: An Oral History of Brigade 2506* (Gainesville, Florida, 2001), 87.

39. Ibid., 87; Martin, *A Hero for Our Time*, 307; Triay, *Bay of Pigs*, 97.

40. Christopher Andrew, *For the President's Eyes Only: Secret Intelligence and the American Presidency* (New York, 1995), 265; Strober and Strober, *"Let Us Begin Anew,"* 346; Nixon, *RN*, 235.

41. Arthur M. Schlesinger Jr., *Journals, 1952-2000* (New York, 2007), 111; Trumball Higgins, *The Perfect Failure: Kennedy, Eisenhower, and the CIA at the Bay of Pigs* (New York, 1989), 13.

42. Geyer, *Guerrilla Prince*, 276; Martin, *A Hero for Our Time*, 301.

43. Nixon, *RN*, 233; Porter McKeever, *Adlai Stevenson: His Life and Legacy* (New York, 1989), 488–89.

44. Hilty, *Brother Protector*, 414; Martin, *A Hero for Our Time*, 308; Arthur Schlesinger Jr., *Robert F. Kennedy and His Times* (Boston, 1978), 471.

45. Jacqueline Kennedy, *Historic Conversations on Life with John F. Kennedy* (New York, 2011), 185–86.

46. Rasenberger, *The Brilliant Disaster*, 342.

47. *Look*, May 21, 1963; Rasenberger, *The Brilliant Disaster*, 402.

48. Arthur Schlesinger Jr., *A Thousand Days: John F. Kennedy in the White House* (Boston, 1965), 290; *Washington Star*, April 24, 1961; *Life*, April 28, 1961; *Newsweek*, May 1, 1961.

49. *Washington Star*, April 25–26, 1961.

50. Nixon, *RN*, 234–35.

51. Andrew, *For the President's Eyes Only*, 266.

52. Bissell Jr. with Lewis and Pudlo, *Reflections of a Cold Warrior*, 191.

53. Mahoney, *The Kennedy Brothers*, 167; Beschloss, *The Crisis Years*, 376.

54. Castro, *Fidel Castro*, 253.

55. Brian Latell, *Castro's Secrets: The CIA and Cuba's Intelligence Machine* (New York, 2012), 54.

56. Nikita Khrushchev, *Khrushchev Remembers: The Glasnost Tapes* (Boston, 1990), 183.

57. John F. Kennedy, "Address and Question and Answer Period in Tampa Before the Florida Chamber of Commerce (November 18, 1963)," *Public Papers of the Presidents: John F. Kennedy 1963*, 867; William Atwood, "Memorandum from U.S. Delegate at the UN William Atwood to Gordon Chase of the National Security Staff," November 8, 1963 in White, *The Kennedys and Cuba*, 337.

58. John F. Kennedy, "Address in Miami before the Inter-American Press Association (November 18, 1963)," *Public Papers of the Presidents: John F. Kennedy 1963*, 876.

59. Ibid.

60. *Newsweek*, December 9, 1963.

61. Ibid., 683.

62. Alex von Tunzelmann, *Red Heat: Conspiracy, Murder, and the Cold War in the Caribbean* (New York, 2011), 334.

63. W. J. Rorabaugh, *Kennedy and the Promise of the Sixties* (New York, 2002), 223; Tunzelmann, *Red Heat*, 317.

64. Beschloss, *The Crisis Years*, 678.

65. *BBC News*, February 19, 2008, http://news.bbc.co.uk/2/hi/americas/7252109.stm; *Fox News Latino*, April 15, 2011, http://latino.foxnews.com/latino/latino/politics/2011/04/15/fidel-castro-remembers-bay-pigs-50th-anniversary/.

66. Kennedy, "Inaugural Address (January 20, 1961)," *Public Papers of the Presidents: John F. Kennedy 1961*, 1–3.

SIX

To the Brink

Nikita Khrushchev and the 1962 Cuban Missile Crisis

In the aftermath of the Bay of Pigs catastrophe, a sheepish John F. Kennedy staged a "unity meeting" with Dwight Eisenhower at Camp David, the remote presidential retreat in Frederick County, Maryland, that Ike had named after his grandson. "No one knows how tough this job is until after he has been in it a few months," Kennedy told his Republican predecessor.[1] If he was expecting a sympathetic hearing, he was gravely mistaken.

Eisenhower immediately lit into him for his failure to provide adequate air support for the operation. When Kennedy responded that he was only trying to keep American involvement in the affair concealed, Eisenhower dressed him down as he would an errant junior officer under his command during the Second World War. "Mr. President," he lectured, "how could you expect the world to believe that we had nothing to do with it? Where did these people get the ships to go from Central America to Cuba? Where did they get the weapons? Where did they get all the communications and all the other things that they would need? How could you possibly have kept from the world any knowledge that the United States had been involved? I believe there is only one thing to do when you go into this kind of thing, it must be a success."[2]

Although Kennedy assured Eisenhower that he had learned his lesson and that there would be no further Bay of Pigs in his administration, the former Supreme Allied Commander remained unconvinced. He privately ridiculed Kennedy for being a "Profile in Timidity and Indecision." He was not alone in expressing such reservations. Former Truman Secretary of State Dean Acheson, who had earlier dismissed the notion of invading Cuba as "a wild idea," now thought Kennedy resembled "a gifted young amateur" with a boomerang who had knocked himself out. "It was such a completely unthoughtout, irresponsible thing to do," he said. Kennedy was even more unsparing. "How could I have been so stupid?" he groaned.[3]

Watching this "perfect failure" unfold from afar with increasing puzzlement was Nikita Khrushchev. The Soviet leader had expected some sort of US military intervention in Cuba due to the Castro regime's embrace of socialism, but in his wildest imagination he could not have foreseen the inept operation that finally emerged. "I don't understand Kennedy," Khrushchev said. "Can he really be that indecisive?"[4]

Decisiveness had never been an issue for Khrushchev. The son of a miner, Khrushchev had grown up amidst grinding poverty in the rural countryside of southern Russia at the end of the nineteenth century. Though he enjoyed a year or two of formal education, he had to quit to support his family financially. "I had learnt to count up to thirty and my father decided that was enough of schooling," he remembered. "He said that all I needed was to be able to count money, and I would never have more than thirty rubles to count anyway." Young Nikita labored at a number of jobs, including sheep herding, coal mining, and metalworking. The hours were long and the wages barely at subsistence level, but the experience itself was politically eye-opening. "I worked at a factory owned by the Germans, at coal pits owned by Frenchmen and a chemical plant owned by Belgians," he said. "There I discovered something about capitalists. They are all alike, whatever their nationality. All they wanted from me was the most work for the least money that would keep me alive."[5]

Given this attitude, it wasn't much of a stretch for Khrushchev to embrace communism and its promise of a better life for the working masses after Lenin and the Bolsheviks seized power in 1917. He became an enthusiastic member of the Communist Party and served with a construction battalion in the Red Army during the Russian Civil War of 1918–1921. But his personal life became embroiled in tragedy when he lost his first wife, the former Yefrosinia Pisareva, to typhus while still on active duty. Although he would remarry two more times, Yefrosinia appears to have been the love of his life. "Her death was a great sadness to me," he later wrote.[6]

Putting aside his grief, Khrushchev drove himself relentlessly in party affairs in the years to follow, eventually catching the eye of Joseph Stalin. Impressed by his unquestioning loyalty, the First Secretary made Khrushchev a member of his ruling inner circle and placed him in a number of high-profile positions of responsibility, including head of the Moscow Communist Party in 1935. Indeed, it was from this perch that Khrushchev got a firsthand view of the purges Stalin arbitrarily launched against tens of thousands of perceived enemies within the party. "It is asked, did the leading cadres of the party know of, let us say, the arrests of people at the time?" Khrushchev later said. "Yes, they knew. But did they know that people who were innocent of any wrongdoing were arrested? No. This they did not know. They believed Stalin and did not admit the thought that repression could be applied to honest people devoted to our cause."[7]

After serving lengthy stints as a political commissar of the Ukraine and as a political officer with the Red Army during the Second World War, Khrushchev returned to his old duties as Moscow party boss in the late 1940s. While it would have been perfectly understandable of him to want to catch his breath after so many years of weighty responsibility, he received no such respite. For when Stalin passed away in 1953, he found himself in the middle of a fierce power struggle that pitted him against the formidable likes of longtime secret police chief Lavrenti Beria. A man of boundless ambition and questionable personal scruples, Beria saw himself as Stalin's heir and was willing to do anything to ensure what he believed to be his rightful place as head of the Soviet regime. "To put it crudely," Khrushchev wrote, "he had a housewarming over Stalin's corpse before it was even put in its coffin. Beria was sure that the moment he had long been waiting for had finally arrived. There was no power on earth that could hold him back now."[8]

Realizing he had little time to lose, Khrushchev mounted a major push inside the Kremlin to defeat Beria, all the while bolstering his own claim for top leadership honors. He was successful on both counts, as he was able to secure Beria's arrest and subsequent execution and gain enough popular support among the party's rank and file to claim the premiership. "His elevation came from his daring," asserted the historian Robert Service.[9]

Khrushchev's penchant for living on the political edge continued when he took on the memory of Stalin directly in early 1956. Concluding that he could not move forward as a leader until he addressed the shortcomings of his predecessor, Khrushchev decided to air his feelings at a session of the Twentieth Congress of the Communist Party of the Soviet Union. What followed was an unusually candid discussion of Stalin's character and his many abuses of power. "Stalin was a very distrustful man, sickly suspicious; we knew this from our work with him," Khrushchev told the surprised gathering. "He could look at a man and say: 'Why are your eyes so shifty today,' or 'Why are you turning so much today and avoiding to look me directly in the eyes?' The sickly suspicion created in him a general distrust even toward eminent Party workers whom he had known for years. Everywhere and in everything he saw 'enemies.' . . . Possessing unlimited power he indulged in great willfulness and chocked a person morally and physically. A situation was created where one could not express one's own will."[10]

The speech sent shockwaves through Soviet society and led directly to millions of political prisoners being released from the Siberian gulags that Stalin had unjustly sentenced them to in the 1920s and 1930s. Other "de-Stalinization" reforms followed, including a general easing of censorship rules, the elimination of purge tribunals, a greater transparency in party proceedings, and the introduction of free market–style incentives to boost lagging domestic agricultural production. "Communist society cannot be built without an abundance of bread, meat, milk, butter, and other agricultural products," Khrushchev liked to point out. [11]

Another unexpected consequence of the speech was that its implicit call for change encouraged many living behind the Iron Curtain in Eastern Europe to rise up and question the political legitimacy of their Soviet puppet rulers. In Hungary, for instance, a full-scale rebellion broke out in the fall of 1956 that resulted in Khrushchev having to order a general military crackdown to restore order. Twenty thousand Hungarians lost their lives as a result, but Khrushchev remained unapologetic. In his mind, the action was deemed necessary to prevent Russia's capitalist enemies from taking undue advantage. "If we depart from Hungary," he warned, "it will give a boost to the Americans, English and French—the imperialists. They will perceive it as weakness on our part and will go on the offensive. We would then be exposing the weakness of our positions. . . . We have no other choice." [12]

Hungary's brutal subjugation did not seem to interfere with Khrushchev's efforts to establish better Cold War relations with the United States and the West. In 1955 he and Dwight Eisenhower met in Geneva, Switzerland, to resolve long-standing East-West differences and to gain a feel for one another as leaders. Although nothing substantial emerged from these high-level diplomatic talks, the "spirit of Geneva" did encourage future dialogue between the two superpowers and a number of cultural exchanges. But Khrushchev did not come away impressed with the American president. "He was a good man, but he wasn't very tough," Khrushchev later wrote. "There was something soft about his character. As I discovered in Geneva, he was much too dependent on his advisors. It was always obvious to me that being President of the United States was a great burden for him." [13]

Eisenhower was none too enamored with Khrushchev either. "He is blinded by his dedication to the Marxist theory of world revolution and Communist domination," Ike observed. "He cares nothing for the future happiness of the peoples of the world—only their regimented employment to fulfill the Communist concept of world destiny. In our use of the word, he is not, therefore, a statesman, but rather a powerful, skillful, ruthless, and highly ambitious politician." [14]

Nevertheless, the two leaders got along well enough to make possible Khrushchev's memorable goodwill tour of America in 1959. Arranged by the US State Department, the tour got off to a bumpy start when a Soviet security guard mistook Khrushchev's designated American escort, the tall and aristocratic UN Ambassador Henry Cabot Lodge Jr., for a journalist and rudely manhandled him at a train station in San Luis Obispo, California. Lodge responded by picking up the guard and tossing him into a corner. "Don't ever lay a hand on me again," he warned his assailant. Khrushchev could not help but be impressed by his host's display of raw physical courage. "I hear you have been beating up one of my guards," he jokingly admonished Lodge.[15]

The diplomatic ice thus broken, Lodge and Khrushchev went on to have a cordial if pleasant time together as they conversed with American union leaders in San Francisco, toured a farmer's cornfield near Coon Rapids, Iowa, and visited a steel mill in Pittsburgh, Pennsylvania. "Looking back over his American journey, it was clear that Khrushchev had seen and learned a great deal," Lodge wrote. "He was most observant, intelligent, and perspicacious." Not everything went according to script. Khrushchev became enraged when he and his party were denied admission to Disneyland due to security concerns. "What is it?" Khrushchev demanded. "Have gangsters taken hold of the place? Your policemen are so tough they can lift a bull by the horns. Surely they can restore order if there are any gangsters around. I say, 'I would very much like to see Disneyland.' They say, 'We cannot guarantee your security.' Then what must I do, commit suicide?"[16]

Khrushchev appeared to have calmed down by the time he met with President Eisenhower at Camp David for the final leg of the journey. There the two leaders laid the diplomatic groundwork for what would become the Paris Summit Conference the following spring. Expectations were high on both sides that breakthrough arms control agreements were within reach. But these hopes went unrealized as the downing of an American U-2 spy plane in Soviet airspace on the eve of the summit doomed any chances for success. Interpreting the incident as an affront to Soviet honor, Khrushchev stormed out of Paris in a rage. "Frankly, I was all worked up, feeling combative and exhilarated," he later admitted. "As my kind of simple folk would say, I was spoiling for a fight."[17]

His explosive temper would flare again on October 12 when he attended a routine session of the United Nations General Assembly in New York City. Protesting an anti-Soviet remark made by a Filipino delegate, Khrushchev took off his right shoe and began violently pounding the podium in front of him. While he made light of his antics afterward, members of his own diplomatic delegation were far from amused. "We were stunned at Khrushchev's behavior," admitted one official. "He was laughing loudly and joking. He said that it had been necessary to 'inject a little life into the stuffy atmosphere of the UN.' He did not seem to realize or care what the other UN members would think about him in the wake of the escapade."[18]

Khrushchev spent the remainder of the fall keeping close tabs on the 1960 presidential campaign. No fan of Richard Nixon, whom he dismissed as "a puppet of the most reactionary circles in the United States,"

Khrushchev was personally delighted to see Kennedy pull out a narrow victory. The two had met briefly at a Senate Foreign Relations Committee reception in 1959 when Khrushchev was making the Washington rounds during his American tour, and he was impressed by what he saw. "I remember liking his face, which was sometimes stern but which often broke into a good-natured smile," Khrushchev recalled. He even playfully passed along an autographed note to Kennedy a few weeks later. "Maybe this will enable you to get out of jail when the revolution comes, but it may have some other value that I do not now recognize," he wrote.[19]

Khrushchev would go on to claim in his memoirs that he had played a decisive role in getting Kennedy elected president when he delayed the release of Francis Gary Powers, the captured American pilot involved in the U-2 affair, until after the election. "We kept Nixon from being able to claim that he could deal with the Russians; our ploy made a difference of at least half a million votes, which gave Kennedy the edge he needed."[20]

Regardless of who was responsible for his ascension to the Oval Office, Kennedy was determined to be his own secretary of state. That is why he insisted on meeting Khrushchev for a two-day superpower summit meeting in Vienna, Austria, in early June. He wanted to gain a full measure of the man who represented his greatest rival on the international stage. "The president prepared more [for that summit] than anything in his life," remembered press secretary Pierre Salinger. Not that it mattered. Contemptuously dismissing Kennedy as "a young man in short pants" for his relative inexperience and exhibited indecisiveness at the Bay of Pigs, Khrushchev spent the bulk of the conference browbeating his younger counterpart and making idle threats of war.[21]

Kennedy came away shaken. "Roughest thing in my life," he confided to journalist James Reston afterward. "He just beat the hell out of me." Having spent his political career figuratively charming the pants off people, Kennedy was unnerved to be finally meeting someone immune to his charismatic personality. "I think the idea that somehow or other the president had received a blow to his psychological solar plexus is a correct interpretation of his reaction," confirmed state department official Martin Hillenbrand. Vice President Lyndon Johnson was even more to the point. "Khrushchev scared the poor little fellow dead," he said.[22]

Kennedy became particularly alarmed when Khrushchev demanded that Berlin become a "free city." Since the end of World War II, Berlin, like the rest of Germany, had been divided up by the triumphant superpowers, with the western portions of the city controlled by the United States and its democratic allies and the eastern portions falling under the domain of the Soviet Union and its East German puppet government. By declaring Berlin "free," the United States and the West would, in effect, be giving up their postwar access rights to the city under international

law, thereby placing the ancient German capital under Communist control, as it lay more than one hundred miles inside East German territory.

Kennedy was adamantly opposed to such a move, as he and other
European leaders viewed Berlin as an important symbol of Western resolve against perceived Soviet expansionism. As Kennedy told Finland
President Urho Kekkonen, "All Europe is at stake in West Berlin."[23] But
Khrushchev had an equally pressing reason to force the issue. Berlin was
an "open city" with no effective border control between its eastern and
western sectors. As a result, tens of thousands of educated professionals
and skilled workers from East Berlin were encountering little difficulty
defecting to the more open and economically vibrant West. For sure, this
"brain drain" was crippling the East German regime to the point where
its very existence was being put into question.

Khrushchev hectored Kennedy on Berlin up to the closing moments of
the summit. "I'll step on your corns any time I want," the former peasant
warned. Weary yet resolved, Kennedy refused to yield any ground. "It is
you, and not I, who wants to force a change," he said in response to a
Khrushchev charge that the United States desired a war over the issue.
As they made their final exit from the summit meeting, Kennedy could
not help but observe ominously that "a cold winter" lay ahead.[24]

Adding to Kennedy's problems at Vienna was the fact that he was not
in the best of shape physically. Prior to the summit meeting, he had
reinjured his chronically bad back at a tree-planting ceremony in Ottawa,
Canada. "Kennedy took the silver shovel handed to him and leaned over
to shovel up some of the neat pile of black earth," journalist Hugh Sidey
recalled years later. "Then it happened. As he bent to scoop, there was a
sharp pain in his back, deep in the lower lumbar region. It was not a
severe pain; the horde of photographers and reporters and visitors did
not see a wince. Yet the pain was an unmistakable signal that his back
was to trouble him again."[25] Desperately wanting to project a robust and
vital image to Khrushchev as the leader of the Free World, Kennedy now
privately feared he would come off as a "cripple."

To avoid such an unappealing scenario, Kennedy turned to a controversial physician named Dr. Max Jacobson or "Dr. Feelgood," as he was
more popularly known. Jacobson, an eccentric German émigré who
worked out of a seedy office in New York City, was by many accounts a
quack. In fact, his license to practice medicine was later revoked by the
state of New York. But in the early 1960s "Mighty Max" was at the height
of his notoriety, acquiring a reputation for being a minor miracle worker
among a jet-set clientele that included Hollywood movie actors, Broad-
way playwrights, and best-selling authors like Truman Capote.

His specialty was giving patients amphetamine injections, i.e., speed,
to see them through whatever perceived health problems they were experiencing at the time. "I went over the top of the building!" recalled one of
his more satisfied former patients. "I felt wonderful, full of energy, ca-

pable of doing just about anything. I didn't know what exactly he was giving me, but it was a magic potion." Not everyone came away as pleased. New York Yankees star outfielder Mickey Mantle went to him for an injection to rid himself of the flu and likened the experience to being "sucked dry by a vampire." He particularly was put off by the unsterilized needle Jacobson used and the sight of blood on the latter's coat.[26]

"Max was out of his mind," claimed a former nurse under his employ. While Kennedy was aware of the concerns surrounding Jacobson's highly unorthodox medical treatments, he dismissed them out of hand. "I don't care if it's horse piss. It works," he said. Whether it worked for the president at Vienna is debatable. As has been pointed out by the historian Michael Beschloss, one of the side effects of this kind of treatment can be "impaired judgment" or even "depression," alarming symptoms that Kennedy exhibited both during and immediately following the summit. Indeed, British Prime Minister Harold Macmillan, who met privately with Kennedy in London afterward, observed that "the President was completely overwhelmed by the ruthlessness and barbarity of the Russian Premier."[27]

Back in Washington, Kennedy tried to regain his bearings, as he now saw Khrushchev as an individual "who doesn't pay much attention to words, the son of a bitch has to see you move." He announced in a July 25 televised address to the nation that he was increasing overall defense spending by $3.2 billion, enlarging military draft lists, calling up reservists, and implementing a broad-based civil defense program. The United States would not knuckle under to Khrushchev's summit threat of making West Berlin communist. "We don't want a fight—but we have fought before," Kennedy indicated. "And others in earlier times have made the same dangerous mistake of assuming that the West was too selfish and too soft and too divided to resist invasions of freedom in other lands. Those who threaten to unleash the forces of war on a dispute over West Berlin should recall the words of the ancient philosopher: 'A man who causes fear cannot be free from fear.'"[28]

Alone, Kennedy was less sanguine. "God knows I'm not an isolationist," he informed aide Kenneth O'Donnell after Vienna, "but it seems particularly stupid to risk killing a million Americans over an argument about access rights on an Autobahn in the Soviet zone of Germany, or because the Germans want Germany reunified. If I'm going to threaten Russia with a nuclear war, it will have to be for much bigger and more important reasons than that." He added that if he was to back Khrushchev against a wall in "a final test" of wills, the peace and security of the entire Western alliance would have to be at stake. "I don't think that President Kennedy had any intention of trying to start World War III and I think it could have been very dicey if we had put a lot of troops in there to face the Red Army," said Richard Helms, the CIA's then-deputy for plans. "They had a lot of forces in East Germany, and they could have put up one hell of a battle."[29]

Khrushchev, however, was livid over Kennedy's public "call to arms," likening the stance to a preliminary declaration of war. "Please tell your president we accept his ultimatum and his terms and will respond in kind," he darkly warned John McCloy, Kennedy's top arms control negotiator, who was visiting the Soviet leader at his dacha on the Black Sea. Khrushchev now thought of Kennedy as "a son of a bitch," whose words and actions were tantamount to "turning back the clock" to the tense early days of the Cold War in the late 1940s. An outbreak of hostilities had been avoided then, but there was no guarantee the same would be true this time around, given the seemingly intractable positions of both sides.[30]

The situation seemed so dire that former American ambassador to the Soviet Union George Kennan approached White House aide Arthur Schlesinger Jr. to say he was willing to sacrifice everything to prevent a war. "You and I are historians—or rather you are a real historian and I am a pseudo-historian," he told the Pulitzer Prize–winning biographer of Andrew Jackson and Franklin Roosevelt. "We both know how tenuous a relation there is between a man's intentions and the consequences of his actions. There is no presumption more terrifying than those who would blow up the world on the basis on their personal judgment of a transient position." Kennan concluded his uncharacteristic emotional outburst by voicing concern for his children's future and declaring he did not propose to let the fate of humanity "be settled or ended by a group of men operating on the basis of limited perspectives and short-run calculations."[31]

Unbeknownst to Kennan, Khrushchev had already been in close secret contact with East German communist leader Walter Ulbricht to resolve the crisis along lines that would ultimately prove acceptable to the US and USSR. It all began without advance notice in the early morning hours of August 13, when East German military units blocked off access to West Berlin and began constructing "The Wall."

The Berlin Wall, which Khrushchev euphemistically referred to as "border control," was a hundred-mile expanse of concrete barriers and barbed wire that cut through the heart of the city like a raging river. Its purpose, in the words of future West German chancellor Willy Brandt, was "to consolidate the East German communist state, which had to be safeguarded against the loss of its major capital: large numbers of able-bodied workers."[32] For sure, the Wall accomplished precisely that goal as the steady flow of East German émigrés to the West, which had grown to as many as 1,500 a day in early August, came to an abrupt halt.

But it did more than that. The fact that the Wall was built on the East German side removed any reason for a US military response, as it posed no direct threat to vital American interests in West Berlin. Kennedy

Figure 6.1.   1961 Vienna Summit Meeting. Kennedy privately admitted that the Soviet leader "just beat the hell out of me." JFK Library PX 96-33:26

seemed to grasp this right away. "Why would Khrushchev put up a Wall, if he intended to seize West Berlin?" he asked. "There wouldn't be any need of a wall if he occupied the whole city. This is his way out of the predicament. It's not a nice solution, but it's a hell of a lot better than a war."[33]

In his memoirs, Khrushchev confirmed this analysis. "We assumed that the West didn't want to start a war and our assumption turned out to be correct," he wrote. "Starting a war over Berlin would have been stupid. There was no reason to do so. Our establishment of border control in [East Germany] didn't give the West either the right or the pretext to resolve our dispute by war."[34]

While Kennedy had managed to avoid a nuclear showdown with Khrushchev over Berlin, he would not be so fortunate with regard to Cuba a year later. On the morning of October 15, 1962, National Security Advisor McGeorge Bundy informed a still pajama-clad Kennedy of the findings of two recent top-secret U-2 surveillance flights over the former American protectorate. The evidence gathered revealed that sites for offensive intermediate and medium-range nuclear missiles were being constructed on the western side of the island by Soviet military and technical personnel. Khrushchev "can't do this to me," exclaimed Kennedy. His sense of outrage was understandable. Over the previous six months, Kennedy had received repeated public and private assurances from the Russian leader that no such activity would take place. In fact, in an official statement released on September 11, the Soviet government boasted of having such powerful nuclear missiles that there was "no need to seek sites for them somewhere beyond the boundaries of the Soviet Union."[35]

Khrushchev had his reasons for partaking in such a bold gambit. First of all, he was responding to fears voiced by Fidel Castro that the United States was planning another invasion of his homeland. The Cuban dictator had good cause to be concerned. Operation Mongoose was in full swing, and the CIA-directed covert warfare operation was doing significant damage to Cuba's economy and infrastructure, not to mention posing a direct threat to Castro's life. "We were quite certain that the [Bay of Pigs invasion] was only the beginning and that the Americans would not let Cuba alone," Khrushchev later wrote.[36]

Secondly, Khrushchev was looking to narrow the strategic gap his country had with the United States when it came to nuclear weapons. As a presidential candidate, Kennedy had loudly proclaimed there was a "missile gap" favoring the Soviets. But upon taking office, he soon found the opposite was true. Instead of openly admitting his error and facing the embarrassing political consequences, Kennedy behaved as if nothing had changed and embarked on an unprecedented nuclear arms buildup. Under his administration the number of American intercontinental ballistic missiles rose from 63 in 1961 to an astonishing 423 by 1963. Predictably, Khrushchev grew alarmed, especially when Kennedy's Deputy Secretary of Defense, Roswell Gilpatric, gave a public speech in late 1961 extolling US superiority. "We have a second-strike capability which is at least as extensive as what the Soviets can deliver by striking first," he said. By placing intermediate and medium-range nuclear missiles in Cuba then, Khrushchev felt confident he could significantly reduce the US advantage. The missiles would be located only ninety miles off the coast of Florida and therefore be able to reach their targets in a much shorter period of time than if they were launched from Russian soil. As Khrushchev remarked, "Why not throw a hedgehog at Uncle Sam's pants."[37]

Lastly, Khrushchev felt he could get away with such a provocative move because Kennedy, from the Bay of Pigs onward, had proven himself to be something of an inept pushover. True, he had held his ground over the issue of Western access rights to Berlin, but he had also not lifted a finger to prevent the construction of the Berlin Wall. If anything, he welcomed it. This was simply the wrong tack to take against someone like Khrushchev, whose own earthy roots valued personal toughness and grit. "As a president," he revealingly told a visiting American official around this time, "[Kennedy] has understanding, but what he lacks is courage."[38]

Having been so clearly "double-crossed" by Khrushchev, an angry Kennedy scrambled to come up with an appropriate US response. He immediately turned to his brother Robert for advice. "Shit," was how the younger Kennedy responded when apprised of the news.[39] The air thus cleared, it was determined that the President needed to convene a special task force of trusted cabinet officials and outside advisors to tackle the crisis. Known officially as the Executive Committee of the National Security Council (ExComm), the group consisted of such notables as Secretary of State Dean Rusk, Secretary of Defense Robert McNamara, CIA Director John McCone, Secretary of the Treasury Douglas Dillon, Dean Acheson, Undersecretary of State George Ball, Vice President Lyndon Johnson, and UN Ambassador Adlai Stevenson. In the tense two weeks ahead, the ExComm met secretly at regular intervals to monitor events and debate probable policy outcomes.

One valued longtime advisor conspicuously absent from these proceedings was the "Founding Father." Joseph P. Kennedy had suffered a debilitating stroke the previous December, which confined him to a wheelchair and deprived him of the ability to speak. "He had been so strong, so vital, so important in all our lives," Edward Kennedy lamented.[40] Now he was a shell of his former self, removed from the very center of political action he had so assiduously spent his adult life striving for and eventually achieving with his son's ascension to the White House.

Just communicating his everyday needs to family members and staff attendants became an arduous task. "He tried to write with his left hand, to give instructions, and tell us what he wanted, but it frustrated him," recalled his chauffeur Frank Saunders. "I would see this look of fear creep into his eyes too—the look you can get from a wild caged animal." The situation had the air of a Greek tragedy. "He's the one who made all of this possible," John Kennedy noted sadly, "and look at him now."[41]

The ExComm came up with two possible courses of action. The first prescribed an all-out military attack on Cuba, involving a preemptive surgical airstrike of the missile sites before they became fully operational. "U.S. bombers could swoop in, eliminate the sites, and fly away, leaving the problem swiftly, magically ended," remembered advisor Theodore Sorensen. But Kennedy became skeptical of this option when the Joint Chiefs of Staff could not guarantee that all the missiles would be destroyed. "No cruise missiles or smart bombs existed in those days to assure the precision and success of the strike," Sorensen explained. Adding to Kennedy's skepticism was the fact that such a military response seemed to go against long-held American traditions that frowned upon "a surprise attack by a very large nation against a very small one." Robert Kennedy forcibly drove this point home to his brother when he passed him a note that read: "I know how Tojo felt when he was planning Pearl Harbor."[42]

The second option called for a naval blockade of Cuba preventing any additional Soviet weapons from reaching the island. The main advantage to this approach was that it would theoretically give Kennedy the time to gradually increase military and diplomatic pressure on the Soviets to abandon their aggressive course of action. But there were also serious drawbacks. According to national security advisor McGeorge Bundy, the blockade "would not remove the missiles; it would not prevent the Russians from completing their installations if they had all the necessary materials at hand, and while the evidence was incomplete, no one could assume they did not." Furthermore, Bundy worried that the blockade might trigger "a deeply embarrassing counterblockade" by the Soviets on some other vital American interest around the world requiring "deadly force in its application."[43]

After carefully weighing the pros and cons, Kennedy came down in favor of the naval blockade. In his mind, it was the most prudent and least provocative action to take, as it would present Khrushchev with a face-saving opportunity to withdraw the missiles. "I'm not going to push the Russians an inch beyond what is necessary," he said. Influencing his thinking was Barbara Tuchman's *The Guns of August*, the 1962 best seller that painstakingly documented the reasons why World War I erupted between the European great powers in 1914. Kennedy read the book and had been struck by how mutual distrust, precipitous decision making, reckless fears, and faulty leadership had led to this calamity. He had no desire to see history repeated. "The great danger and risk in all of this is a miscalculation—a mistake in judgment," he said.[44]

Having settled on a course of action, Kennedy took to the radio and television airwaves on October 22 to inform the nation of the grave situation and what his administration intended to do about it. "Within the past week, unmistakable evidence has established the fact that a series of offensive missile sites is now in preparation on [Cuba]," he solemnly began from a text prepared by presidential speechwriter Theodore Sorensen. "The purpose of these bases can be none other than to provide a nuclear strike capability against the Western Hemisphere." After explaining the United States would not tolerate the existence of such a provocative military threat so close to its own shores, he announced his decision to "quarantine" the island. "All ships of any kind bound for Cuba from whatever nation or port will, if found to contain cargoes of offensive weapons, be turned back," he said.[45]

He also took the opportunity to remind his audience of the price of inaction, by directly alluding to the ineffectual appeasement policies pursued by Western democratic leaders prior to the outbreak of World War II. "The 1930s taught us a clear lesson: aggressive conduct, if allowed to go unchecked and unchallenged, ultimately leads to war," he said. "We are also true to our word. Our unswerving objective, therefore, must be to prevent the use of these missiles against this or any other country, and to secure their withdrawal or elimination from the Western hemisphere." In closing, Kennedy went out of his way to say the United States did not desire or expect a war. "We are a peaceful people who desire to live in peace with all other peoples," he maintained. Yet this reluctance to take up arms did not preclude using force when the country's vital interests were at stake. "The cost of freedom is always high—but Americans have always paid it," he said. "And one path we will never choose, and that is the path of surrender or submission." [46]

Now it was Khrushchev's turn to voice moral outrage, lashing out at what he considered American perfidy. "I must say frankly that the measures indicated in your statement constitute a serious threat to the peace and security of nations," he testily responded to Kennedy the next day. While admitting that his government had provided Cuba with "armaments," he maintained they were "intended solely for defensive purposes," i.e., to protect the Castro regime from an American invasion. "I hope that the United States government will display wisdom and renounce the reactions pursued by you, which may lead to catastrophic consequences for world peace," he concluded. [47]

Despite Khrushchev's harsh-sounding rhetoric, Soviet vessels did honor the Cuban blockade line, thus avoiding a major confrontation with the U.S. Navy on the high seas. "We were eyeball to eyeball, and the other fellow just blinked," Dean Rusk famously remarked. But the crisis was far from over. There still remained the problem of the missile sites, which the Soviets were working feverishly on to complete. "Each hour the situation grew steadily more serious," Robert Kennedy recalled. "The feeling grew that this cup was not going to pass and that a direct military confrontation between the two great nuclear powers was inevitable." [48]

That sense of fatalism only intensified when a U-2 surveillance plane was shot down over Cuban airspace on October 27. The plane's pilot, thirty-five-year-old Air Force Major and decorated Korean War veteran Rudolf Anderson Jr., had participated in the original aerial surveillance mission that had discovered the missiles. Now he was dead, the victim of a Soviet surface-to-air missile. "This is much of an escalation by them, isn't it?" Kennedy said upon hearing the news. [49]

As he would throughout the entire crisis, the president kept his cool and refrained from taking retaliatory military action. "His actions were never jerky," remembered his secretary Evelyn Lincoln. "He never banged on the desk, waved his arms, or raised his voice in a shrill shout. Instead he would sit crouched at his desk, push his hair to one side, stand up, turn around and stare out the window, sit down, pick up the telephone and place a call, then hang up the receiver and wait for the operator to get his party." [50]

Khrushchev was the direct opposite. Excitable by nature, the stocky, loud-spoken Russian demonstrated disturbing signs that he was cracking under the pressure. The clearest example of this can be seen in the wildly conflicting diplomatic signals he sent Kennedy during this period. On October 26, he indicated in a highly conciliatory letter to the president that he was amenable to ending the crisis if Kennedy agreed to make a public statement declaring the United States would not invade Cuba. "Then the necessity for the presence of our military specialists in Cuba would disappear," he wrote.[51] But before Kennedy had a chance to respond, Khrushchev fired off another missive, this one far more menacing in tone and substance.

He now insisted that the United States not only issue a no-invasion pledge of Cuba but remove the fifteen Jupiter intermediate-range nuclear missiles it had earlier deployed to Turkey. Otherwise, war was a certainty. "You are disturbed over Cuba," he admonished Kennedy. "You say that this disturbs you because it is 90 miles by sea from the coast of the United States of America. But Turkey adjoins us; our sentries patrol back and forth and see each other. Do you consider, then, that you have the right to demand security for your own country and the removal of the weapons you call offensive, but do not accord the same right to us? You have placed destructive missile weapons, which you call offensive, in Turkey, literally next to us."[52]

Kennedy and the ExComm had discussed the possibility of trading the Turkish for Cuban missiles, but dismissed the idea out of hand. "The Jupiters were in Turkey as part of our whole [North Atlantic Treaty Organization] commitment, and the U.S. could not trade off equipment committed by NATO to serve interests of its own without undercutting the confidence of our Western allies," George Ball wrote.[53]

With the prospect of World War III hanging in the balance, however, Kennedy had to rethink his position. He dispatched his brother Robert to sound out Soviet ambassador Anatoly Dobrynin in his cavernous wood-paneled Justice Department office on the evening of October 27. According to Dobrynin, the younger Kennedy looked positively haggard. "One could see from his eyes that he had not slept for days," he recounted. "[Kennedy] himself said that he had not been home for six days and nights." Be that as it may, Kennedy wasted little time in getting down to business. He told Dobrynin that while his brother did not desire a war, he was willing to take "retaliatory action" unless he received a concrete assurance from the Soviet government the missiles would be removed soon. "I was not giving them an ultimatum but a statement of fact," Kennedy wrote afterward.[54]

Undeterred, Dobrynin pressed on the issue of the Turkish missiles, suggesting that their removal would end the diplomatic impasse. Kennedy responded by saying there could be "no quid pro quo" or "any arrangement made under this kind of threat or pressure." But he then

Figure 6.2.   Khrushchev working the crowd with his new ally. Reproduction Number: LC-USZ62-127233

proceeded to soften his stance, assuring Dobrynin that the President intended to have the Jupiters removed from Turkey within six months. The catch was none of this could be made public as part of any final deal. What could be made public, he told Dobrynin, was that the United States was willing to make a pledge not to invade Cuba if the Soviets agreed to dismantle their missile sites. "Time was running out," Kennedy said.[55]

Uncertain that he had made any diplomatic headway, Kennedy returned to the White House and relayed his pessimism. The president did not seem surprised. He too was of the opinion that the Soviets were unlikely to budge from their position, and preparations for war were required. "He ordered twenty-four troop-carrier squadrons of the Air Force Reserve to active duty," Robert Kennedy wrote. "They would be necessary for an invasion [of Cuba]." [56]

The squadrons were not needed. A clearly rattled Khrushchev decided to end the crisis he had so unwisely precipitated by agreeing to Kennedy's terms. "In order to eliminate as rapidly as possible the conflict which endangers the cause of peace [between the US and USSR]," he announced to the president in a special Radio Moscow broadcast on October 28, "the Soviet government, in addition to earlier instructions on the discontinuation of further work on weapons construction sites, has given a new order to dismantle the arms which you described as offensive, and to crate and return them to the Soviet Union." [57]

Kennedy and the world heaved a sigh of relief. "This is an important and constructive contribution to peace," read the official White House response. In private, Kennedy was considerably more effusive. "Dave," he told longtime friend and political aide David Powers, "we have extra reason to pray." British Prime Minister Harold Macmillan did not disagree. "When we recall the many occasions in history where hesitation and self-deception have led to war," he wrote, "our admiration [for Kennedy's peaceful resolution of the crisis] is correspondingly increased." Washington journalists had a slightly different take, preferring to characterize the outcome as a resounding Soviet defeat. Kennedy did his best to tamp down on such sentiment, fearing that any public gloating might backfire diplomatically and give his always unpredictable Russian counterpart a reason to change his mind. "Khrushchev has eaten enough crow," he said. "Let's not rub it in." [58]

Having narrowly avoided a nuclear war, Kennedy and Khrushchev decided to step back from the brink in the months ahead and make a concerted effort to ratchet down the tension level that existed between their two countries. To this end, a "hotline" was installed between Moscow and Washington to improve overall communication. In the event of another major nuclear crisis, American and Soviet leaders would be given the opportunity to communicate with one another directly to avoid any misunderstandings or potential miscalculations.

As welcomed as this development was, however, its significance paled next to the signing of the Limited Nuclear Test Ban Treaty in July 1963. For this groundbreaking accord mandated that both superpowers in conjunction with Great Britain bar all atmospheric and underwater nuclear testing. "The agreement, as millions of people appreciated, marked a pause in Cold War tensions that, in the early sixties, seemed to make a global conflict all too likely," Kennedy biographer Robert Dallek noted. Eventually leaders from over a hundred other nations would affix their signatures to this agreement, which Kennedy labeled the greatest accomplishment of his administration. "This treaty is not the millennium," he said. "It will not reduce our need for arms or allies or programs of assistance for others. But it is an important first step—a step toward peace—a step toward reason—a step away from war." [59]

Kennedy had set the stage for the treaty's enactment on June 10, when he told graduating seniors at Washington, DC's American University that the United States and the Soviet Union had "a mutually deep interest" in creating "a just and genuine peace." "Total war makes no sense in an age when great powers can maintain large and relatively invulnerable nuclear forces without resort to these forces," he explained. But in order to avoid such a tragic outcome, both sides needed to put aside their differences and work together in a constructive and mutually enlightened manner. "The problems of man are man-made; they can be solved by man," he asserted. "And man can be as big as he wants. No problem of human destiny is beyond human beings. Man's reason and spirit have often solved the seemingly insolvable—and we believe they can do it again." [60]

In speaking along these conciliatory lines, Kennedy was making a major departure from the "hour of maximum danger" rhetoric he had employed during the first two and half years of his presidency. The Russians were no longer seen as malefactors of the "Red Peril," but as potential partners in peace who had heroically turned the tide of battle against Hitler and the Nazis during the Second World War. "At least twenty million [Soviet citizens] lost their lives," he said. "Countless millions of homes and farms were burned or sacked. A third of the nation's territory, including nearly two thirds of its industrial base, was turned into a wasteland—loss equivalent to the devastation of this country east of Chicago." Given this immense sacrifice, Kennedy thought it prudent to point out that the Russians did not desire war any more than Americans. "For in the final analysis," he said, "our most basic common link is that we all inhabit this small planet. We all breathe the same air. We all cherish our children's future. And we are all mortal." [61]

"In that speech," maintained Theodore Sorensen, "Kennedy became the first American president to demonstrate not only appreciation of Russia as a great power—a recognition Khrushchev dearly wanted—but also empathy for Russia's enormous toll of human casualties in World War II, which the Russians felt had been largely unrecognized in the West." [62]

Khrushchev called the speech the greatest made by an American president since Franklin Roosevelt and voiced satisfaction that Kennedy was sincere about building a détente with his nation. But any hope for further diplomatic breakthroughs ended with Kennedy's assassination in Dallas, Texas, in late November. "His death was a great loss," Khrushchev wrote afterward. "He was gifted with the ability to resolve international conflicts by negotiation, as the whole world learned during [the Cuban Missile Crisis]."[63]

Though he did not realize it at the time, Khrushchev's own days as a global power broker were numbered. Owing to his "humiliating defeat" at the hands of Kennedy during the missile crisis, conservative hardliners within the Kremlin began to secretly plot his ouster. The hammer fell on October 13, 1964, when Khrushchev was summoned before a plenum of leading party officials in Moscow and told to step down. Khrushchev did his best to defend himself, especially from the charge he had unwisely removed the missiles from Cuba. "What do you mean, that we should have started a world war over them?" he retorted. Still, Khrushchev was politically savvy enough to realize his time was up. "Obviously it will now be as you wish," he told his fellow comrades. "What can I say—I got what I deserved. I'm ready for anything. You know, I myself was thinking that it was time for me to go; we face a lot of problems, and at my age it isn't easy to cope with them at all."[64]

In retirement, Khrushchev found the going difficult as he tried in vain to adjust to his newly reduced circumstances. "A pensioner's lot is simply to exist from one day to the next—and to wait for the end," he complained. "An idle old age isn't easy for anyone. It's especially difficult for someone who's lived through as tumultuous a career as mine. Now, after a lifetime of weathering storms, I've run aground." He tried to take up fishing as a way to fill the empty hours, but even this recreational activity failed to engage him. "You sit there feeling like an absolute idiot!" he exclaimed. "You can even hear the fish laughing at you under the water. That's not for me." Nor did it help matters that the ruling Soviet regime, now led by his former top political lieutenant Leonid Brezhnev, had gone out of its way to banish any memory of Khrushchev from the public square. As his son Sergei Khrushchev noted, "He simply vanished— along with all his victories and defeats, all his virtues and shortcomings, all the love of his friends and the hatred of his enemies."[65]

To preserve his place in history as well as give him something to do in his enforced idle, Khrushchev began to secretly compose his memoirs, which would later be smuggled to the West and published under the title *Khrushchev Remembers.* Noted Soviet expert and Khrushchev biographer Edward Crankshaw, who supplied extensive commentary for the work, called it a "remarkable document" that gave an unprecedented peek at "the assumptions, the ignorances, [and] the distorted views" of a Soviet leader that came of age under Stalin in the tumultuous 1930s and 1940s.[66]

Getting wind of what he was up to, Kremlin authorities urged him to abandon the project by threatening to cut off his pension and comfortable Moscow living arrangement. But Khrushchev was characteristically defiant. "You are behaving in a way no government allowed itself to behave even under the Tsars," he told them. "You can take everything away from me; my pension, the dacha, my apartment. That's all within your power, and it wouldn't surprise me if you did." He vowed to bravely soldier on and resort to begging if necessary to survive. "People will give me what I need," he insisted. "But no one would give you a crust of bread. You'd starve."[67]

Khrushchev passed away from heart failure on September 11, 1971, at the age of seventy-seven. At the height of his power, he had boasted Russia would abandon communism when "a shrimp learns to whistle."[68] While the latter never came to pass, the Soviet Union did formally cease to exist on December 25, 1991. Khrushchev had badly misjudged the long-term viability of the Marxist regime, just as he had failed to gauge accurately Kennedy's resolve during the hectic, tension-filled days of the Cuban Missile Crisis.

NOTES

1. Richard Reeves, *President Kennedy: Profile of Power* (New York, 1993), 102.
2. Ibid.
3. Robert H. Ferrell, ed., *The Eisenhower Diaries* (New York, 1981), 390; Dean Acheson Oral History, John F. Kennedy Library (hereinafter cited as JFKL); Reeves, *President Kennedy*, 103.
4. William Taubman, *Khrushchev: The Man and His Era* (New York, 2003), 493.
5. *New York Times*, September 12, 1971.
6. Nikita Khrushchev, *Khrushchev Remembers* (Boston, 1970), 17.
7. *New York Times*, September 12, 1971.
8. Khrushchev, *Khrushchev Remembers*, 322.
9. Robert Service, *A History of Twentieth Century Russia* (Cambridge, Massachusetts, 1997), 335.
10. Khrushchev, *Khrushchev Remembers*, 585.
11. *New York Times*, September 12, 1971.
12. Aleksandr Fursenko and Timothy Naftali, *Khrushchev's Cold War: The Inside Story of an American Adversary* (New York, 2006), 130.
13. Khrushchev, *Khrushchev Remembers*, 397.
14. Dwight D. Eisenhower, *Mandate for Change: The White House Years, 1953–56* (Garden City, New York, 1963), 522.
15. Henry Cabot Lodge, *The Storm Has Many Eyes: A Personal Narrative* (New York, 1973), 170.
16. Ibid., 173; Peter Carlson, *K Blows Top: A Cold War Comic Interlude Starring Nikita Khrushchev, America's Most Unlikely Tourist* (New York, 2009), 159.
17. Ibid., 263–64.
18. Ibid., 286.
19. Ibid., 273; Khrushchev, *Khrushchev Remembers*, 458; Michael Beschloss, *The Crisis Years: Kennedy and Khrushchev, 1960-1963* (New York, 1991), 16.
20. Khrushchev, *Khrushchev Remembers*, 458.
21. Charles Kenney, *John Kennedy: The Presidential Portfolio* (New York, 2000), 73; W. R. Smyser, *Kennedy and the Berlin Wall* (Lanham, 2009), 34.
22. Beschloss, *The Crisis Years*, 224–25; Gerald S. Strober and Deborah H. Strober, *"Let Us Begin Anew": An Oral History of the Kennedy Presidency* (New York, 1993), 358; Ralph G. Martin, *A Hero for Our Time: An Intimate Story of the Kennedy Years* (New York, 1963), 329.
23. Arthur Schlesinger Jr., *A Thousand Days: John F. Kennedy in the White House* (Boston, 1965), 318.

24. Martin, *A Hero for Our Time*, 328; Beschloss, *The Crisis Years*, 223; *Newsweek*, December 2, 1963.

25. Joan Myers, ed., *John Fitzgerald Kennedy As We Remember Him* (New York, 1965), 132.

26. Peter Carlson, "Jack Kennedy and Dr. Feelgood," *American History*, June 2011; Jane Leavy, *The Last Boy: Mickey Mantle and the End of America's Childhood* (New York, 2010), 225.

27. Carlson, "Jack Kennedy and Dr. Feelgood," Reeves, *President Kennedy*, 147; Beschloss, *The Crisis Years*, 191; Alistair Horne, *Harold Macmillan: Volume II: 1957-1986* (New York, 1989), 303.

28. *Look*, November 17, 1964; Kennedy, "Radio and Television Address to the American People on the Berlin Crisis (July 25, 1961)," *Public Papers of the Presidents: John F. Kennedy 1961*, 533.

29. Kenneth P. O'Donnell and David F. Powers with Joe McCarthy. *Johnny, We Hardly Knew Ye: Memories of John F. Kennedy* (Boston, 1972), 299; Strober and Strober, *"Let Us Begin Anew,"* 366.

30. Taubman, *Khrushchev*, 502; Smyser, *Kennedy and the Berlin Wall*, 91; Khrushchev, *Khrushchev Remembers*, 458.

31. Arthur M. Schlesinger Jr., *Journals, 1952-2000* (New York, 2007), 128.

32. Willy Brandt, *People and Politics: The Years 1960-73* (Boston, 1976), 24.

33. O'Donnell and Powers with McCarthy, *Johnny, We Hardly Knew Ye*, 303.

34. Khrushchev, *Khrushchev Remembers*, 458.

35. Michael Dobbs, *One Minute to Midnight: Kennedy, Khrushchev, and Castro on the Brink of Nuclear War* (New York, 2008), 6; The Soviet Government, "The Arms and Military Equipment to Cuba Are Intended Solely for Defensive Purposes," September 11, 1962 in *American Foreign Policy: Current Documents 1960-3* (Washington, 1967), 371.

36. Khrushchev, *Khrushchev Remembers*, 492.

37. Thomas G. Paterson, J. Garry Clifford, and Kenneth J. Hagen, *American Foreign Relations: A History Since 1895, Volume II* (Lexington, Massachusetts, 1995), 386; Elie Abel, *The Missile Crisis* (New York, 1966), 4; John Lewis Gaddis, *The Cold War: A New History* (New York, 2005), 75.

38. Smyser, *John Kennedy and the Berlin Wall*, 189.

39. Reeves, *President Kennedy*, 369.

40. Edward M. Kennedy, *True Compass: A Memoir* (New York, 2009), 178.

41. Frank Saunders with James Southwood, *Torn Lace Curtain* (New York, 1982), 134; Rose Kennedy, *Times to Remember* (New York, 1974), 441.

42. Ted Sorensen, *Counselor: A Life at the Edge of History* (New York, 2009), 288; Robert F. Kennedy, *Thirteen Days: A Memoir of the Cuban Missile Crisis* (New York, 1969), 38, 31.

43. McGeorge Bundy, *Danger and Survival: Choices about the Bomb in the First Fifty Years* (New York, 1990), 138.

44. Martin, *A Hero for Our Time*, 435; Kennedy, *Thirteen Days*, 62.

45. Kennedy, "Radio and Television Report to the American People on the Soviet Arms Buildup in Cuba (October 22, 1962)," *Public Papers of the Presidents: John F. Kennedy 1962*, 806–7.

46. Ibid., 808–9.

47. "Letter from Chairman Nikita Khrushchev to President John F. Kennedy," October 23, 1962, Presidential Office Files, JFKL.

48. Thomas J. Schoenbaum, *Waging Peace and War in the Truman, Kennedy, and Johnson Years* (New York, 1988), 319; Kennedy, *Thirteen Days*, 83.

49. Ernest R. May and Phillip D. Zelikow, eds., *The Kennedy Tapes: Inside the White House During the Cuban Missile Crisis* (Cambridge, Massachusetts, 1970), 571.

50. Martin, *A Hero for Our Time*, 437.

51. "Letter from Chairman Nikita Khrushchev to President John F. Kennedy," October 26, 1962, Presidential Office Files, JFKL.

52. " Letter from Chairman Nikita Khrushchev to President John F. Kennedy," October 27, 1962, Presidential Office Files, JFKL.

53. George Ball, *The Past Has Another Pattern: Memoirs* (New York, 1973), 291.

54. Khrushchev, *Khrushchev Remembers*, 497; Kennedy, *Thirteen Days*, 108.

55. Ibid., 108–9.

56. Ibid.

57. "Message from Chairman Nikita Khrushchev to President John F. Kennedy," October 28, 1962, National Security Files, JFKL; Martin, *A Hero for Our Time*, 440; Kennedy, *Thirteen Days*, 20; Martin, *A Hero for Our Time*, 439.

58. Kennedy, "Statement by the President Following the Soviet Decision To Withdraw Missiles From Cuba (October 28, 1962)," *Public Papers of the Presidents: John F. Kennedy 1962*, 815.

59. Robert Dallek, *An Unfinished Life: John F. Kennedy* (Boston, 2003), 629; Kennedy, "Radio and Television Address to the American People on the Nuclear Test Ban Treaty (July 26, 1963)," *Public Papers of the Presidents: John F. Kennedy 1963*, 602.

60. Kennedy, "Commencement Address at American University in Washington (June 10, 1963)," *Public Papers of the Presidents: John F. Kennedy 1963*, 460–61.

61. Ibid., 461–62.

62. Sorensen, *Counselor*, 327.

63. Khrushchev, *Khrushchev Remembers*, 505.

64. Sergei Khrushchev, *Khrushchev on Khrushchev: An Inside Account of the Man and His Era* (Boston, 1990), 157.

65. William J. Thompson, *Khrushchev: A Political Life* (New York, 1995), 278; Khrushchev, *Khrushchev on Khrushchev*, 400; Beschloss, *The Crisis Years*, 704.

66. Khrushchev, *Khrushchev Remembers*, viii.

67. Thompson *Khrushchev*, 280.

68. *New York Times*, September 12, 1971.

SEVEN

Taking on Jim Crow

George Wallace and the Integration of the University of Alabama

While John F. Kennedy and his top advisors expended most of their energies on meeting Soviet challenges in Berlin and Cuba during the first two years of his presidency, comparatively little time or effort was devoted to domestic affairs. This was no accident. Kennedy believed that the exigencies of fighting the Cold War took precedence over such "mundane" matters as federal aid for education, unemployment relief, or medical care for the aged, issues that were at the core of his domestic reform agenda. "Each day, the [foreign] crises multiply," Kennedy said. "Each day, their solution grows more difficult. Each day, we draw nearer to the hour of maximum danger, as weapons spread and hostile forces grow stronger." It also didn't help that a powerful coalition of conservative southern Democrats and Republicans, who had held sway in Congress since 1938, were adamantly opposed to expanding the federal social safety net. "I can't get a Mother's Day resolution through that goddamn Congress," Kennedy complained.[1]

Kennedy could nevertheless claim some significant accomplishments in the domestic realm. His administration persuaded Congress to raise the minimum wage, increase social security benefits, provide loans and grants to economically depressed areas, reduce tariffs on foreign imports, and enact a Manpower Development and Training Act designed to give unemployed workers with obsolescent skills the necessary educational and technical expertise to land jobs in the private sector. Kennedy was even able to force the steel industry to rescind a potential inflation-inducing price increase when he threatened them with federal antitrust legal action. "My father always told me, [the steel executives] were sons of bitches, but I never believed him till now," he said.[2]

Success advancing civil rights would be more elusive. Starting with the landmark 1954 Supreme Court case of *Brown v. Board of Education of Topeka, Kansas*, which ended legalized segregation in schools, to Rosa Parks' brave refusal to move to the back of the bus in Montgomery, Alabama, in 1955 to the Greensboro, North Carolina, lunch counter sit-ins of 1959, African Americans had demonstrated a willingness to challenge the prevailing status quo. It was the era of "Jim Crow," when "separate but equal" segregation laws barred blacks from attending the same kind of restaurants, stores, theaters, churches, and hotels as whites. The discriminatory laws were put into place by state governments in the South when the last of the federal troops departed at the end of Reconstruction in 1877. By the early 1960s, blacks had become emboldened by the substantial economic and social gains they had made during the First and Second World Wars. They were fighting back through mostly nonviolent means, including lawsuits, economic boycotts, and teach-ins.

"We can never be satisfied as long as the Negro is the victim of the unspeakable horrors of police brutality," said Martin Luther King Jr., the country's foremost civil leader. "We can never be satisfied as long as our bodies, heavy with the fatigue of travel, cannot gain lodging in the motels of the highways and the hotels of the cities. We cannot be satisfied as long as the Negro's basic mobility is from a smaller ghetto to a larger one. We can never be satisfied as long as a Negro in Mississippi cannot vote and a Negro in New York believes he has nothing for which to vote. No, no we are not satisfied, and we will not be satisfied until justice rolls down like waters and righteousness like a mighty stream."[3]

That Kennedy initially appeared tone deaf to these demands for greater racial equality is not surprising. His privileged upbringing had prevented him from having any meaningful contact with blacks throughout his life. Indeed, one longtime family friend observed that JFK had never seen "a Negro on level social terms with the Kennedys. And I never heard the subject mentioned." So obtuse was he on matters of race that he had no problem signing off on a restrictive covenant to his Washington, DC, home that barred him from selling his property to nonwhites. Nor did he take issue with crude racial remarks being used in his presence. When George Jacobs, an African American and the valet for his movie star friend Frank Sinatra, began spouting off about "niggers" at the latter's Palm Springs residence, Kennedy appeared greatly amused. Jacobs recalled, "[Blacks] make too much noise, I said. The Mexicans smell and I can't stand them either." Kennedy pitched over into the pool in laughter. "I think privilege requires a certain measure of ignorance," observed Yale University chaplain and longtime civil rights activist William Sloane Coffin, "and [Kennedy] was a very privileged guy."[4]

Politically, Kennedy had always claimed to be an advocate of civil rights, but because he had few blacks in his constituency back home in Massachusetts and because he had needed white southern backing in his quest to win the Democratic presidential nomination, his support never went much beyond lip service. "He seemed quite oblivious to the impending social revolution," concluded political advisor and future Supreme Court Justice Abe Fortas.[5]

There was one notable exception. In the closing stages of his presidential campaign fight against Nixon, he did place a phone call to Coretta Scott King to express concern about the safety and well-being of her famous husband, who had been imprisoned in Georgia for a minor traffic violation. The King call "helped many to make up their minds that Kennedy would be concerned, at least, about what Dr. King was talking about—trying to get justice for the black people," claimed civil rights leader the Reverend Fred Shuttlesworth.[6] King himself was in accordance with this view, adding that it took "a little political courage" for the Democratic nominee to make the call. Kennedy "didn't know it was politically sound," he said. "It was a risk because he was already grappling with the problem of losing the South [in the general election] on the religion issue. He had to face the fact that this [could] even make his situation worse in the South. And there was no assurance that he would pick up [African American votes] in the North as a result of this, so it was a risk that he took."[7]

A similar demonstration of political courage was sadly missing when Kennedy was forced to confront the first major civil rights crisis of his new administration: the "Freedom Rides." Activists from the Congress of Racial Equality and the Student Nonviolent Coordinating Committee had organized these interracial bus rides into the Deep South in the spring of 1961 to protest the segregated conditions at bus terminals, lunch counters, and roadside lodgings. Mob violence against the Freedom Riders quickly followed, but Kennedy was reluctant to get the federal government involved for two reasons. One, he feared that such action would unduly upset key southerners in Congress who would determine the success or failure of his domestic legislative program, which called for raising the minimum wage, enacting Medicare, and providing federal aid for education. Two, Kennedy was concerned that the unfolding spectacle of violence would make the country look bad in the eyes of the international community, especially when the United States was competing with the Soviet Union for the hearts and minds of dark-skinned people throughout the Third World. Kennedy's immediate response was one of haughty annoyance. As he told his liberal aide Harris Wofford, "Can't you get your goddamned friends off those buses? Stop them." As the crisis deepened, however, Kennedy sent in US Marshals to restore order and to protect the lives of the Freedom Riders. But he wasn't happy about it, particularly with a summit meeting with Soviet leader Nikita Khrushchev in Europe coming up. "I wonder whether [the Freedom Riders] have the best interests of their country at heart," Attorney General Robert Kennedy said.[8]

Supporters of civil rights could have asked the same of JFK, as he tried to placate the southern white political establishment by appointing several segregationist judges to the federal bench. Kennedy had also backpedaled on a highly publicized campaign promise to end discrimination in federally subsidized housing. He said he would do away with such differential treatment "with the stroke of a pen." But as the first year of his administration came to a close, he still had not signed the executive order. As a result, civil rights advocates mailed thousands of pens to the White House, mockingly reminding the president of his earlier pledge. Kennedy signed the order in November 1962, but in a watered down form that applied only to certain areas of federal housing. "It was a good step, but it still wasn't comprehensive enough," King said. "It wasn't retroactive and it didn't cover the loans, the saving and loans associations, and banks where you get a number of houses financed."[9]

Kennedy had better luck promoting civil rights closer to home. After years of refusing to draft or sign talented players of color, prosegregationist Washington Redskins owner George Preston Marshall ("We'll start signing Negroes when the Harlem Globetrotters start signing whites," he once said) finally caved under pressure from Kennedy's Interior Department. The Redskins selected Heisman Trophy–winning running back Ernie Davis from Syracuse University as the first overall pick of the 1962 National Football League Draft. "There were [demands for action] from Secretary of the Interior Stewart Udall and also from Washington fans, wearying of the performances of the Redskins' segregated [roster] which could win only one game in two years," wrote Shirley Povich of the *Washington Post*.[10]

With Kennedy's approval, Udall, a former three-term Democratic congressman from Arizona, had threatened to deny Marshall and his team use of DC Stadium, which had been constructed on public land and therefore subject to federal jurisdiction. "Marshall is one of the few remaining Jim Crow symbols in American sports, and we believe such an action would have a wide impact on the civil rights field," Udall explained. Davis would never suit up for the Redskins. The high salary he commanded as the number-one pick in the nation compelled the notoriously penurious Marshall to trade him to the Cleveland Browns for two lesser players, including halfback Leroy Jackson, who was also an African American. Still, a high-profile segregation barrier had fallen. "The integration success story of the Kennedy administration didn't take place in Mississippi but here in the backyard of the nation's capital," the *Boston Globe* said.[11]

As 1962 gave way to 1963, many black leaders had grown disenchanted with Kennedy's lack of action and began to criticize him openly.

While conceding that Kennedy had done "a little more" for civil rights than his predecessor in the Oval Office, Martin Luther King asserted "the plight of the vast majority of Negroes remains the same." He went on to charge the president with "a failure of leadership and with not living up to his campaign promises." This point was further driven home when Robert F. Kennedy agreed to meet with a group of civil rights activists at his family's apartment in New York City. Initially intended as a friendly exchange of views, the meeting quickly degenerated into a shouting match as the predominantly black audience accused Kennedy of being "just another politician" and the administration itself as needlessly dragging its feet on integration efforts. "Look, man," one angry participant interjected, "I don't want to hear none of your shit." [12]

Tempers had barely cooled when the Birmingham crisis erupted in April 1963. Local activists, in conjunction with Martin Luther King and the Southern Christian Leadership Conference, had decided to take on the Jim Crow establishment of the notoriously segregated Alabama city in a series of well-coordinated demonstrations. "As Birmingham goes, so goes the South," King had said. [13] But the white powers-that-be were in no mood to see their authority questioned, and what ensued was a violent crackdown led by the local commissioner of public safety, Theophilus Eugene "Bull" Connor. While an uneasy truce was eventually brokered between the two sides, televised images of protesters being beaten, clubbed, and set upon by attack dogs left a lasting, indelible impression.

Kennedy became outraged when photographs of the violence arrived at the White House. He said the images made him "sick." More importantly, they forced him to rethink his long-standing position on civil rights and conclude that his administration's strategy of trying to placate white southern opinion and keep "at least one step ahead of the evolving pressures" was no longer a workable policy. Racial warfare seemed ready to break out throughout the entire South. "The situation was rapidly reaching a boil which the President felt the federal government should not permit if it was to lead and not be swamped," Theodore Sorensen wrote later. [14]

Vice President Lyndon Johnson, himself a southerner, was even more to the point. "I think the Southern whites and the Negro share one point of view that's identical," he told Kennedy. "They're not certain that the government is on the side of the Negroes. The whites think we're just playing politics to carry New York. The Negroes feel . . . we're just doing what we got to do. Until that's laid to rest I don't feel you're going to have much of a solution. . . . What Negroes are really seeking is moral force." [15] Indeed, the time appeared ripe for Kennedy to launch what historian Carl M. Brauer later called "the Second Reconstruction," a concerted federal effort "to remove racial barriers and create equal opportunities for all in the political and economic life of the nation." [16] But before embarking on such a crusade, Kennedy had to deal with a new crisis developing at the University of Alabama at Tuscaloosa.

Two black students, James Hood and Vivian Malone, had gained admission to the school, thanks to a federal court desegregation order mandating their matriculation. But Alabama Governor George Wallace threatened to bar their entry, claiming the students' presence on campus would violate states' rights and undo decades of established tradition at the all-white school. "I will never submit myself voluntarily to any integration of any school system in Alabama," he declared. Kennedy took offense at this tack, arguing that Wallace's truculent attitude represented "a violation of accepted standards of public conduct" by an elected state official.[17] Wallace was characteristically unmoved by the criticism.

The son of a struggling farmer, Wallace grew up the eldest of four children in Barbour County, a remote rural section of southeastern Alabama best known for its historic cotton plantations. Life was far from idyllic. "I guess we looked like something out of the *Our Gang* comedies," remembered Gerald Wallace, George's younger brother. "We wore coveralls and Mother made us shirts out of fertilizer sacks, and on Sundays we put on these knicker suits."[18]

Despite the hardscrabble existence, Wallace never let the grinding poverty defeat him. He excelled in his studies and established a reputation for knowing his way around a boxing ring. He won two state Golden Gloves bantamweight titles while still a teenager. Although steeped in the mores of the Jim Crow South, which posited that black people were inferior to whites, Wallace never let such racist sentiment interfere with his need for sparring partners. "He'd resort to any means to find somebody to fight," recalled an acquaintance. "But a fella that'd get into the ring with him was in a helluva fix. None of them nigguh boys ever came back for more—he'd whale the hell out of them. One of them said one time, 'They might draft me, but I ain't volunteerin'. [Wallace] just couldn't find anybody around who was as good as he was."[19]

Wallace got his first real taste of politics in 1937, when he was elected president of his freshman class at the University of Alabama Law School. While this was the only office he would win in college, the early success spurred him to seek a lifelong career in the spotlight. After earning his law degree in 1942, he felt compelled to join other young men of his generation fighting in World War II. He enlisted in the Army Air Corps and became a flight engineer aboard a B-29 bomber dispatched to the Mariana Islands south of Japan. As he awaited orders to be shipped out, he married the former Lurleen Burns, a pretty local sales clerk who would go on to succeed her husband in 1967, becoming Alabama's first female governor. "He had the prettiest dark eyes, and the way he'd cut up!" she later recalled of their first meeting. "Even then, he was talking about politics all the time. That's what seemed to me to be really occupying his mind. He was already talking about running for governor."[20]

In the segregated service, Wallace clung to the predominant racial attitudes and traditions of his home state, often reminding his fellow airmen of the need to keep whites and blacks separate. "You don't know what it's like living in Barbour County, Alabama," he said. "I don't hate them. . . . The colored are fine in their place, don't get me wrong. But they're just like children, and it's not something that's going to change. It's written in stone. It's written in stone."[21] Like John Kennedy, he experienced his share of frontline action as he and his B-29 crewmates participated in a number of devastating bombing raids on civilian Japanese cities. "I'm glad I didn't have to see what those bombs did," he once admitted. "It's awful that folks have to drop bombs on other folks. You know, Japan's a great little country, they are a great little people. But to see all those planes, thousands of bombers, rendezvousing in the morning sun over the coast of a hostile country, glintin' in the sun as far as you could look in any direction—it was the most colossal, tremendous sight I ever seen in my life, and I been on top of the Empire State Building."[22]

By war's end, the strain of combat had taken a toll on Wallace. He lost several pounds and suffered from anxiety. He told his commanding officer that he could no longer fly practice missions with his bomber crew, a situation that put him perilously close to being court-martialed. "I'm not unpatriotic, but I've done my share," he explained. Fortunately for Wallace, he avoided official censure when he was diagnosed with a case of battle fatigue. As he remembered, "I was haggard and worn; the [commanding officer] really didn't want to do anything to harm me because he knew I was in no condition to fly. The bomber crew went ahead and flew the lead-crew training without me; they got a replacement engineer. They all took bets on whether I'd fly again—and the ones who bet that I would not certainly won their money."[23]

All the while, he thought of and prepared for his future political career back home. He sent personalized Christmas cards to Barbour County voters from the Mariana Islands. "It seemed kinda strange," recalled one recipient. Strange but effective. He easily won an open seat in the state legislature after being honorably discharged from the service in 1946. Despite the impressive victory, he did not strike many as a future political leader. "He was just a little gimlet-assed fella in a pair of britches with a buckle in the back," recalled an associate. "I said to myself, 'Good God, is that little boy actually a member of the legislature?'"[24]

Through hard work, an ingratiating personality, and an uncanny ability to get along with his fellow lawmakers, this initially negative impression gave way to a new one: Wallace the consummate politician. "I kept everybody friendly with me by not taking a big part in opposing other people's bills; if I was against something, I just voted that way but didn't make a speech," he later said. This make-no-waves approach was on display at the 1948 Democratic National Convention in Philadelphia. Although opposed to President Truman's endorsement of civil rights, he refused to join other outraged southern "Dixiecrat" delegates who stormed out of the convention in protest. To do so ran the risk of alienating key members of the party's top leadership, who could become politically useful down the road. "The young man from Barbour County was a segregationist in 1948, but he wasn't a stupid segregationist," noted his biographer Dan T. Carter.[25]

In 1953 Wallace was elected a circuit judge to Barbour County and made a name for himself by frequently ruling in favor of "working folks" over powerful regional monied interests. He was also known to be unusually lenient in cases dealing with perpetrators of minor crimes, including persons of color. It was also not out of character for him to reach into his own pocket and instruct the bailiff to buy food for the incarcerated. "George Wallace was for the little man, no doubt about that," recalled African American lawyer J. L. Chestnut, who tried several cases in his courtroom. But his progressive-mindedness had its limits. For when it came to civil rights, "The Fighting Judge," as he came to be known, was adamantly opposed to federal efforts to promote greater legal and social equality between the races. As he later said, "We thought [segregation] was in the best interests of all concerned."[26]

After successfully fighting his way through the thickets of Alabama politics, the top prize still eluded him: the governorship. In 1958 Wallace

Figure 7.1. The famous stand at the schoolhouse door. Deputy US Attorney General Nicholas Katzenbach appears unimpressed. Reproduction Number: LC-DIG-ppmsca-04294

attempted to rectify that by announcing his candidacy for the open office. His chief opponent was John Patterson, the state's photogenic young attorney general who portrayed himself during the campaign as an even stauncher foe of civil rights. Benefiting from the enthusiastic support of the Ku Klux Klan, who appreciated his legal maneuverings against the local NAACP and other high-profile African American organizations, Patterson was able to bury Wallace at the polls. "John Patterson out-nigguhed me," a crushed Wallace reportedly told his friends afterward. "And boys, I'm not to be out-nigguhed again." [27]

True to his word, Wallace embraced a more robust stance against civil rights when he launched a second gubernatorial bid in 1962. "I will continue to fight for segregation in Alabama because it is based on our firm conviction of right, and because it serves the best interests of all our people," he vowed. "I shall act vigorously to outside meddling. We shall fight the federals in the arena of an increasingly sympathetic national public opinion. We shall fight them in the arena of our courts by interposing constitutional questions involving the sovereignty of this state." [28] This message along with Patterson's inability to seek reelection due to a long-standing bar in Alabama against chief executives serving consecutive terms proved decisive. With a relatively weak field opposing him, Wallace easily swept his way to the governor's mansion. "Alabama was still innocent of the consequences of point-blank defiance, and Wallace was an enthralling, giddy, irresistible temptation," explained the journalist and Wallace biographer Marshall Frady. "He vowed he would place his body in the door of any schoolhouse ordered to integrate." [29]

Wallace repeated this racial hard line when he delivered his inaugural address on the steps of the Alabama State House in Montgomery on January 14, 1963. Authored by the veteran speechwriter and Ku Klux Klan devotee Asa Carter, who later went on to best-selling success with his *The Rebel Outlaw: Josie Wales* and *The Education of Little Tree* novels, the address was as politically provocative as it was memorable. Making note of the fact that he was standing exactly where Jefferson Davis had more than a hundred years earlier when he took the oath of office as president of the Confederate States of America, Wallace launched into a searing attack on federal integration efforts. "Let us rise to the call of freedom-loving blood that is in us and send our answer to the tyranny that clanks its chains upon the South," he thundered. "In the name of the greatest people that ever trod upon this earth, I draw the line in the dust and toss the gauntlet before the feet of tyranny, and I say: segregation now, segregation tomorrow, segregation forever." [30]

Having reached an impasse with Kennedy over the question of integrating the University of Alabama, Wallace now braced himself for an inevitable public showdown. It occurred on the morning of June 11, when Deputy US Attorney General Nicholas Katzenbach arrived on the Tuscaloosa campus to confront Wallace on the front steps of Foster Auditorium, a three-story red-bricked building that housed the university's registrar's office. Katzenbach told Wallace he had come bearing an official proclamation from the president directing the governor to comply with the federal court order allowing Vivian Malone and James Hood admission into the school. "I am asking from you," Katzenbach, said, "an unequivocal assurance that you will not bar entry to these students . . . and that you will step aside peacefully, do your constitutional duty as governor of this state, and as officer of the court, as you are a member of the bar, and that nobody acting under you will bar their entrance physically or by any other means. May I have [your] assurance?"[31]

Wallace refused to give any, preferring instead to read from a prepared statement attacking the federal government for exceeding its constitutional authority. "The unwelcome, unwanted, unwarranted and force-induced intrusion upon the campus of the University of Alabama today of the might of the central government offers frightful example of the suppression of the rights, privileges and sovereignty of this state by officers of the Federal Government," he contended. Unimpressed with Wallace's show of defiance, Katzenbach asked the governor two more times to step aside. "The two students who simply have been seeking an education on this campus are presently on this campus," he said. "They have a right to be here, protected by that court order. They have the right to register here. It is a simple problem, scarcely worth this kind of tension in my judgment. These students will remain on this campus. They will register today. They go to school tomorrow, and they will go to school at this university for the summer session of the university. The university has indicated its willingness to accept them. From the outset governor, all of us have known that the final chapter of this history will be the admission of these students."[32]

When Wallace responded to Katzenbach's entreaties with stony silence, the justice department official turned away and escorted Malone and Hood to their dormitories on campus. The next move belonged to Kennedy back in Washington, and he acted accordingly by issuing an executive order federalizing the Alabama National Guard to carry out the court order. The troops arrived on campus late in the afternoon under the leadership of Brigadier General Harry Graham, assistant commander of the Guard's 31st infantry division. Graham marched up to Wallace at the doorway and greeted him with a respectful salute. "It is my sad duty to inform you," Graham said to the man who had been his boss just a few hours earlier, "that the National Guard has been federalized. Please step or stand aside so that the order of the court may be accomplished."[33] This time Wallace did as he was told, but not before denouncing the Kennedy administration for what he called a trend toward "military dictatorship."[34] Malone and Hood were officially registered as University of Alabama students shortly thereafter.

Yet the true climax to the affair took place that evening, when Kennedy addressed the nation from the Oval Office for thirteen minutes of prime time. He began his remarks by urging his fellow countrymen not to view the events in Tuscaloosa as merely a sectional issue. "Difficulties over segregation and discrimination exist in every city, in every state of the Union, producing in many cities a rising tide of discontent that threatens the public safety," he said. Nor could the events be defined solely as a partisan issue or as a matter of strict legality, even though, he conceded, new laws were needed "at every level" to address the situation. "We are confronted primarily with a moral issue," he insisted. "It is as old as the Scriptures and is as clear as the American Constitution. The heart of the question is whether all Americans are to be afforded equal rights and equal opportunities, whether we are going to treat our fellow Americans as we want to be treated."[35]

He continued: "If an American, because his skin is dark, cannot eat lunch in a restaurant open to the public, if he cannot send his children to the best public school available, if he cannot vote for the public officials who represent him, if, in short, he cannot enjoy the full and free life which all of us want, then who among us would be content to have the color of his skin changed and stand in his place? Who among us would then be content with the counsels of patience and delay?" Noting that a hundred years had passed since President Lincoln had freed the slaves, Kennedy poignantly reminded his radio and television audience that their grandsons were still "not fully free." "They are not yet freed from the bonds of injustice," he said. "They are not yet freed from social and economic oppression; and this nation, for all its hopes and all its boasts, will not be fully free until all its citizens are free." Now, he declared, the time had come for the country to "fulfill its promises" to the African American community: "The events in Birmingham and elsewhere have so increased the cries for equality that no city or state or legislative body can prudently choose to ignore them." Indeed, the "fires of frustration and discord" were already "burning" in every major American city, North and South.[36]

"We face, therefore, a moral crisis as a country and as a people," Kennedy concluded. "It cannot be met by repressive police action. It cannot be left to increased demonstrations in the streets. It cannot be quieted by token moves or talk. It is a time to act in the Congress, in your state and local legislative body, and, above all, in all of our daily lives." He promised that he would ask Congress to enact sweeping new civil rights legislation dedicated to the proposition that "race has no place in American life or law."[37]

Yet, he cautioned, legislation alone would not be enough to redress the age-old problem of prejudice and discrimination. "It must be solved in the homes of every American in every community across the country. . . . This is one country. It has become one country because all of us and all the people who come here had an equal chance to develop their talents. We cannot say to 10 percent of the population that you cannot have that right; that your children can't have the chance to develop whatever talents they have; that the only way that they are going to get their rights is to go into the streets and demonstrate. I think we owe them and we owe ourselves a better country than that." 38

The speech marked a major turning point. No president since Lincoln had taken the bold step of placing the full legal and moral authority of the executive branch behind the cause of black civil rights. Now Kennedy had done so, and the country would never be the same. Henceforward, the federal government would play a proactive role in integrating American society, regardless of a person's skin color or ethnicity. "It was . . . by far the strongest speech that had ever been made in support of civil rights by any president," Nicholas Katzenbach later related. It "committed the Kennedy Administration and [other successor administrations to follow] to that road and I think it is a very proud moment in our history." 39

Not surprisingly, given their many years of sacrifice and toil for the cause, civil rights leaders were among the first to grasp the historic significance of Kennedy's remarks. "Your speech last night to the nation on the civil rights crisis was a clear, resolute exposition of basic Americanism and a call to all our citizens to rally in support of the high traditions of our nation's dedication to human rights," Roy Wilkins wrote to Kennedy on June 12. Martin Luther King Jr. was equally effusive. "Walter," he told his friend and fellow civil rights activist Walter E. Fauntroy, "can you believe that white man not only stepped up to the plate, he hit it over the fence." Publicly, King's praise took a more prudent tone. "I am sure," he telegrammed Kennedy, "that your encouraging words will bring a new sense of hope to the millions of disinherited people of our country. Your message will become a hallmark in the annals of history. The legislation which you will propose, if enacted and implemented, will move our nation considerably closer to the American dream." 40

Not everyone was sympathetic to these pleas for justice. Critical letters addressed to Kennedy poured into the White House from irate whites below the Mason-Dixon Line. A common example was the following June 11 missive from a "hot tempered" Huntsville, Texas, resident. "I want you to know that I agree 100% with Gov. Wallace," wrote Debbie Terrell. "I also want you to know this: when you were first elected as President of the United States, I respected you very much. Now I am sorely disappointed. Can't you see what will happen if we let Negros go to our schools, swimming pools, and other places. Soon they will take over." A Gallup Poll taken on June 16 showed that 62 percent of all white southerners felt Kennedy was moving "too fast" on racial integration, while only 32 percent from the same sampling approved of his performance as president. These results were particularly worrisome to Kennedy, given how vital an electoral role the "Solid South" had played in his razor-thin victory over Nixon in 1960. He had carried six southern states in that election, and now it seemed quite possible he would carry none if he ran again in 1964. "He always felt that maybe that was going to be his political swan song," Robert Kennedy said. George Wallace did not disagree. "The South next year will decide who the next president is," he told reporters after the Tuscaloosa showdown. "Whoever the South votes for will be the next president, because you can't win without the South. And you're going to see that the South is going to be against some folks."[41]

If this wasn't cause enough for concern, the very night Kennedy delivered his civil rights address to the nation, Medgar Evers, the first field secretary for the Mississippi NAACP, was gunned down on the front doorstep of his home. "Medgar was lying there . . . in a pool of blood," his grief-stricken wife Myrlie said afterward. "I tried to get the children away. But they saw it all—the blood and the bullet hole that went right through him." Evers had been carrying an armful of NAACP sweatshirts emblazoned with the slogan "JIM CROW MUST GO" when a sniper fatally shot him in the back. His final words were, "Turn me loose!" Bernard Lafayette, a charismatic young organizer for the Student Nonviolent Coordinating Committee in Selma, Alabama, was also the target of an assassination attempt that evening. He managed to escape with his life when a neighbor intervened to help ward off his attackers. "I didn't know Medgar was killed until the next day because I was in the hospital [with serious head wounds]," he said.[42]

To his credit, Kennedy did not retreat from his administration's commitment to civil rights in the wake of these sobering developments. If anything, he became even more determined to see the issue through to its conclusion, whatever the outcome. As he had earlier told Luther Hodges, his Secretary of Commerce, "There comes a time when a man has to take a stand and history will record that he has to meet these tough situations and ultimately make a decision."[43]

One way Kennedy demonstrated this resolve was by giving official approval to a planned march on Washington by civil rights leaders on August 28. "I think that's in the great [American] tradition," he told reporters at the time. "We want citizens to come to Washington if they feel they are not having their rights expressed."[44] And come they did in what was one of the most memorable displays of nonviolent protest in the country's history.

More than 250,000 people descended upon the Lincoln Memorial to hear Martin Luther King Jr. deliver his stirring "I Have a Dream" speech. "I say to you today, my friends, that in spite of the difficulties and frustrations of the moment I still have a dream," King told the multitudinous gathering. "It is a dream deeply rooted in the American dream. I have a dream that one day this nation will rise up and live out the true meaning of its creed: 'We hold these truths to be self-evident; that all men are created equal. . . . I have a dream that my four little children will one day live in a nation where they will not be judged by the color of their skin but by the content of their character. I have a dream today. . . . This is our hope. This is the faith which I return to the South. With this faith we will be able to hew out of the mountain of despair a stone of hope. With this faith we will be able to transform the jangling discords of our nation into a symphony of brotherhood. With this faith we will be able to work together, to pray together, to struggle together, to go to jail together, to stand together, to stand up for freedom together, knowing that we will be free one day." Conversing with King at a Cabinet Room reception afterward, a clearly impressed Kennedy shook his hand and said, "I have a dream." [45]

In the early planning stages of the March on Washington, Kennedy had met with King and other prominent black leaders at the White House to candidly discuss the stakes involved. "Okay, we're in this up to our necks," he informed them. "A good many programs I care about may go down the drain because of this. I may lose the next election because of this. We may all go down the drain as a result of this—so we are putting a lot on the line. What is important is that we preserve confidence in the good faith of each other." [46]

As a sign of his own good faith, Kennedy formally introduced his civil rights bill to Congress on June 19. Described by a *New York Times* editorial as "a bold and admirable attempt to erase the barriers that now stand in the way of the full enjoyment by every American of the constitutional guarantees that are his birthright," the bill outlawed "racial segregation and discrimination" in all public and privately owned facilities while strengthening voting rights protection. "The legal remedies I have proposed are the embodiment of this Nation's basic posture of common sense and common justice," Kennedy said. "They involve every American's right to vote, to go to school, to get a job and to be served in a public place without arbitrary discrimination—rights which most Americans take for granted. . . . It will go far toward providing reasonable men with the reasonable means of meeting these problems, and it will thus help end the kind of racial strife which this nation can hardly afford. . . . To paraphrase Lincoln: 'In giving freedom to the Negro, we assure freedom to the free—honorable alike in what we give and what we preserve.'" [47]

Kennedy would never learn the fate of his civil rights bill. His assassination in Dallas on November 22, 1963, shocked the nation and the world, but within the African American community the grieving was particularly intense and heartfelt. "It was the first time I cried with white people," remarked one New York City cab driver. Future best-selling author Anne Moody became so emotionally distraught upon hearing the news that she fainted in the New Orleans restaurant where she worked.

Boarding a public streetcar afterward and looking at the grief-stricken black faces around her, she observed, "I knew they must feel as though they lost their best friend—one who was in a position to help determine their destiny. To most Negroes, especially to me, the President had made 'Real Freedom' a hope."[48]

Civil rights activist Andrew Young became similarly distraught when he first learned of the tragedy during an educational workshop he was conducting in South Carolina. "We gathered everyone in the chapel and there we shared the sorrowful news," he remembered. "The chapel was comforting in its Quaker simplicity; the bare wooden floors and angular lines suited the somber mood that fell over the group. Somebody began to pray. This was not prayer as performance, standing regally in front of the gathered community grasping the security of a podium. This was heart-baring prayer. When it was your time to pray you got down on your knees, put your elbows on the seat of one of the cold, metal folding chairs and your head on your hands and begged for the comfort that only God can provide. The folk gathered there knew something had happened that could potentially change the course of the country and particularly their own lives."[49]

Ironically, Kennedy's death would serve as a catalyst in getting his civil rights bill through Congress. Seeking to capitalize on the enormous outpouring of public grief and sympathy the tragedy had engendered, newly sworn-in President Lyndon Johnson portrayed himself as the executor of Kennedy's political will. He pledged to enact into law every piece of New Frontier legislation still pending before Congress. Topping the list was civil rights. "First," Johnson declared, "no memorial or oration or eulogy could more eloquently honor President Kennedy's memory than the earliest possible passage of the civil rights bill for which he fought so long. We have talked for one hundred years or more. It is time now to write the next chapter and write it in the books of law."[50] Working closely with civil rights leaders and making full use of his talents as a backroom political operator, Johnson was able to get the legislation past an initially reluctant Congress.

The final product was the landmark Civil Rights Act of 1964, which for all intents and purposes marked the beginning of the end for the decades-old Jim Crow system of racial injustice in the South. "The purpose of this law is simple," Johnson announced. "It does not restrict the freedom of any American so long as he respects the rights of others. It does not give any special treatment to any citizen. It does say the only limit to a man's hope for happiness and for the future of his children shall be his own ability. It does say that those who are equal before God shall now also be equal in the polling booths, in the classrooms, in the factories, and in the hotels and restaurants, and movie theatres, and other places that provide service to the public." In making these comments, Johnson was also careful to pay special tribute to "our late and beloved president John F. Kennedy" for initially conceiving and introducing the legislation to Congress. "It has received the thoughtful support of tens of thousands of civic and religious leaders in all parts of this nation, and it is supported by the great majority of the American people," he said.[51]

George Wallace did not include himself in that majority. He vehemently opposed the legislation, claiming it to be a violation of individual constitutional rights and communist-inspired. "The bill," Wallace warned, "has been endorsed and pushed by *The Communist Daily Worker* in every section of it and not a one of them believes man has a soul or has any afterlife and doesn't believe that man is made in the image of God. Every left-wing organization in America who doesn't believe in the existence of God is behind this bill." Religion aside, Wallace had by this time grown alarmed at the increasingly liberal, bureaucratic, and anti–Vietnam War drift of the national Democratic Party. "Our lives are being taken over by bureaucrats, and most of them have beards!" he charged. To provide a nationwide forum for his opposition as well as satisfy a growing personal ambition to achieve higher office, Wallace decided to launch an independent bid for the presidency in 1968. "We're going to shake 'em up good in November," he pledged.[52]

Wallace had tested the presidential waters as a Democratic candidate in 1964, but dropped out early owing to the inevitability of Johnson's nomination and victory that year. He thought 1968 would be different. "Lincoln was a plurality winner, and I'll be a plurality winner," he said. "In a four-man race he didn't get a majority of the people's votes, but he had enough to get a majority of the electoral votes. Well, if I run, this will be at least a three-man race, and the same thing could happen." Denouncing big government, student protesters, court-ordered busing, voting rights, and expanded federal social welfare programs for the poor, Wallace's "politics of rage" was warmly received by disaffected white working-class voters across the land. In fact, this approach would become a template for future conservative candidates like Ronald Reagan and George W. Bush, who made a point of articulating similar reactionary themes in their presidential campaigns. "He's gonna turn this country around," one enthusiastic supporter told a *Newsweek* reporter. "It's not that we dislike niggers—we hate 'em."[53]

For his part, Wallace relished the opportunity of tweaking the nose of the liberal Democratic establishment, whom he believed had unfairly treated him. "I'm sick and tired of some professors and some judges and some newspaper editors having more to say about my everyday life . . . than I have to say about it myself," he thundered. "I am going to give the moral support of the presidency to the police and firemen in your city and through your state. Let me tell you something: if it wasn't for the police and firemen in your city, you wouldn't be able to even ride down your streets, much less walk down them." As for those "anarchists in the street" who were protesting against the war and general societal injustice,

Wallace also had a special message. "[I]f any *demonstrator* ever lays down in front of *my* car, it will be the *last* car he'll ever lay down for," he promised.[54]

On Election Day, however, it was Wallace who felt run over. Even though he had finished better than any third-party candidate since 1912 with more than nine million votes and forty-six electoral votes from five southern states [Louisiana, Mississippi, Arkansas, Alabama, and Georgia], he still ended up a distant third to Republican standard-bearer Richard Nixon and his Democratic challenger Hubert H. Humphrey. "Wallace is a campaigner, and a good one," praised former presidential advisor Richard Scammon afterward.[55] Just not good enough, he might have added.

Wallace declined another third-party challenge in 1972, instead opting for a return to his partisan political roots. An independent candidacy "didn't have a chance in hell," explained a top campaign advisor. "[Wallace] decided he'd run in the Democratic primaries." Though many Democrats treated him like a prodigal son and kept him at arm's length, he notched a second-place finish in Wisconsin and reeled off impressive victories in Maryland, Michigan, Florida, North Carolina, and Tennessee. But his presidential campaign was brutally cut short in May when a deranged twenty-one-year-old busboy named Arthur Bremer shot Wallace at a campaign rally in Laurel, Maryland. Bremer "kept yelling 'Hey George! Hey George!'" an eyewitness said. "The man stuck his gun in his stomach and fired." Several gunshots were fired, and one bullet pierced Wallace's spinal cord, leaving him without the use of his legs and permanently confined to a wheelchair. "I have to kill somebody," Bremer had written in his diary. "I am one sick assassin."[56]

Despite suffering frequent episodes of severe pain, Wallace gamely refused to let the disability end his political career. He won two more terms to the Alabama governorship in 1974 and 1982 and tried yet again to become the Democratic nominee for the presidency in 1976. He told a close supporter that his diminished physical status prevented him from fulfilling his White House ambitions. When the supporter mentioned how Franklin Roosevelt had overcome similar limitations decades earlier, Wallace remained unconvinced. "Yeah," he responded, "they elected Roosevelt, but they didn't watch him on television every night getting hauled on a plane like he was half-dead."[57]

Having become a born-again Christian in his later years, Wallace found it prudent to apologize to the African American community of Alabama for his race-baiting past, especially his 1963 call for "segregation forever." "I never should have said it, because it wasn't true," he told the journalist Carl T. Rowan a few years prior to his death by septic shock in 1998. "That statement in 1963 . . . and my stand in the classroom door reflected my vehemence, my belligerence, against the federal court system that seemed to be taking over everything in the South. I didn't write those words about segregation now, tomorrow and forever. I saw them in the speech written for me and planned to skip over them. But the wind-chill factor was [five] below zero when I gave that speech. I started reading just to get it over and read those words without thinking. I have regretted it all my life." He added disingenuously that he had never supported "white supremacy" and that his political actions were no worse than those of Lyndon Johnson. "He was for segregation when he thought he had to be," Wallace explained. "I was for segregation, and I was wrong. The media has rehabilitated Johnson, why won't it rehabilitate me?"[58]

Historians cast an equally reproachful eye on Kennedy's involvement with the civil rights movement in the early 1960s. His actions during this crucial period were dismissed as tardy and ineffectual, not to mention overly timid. "He almost always allowed the voice of political expedience to drown out the better angels of his nature," claimed Nick Bryant, the author of the scathing 2006 study *The Bystander: John F. Kennedy and the Struggle for Black Equality*. Even sympathetic biographers like Robert Dallek expressed strong reservations. Kennedy, Dallek wrote, "was slow to recognize the extent of the social revolution fostered by Martin Luther King and African Americans, and he repeatedly deferred to southern sensibilities on racial matters, including appointments of segregationist

Reproduction Number: DIG-ppmsca-19605

Figure 7.2.   Articulating the "politics of rage": Wallace made his second ill-fated run for the White House in 1968.

judges in federal districts."[59] While most of these criticisms are valid for the first two and half years of his presidency, they fail to account for the dramatic transformation Kennedy underwent in the final months of his life.

Deeply moved by the events in Birmingham, he concluded that drastic change was needed if the nation was ever to surmount the bitter racial divisions that had plagued it since the end of Reconstruction. His decision to confront George Wallace over the integration of the University of Alabama afforded him the opportunity to lay the moral and legal groundwork for such change. "Historians will record that he vacillated like Lincoln," Martin Luther King Jr. said later, "but he lifted the cause far above the political level."[60]

He had "The Fighting Judge" to thank for that.

NOTES

1. Kennedy, "Annual Message to the Congress on the State of the Union (January 30, 1961)," *Public Papers of the Presidents: John F. Kennedy 1961*, 22; Gerald S. Strober and Deborah H. Strober, *"Let Us Begin Anew": An Oral History of the Kennedy Presidency* (New York, 1993), 287.

2. *New York Times*, October 18, 1985.

3. Martin Luther King Jr., "I Have a Dream," August 28, 1963, in *Great Issues in American History: From Reconstruction to the Present Day, 1864-1981* (New York, 1982), Volume III, Richard Hofstadter and Beatrice K. Hofstadter, 451.

4. James N. Giglio, *The Presidency of John F. Kennedy* (Lawrence, Kansas, 1991), 159; David Burner, *John F. Kennedy and a New Generation* (Boston, 1988), 55; Shawn Levy, *Rat Pack Confidential: Frank, Dean, Sammy, Joey, and the Last Great Showbiz Party* (New York, 1998), 72; Strober and Strober, *"Let Us Begin Anew,"* 275.

5. Ralph G. Martin, *A Hero for Our Time: An Intimate Story of the Kennedy Years* (New York, 1963), 72.

6. Strober and Strober, *"Let Us Begin Anew,"* 36.

7. Martin Luther King Jr. Oral History, John F. Kennedy Library (hereinafter cited as JFKL).

8. Robert Dallek, *An Unfinished Life: John F. Kennedy* (Boston, 2003), 384; Alan Brinkley, *John F. Kennedy* (New York, 2012), 101.

9. Harris Wofford, *Of Kennedy and Kings: Making Sense of the Sixties* (New York, 1980), 124; Martin Luther King Jr. Oral History, JFKL.

10. Thomas Smith, *Showdown: JFK and the Integration of the Washington Redskins* (Boston, 2011), viii; *Washington Post*, December 15, 1961.

11. Smith, *Showdown*, 171, 151.

12. *New York Times*, June 10, 1963; Arthur Schlesinger Jr., *Robert Kennedy and His Times* (Boston, 1978), 909.

13. Juan Williams, *Eyes on the Prize: America's Civil Rights Years 1954-1965* (New York, 1987), 182.

14. Geoffrey Perret, *Jack: A Life Like No Other* (New York, 2002), 368; Theodore C. Sorensen, *Kennedy* (New York, 1965), 494; Carl M. Brauer, *John F. Kennedy and the Second Reconstruction* (New York, 1977), 246.

15. Mark Stern, *Calculating Visions: Kennedy, Johnson, and Civil Rights* (New Brunswick, New Jersey, 1992), 88.

16. Brauer, *John F. Kennedy and the Second Revolution*, viii.

17. Marshall Frady, *Wallace* (New York, 1968), 153; Kennedy, *Washington Post*, June 11, 1963.

18. Frady, *Wallace*, 64.

19. Ibid., 69–70.

20. Stephan Lesher, *George Wallace: American Populist* (Reading, Massachusetts, 1994), 44–45.

21. Dan T.Carter, *The Politics of Rage: George Wallace, The Origins of the New Conservatism, and the Transformation of American Politics* (New York, 1995), 62.

22. Frady, *Wallace*, 87.

23. Carter, *The Politics of Rage*, 66; Lesher, *George Wallace*, 60.

24. Frady, *Wallace*, 88, 92.

25. Lesher, *George Wallace*, 71; Carter, *The Politics of Rage*, 88.

26. J. L. Chestnut Jr. and Julia Cass, *Black in Selma: The Uncommon Life of J.L. Chestnut Jr.: Politics and Power in a Small American City* (New York, 1990), 126; *Washington Post*, September 14, 1998.

27. Frady, *Wallace*, 127.

28. Lesher, *George Wallace*, 157; Frady, *Wallace*, 157.

29. Ibid., 133.

30. George Wallace, "The Inaugural Address of Governor George C. Wallace," January 14, 1963, Alabama Department of Archives and History, Montgomery, Alabama, http:www.archives.state.al.us/govs_list/inauguralspeech.html.

31. *Boston Globe*, June 12, 1963.

32. Ibid.

33. *Time*, June 21, 1963.

34. *Boston Globe*, June 12, 1963.

35. Kennedy, "Radio and Television Address to the American People on Civil Rights (June 11, 1963), *Public Papers of the Presidents: John F. Kennedy 1963*, 469.

36. Ibid.

37. Ibid.

38. Ibid., 470.

39. *Kennedy vs. Wallace: A Crisis Up Close*, video documentary, Drew Associates, 1988.

40. Stern, *Calculating Visions*, 88; Ted Sorensen, *Counselor: A Life at the Edge of History* (New York, 2009), 282; *Washington Post*, June 12, 1963.

41. "Letter from Debbie Terrell to President Kennedy," June 11, 1963, Presidential Papers, White House Central Subject Files, JFKL; Brauer, *John F. Kennedy and the Second Reconstruction*, 263; Dallek, *An Unfinished Life*, 605; *Kennedy vs. Wallace*.

42. *Time*, June 21, 1963; *Newsweek*, June 24, 1963; Bernard Lafayette interview with author.

43. Brauer, *John F. Kennedy and the Second Revolution*, 247.

44. Kennedy, "The President's News Conference of July 17, 1963," *Public Papers of the Presidents: John F. Kennedy 1963*, 572.

45. *King Jr., "I Have a Dream," Great Issues in American History*, Hofstadter and Hofstadter, eds., 452–53; *Look*, November 17, 1964.

46. Charles Kenney, *John F. Kennedy: The Presidential Portfolio* (New York, 2000), 202; *New York Times*, August 29, 1963.

47. Ibid., June 20, 1963; Kennedy, "Special Message to the Congress on Civil Rights and Job Opportunities (June 19, 1963), *Public Papers of the Presidents: John F. Kennedy 1963*, 493–94.

48. *Life*, November 29, 1963; Anne Moody, *Coming of Age in Mississippi* (New York, 1968), 320.

49. Andrew Young, *An Easy Burden: The Civil Rights Movement and the Transformation of America* (New York, 1996), 278–79.

50. *New York Times*, November 28, 1963.

51. Ibid., July 3, 1964.

52. Lesher, *George Wallace*, 294; Lewis L. Gould, *1968: The Election That Changed America* (Chicago, 1993), 31; *Newsweek*, September 16, 1968.

53. Rick Perlstein, *Nixonland: The Rise of a President and the Fracturing of America* (New York, 2008), 224; *Newsweek*, September 16, 1968.

54. Lesher, *George Wallace*, 420; *Newsweek*, September 16, 1968.

55. *Washington Post*, September 22, 1968.

56. Lesher, *George Wallace*, 460; *Washington Post*, May 16, 1972; *Time*, August 14, 1972.

57. *New York Times*, September 14, 1998.

58. *Washington Post*, September 5, 1991.

59. Nick Bryant, *The Bystander: John F. Kennedy and the Struggle for Black Equality* (New York, 2006), 470; Dallek, *An Unfinished Life*, 707.

60. *Look*, November 17, 1964.

EIGHT

A Lesson to All

J. Edgar Hoover, Lee Harvey Oswalk, and the Death of a President

As the shadows lengthened and the leaves began to fall outside the Oval Office in the autumn of 1963, John Kennedy's thoughts turned more and more to one subject: South Vietnam. Under the authoritarian leadership of Ngo Dinh Diem, the small Southeast Asian country had been waging a losing three-year battle against North Vietnamese communists, who were conducting large-scale guerrilla warfare operations in the south. Unless the military situation showed marked improvement, the former French colony appeared destined for communist subjugation, a prospect that deeply offended the Cold War sensibilities of the president. "It doesn't do us any good to say, 'Well, why don't we all just go home and leave the world to our enemies,'" he said.[1]

On the advice of Secretary of State Dean Rusk, Kennedy appointed his old political rival Henry Cabot Lodge Jr. to the ambassadorship of South Vietnam. In recommending a distinguished Republican such as Lodge for the Saigon post, Rusk hoped to win bipartisan support for the administration's Vietnam policy, which called for massive amounts of military and economic aid to the south. Kennedy wasted little time in signing off on this choice, perhaps sensing as well that the GOP leader would act as "asbestos against the heat of possible future criticism of his foreign policy." Only the president didn't phrase it that way when he met with Lodge on June 12 to discuss the latter's availability for the job. "Cabot," he said, "I am beginning to spend more of my time on Vietnam than anything else. The Diem government seems to be in the terminal phase. . . . I'd like to persuade you to go out there as Ambassador and as my personal representative."[2]

Lodge accepted, and the South Vietnam he went to was a seething cauldron of political unrest. In previous months, Diem, a devout Roman Catholic, had embarked on a ruthless campaign of oppression against the country's majority Buddhist population. Measures taken included the arrest and torture of several hundred monks and nuns and the wanton destruction of religious shrines and pagodas. The raids were carried out by Diem's brother, Ngo Dinh Nhu, whose reputation for brutality was surpassed only by his appetite for power.

To correct the situation, Kennedy instructed Lodge to put pressure on Diem to reform his ways. "If, in spite of your efforts, Diem remains obdurate and refuses," the president cabled his ambassador on August 24, "then we must face the possibility that Diem himself cannot be preserved." Lodge, who had a thinly disguised contempt for the Vietnamese leader, found no fault with this policy, especially when Diem refused to make the requested changes to his regime. "We are launched on a course from which there is no responsible turning back: the overthrow of the Diem government," Lodge wrote Kennedy five days later. "We should make an all-out effort to get the generals to move promptly."[3] The "generals" Lodge referred to were disgruntled field commanders in the South Vietnamese army who had grown weary of Diem's excesses and his failure to decisively meet the communist threat from the north.

Under the direction of major General Duong Van Minh, the military leaders staged a successful coup d'etat on November 1 that resulted in the executions of Diem and Nhu. Though Lodge made a half-hearted effort to secure Diem safe passage during the crisis ("If I can do anything for your physical safety, please call me," he told him), he shed no tears over the Vietnamese leader's passing. "When we read in our newspapers about a coup in Vietnam," he told journalist Charles Bartlett in 1965, "we think in terms of a coup in the White House, and we're horrified. But it doesn't horrify the Vietnamese. In fact, when the coup came there were smiles on everybody's faces, and they just wanted to be sure that some of these officials, who'd been torturing people and incarcerating them, were going to get punished." As for Kennedy's handling of the affair, Lodge opined, "I think he was sophisticated in his realization that he was dealing with a different kind of civilization, with a different kind of culture."[4] However patronizing and culturally insensitive these remarks now appear, they are representative of the type of paternalistic mind-set that dominated Washington policy-making circles in the early 1960s. The Vietnamese were viewed as children, supposedly not sufficiently schooled in the tenets of democracy to know the difference between liberty and dictatorship.

When official word of Diem's murder reached the White House, a horrified Kennedy could barely contain his emotions. He bolted from his chair in the middle of a meeting and rushed to the door "with a look of shock and dismay on his face." "He had always insisted that Diem must never suffer more than exile and had been led to believe or had persuaded himself that a change in government could be carried out without bloodshed," remembered Maxwell Taylor, chairman of the Joint Chiefs of Staff. Burdened with a deep sense of personal guilt, Kennedy settled down afterward to dictate a memorandum on the unexpected turn of events. "The way [Diem] was killed makes it particularly abhorrent," he said. "The question now is whether the [South Vietnamese] generals can stay together and build a stable government, or whether . . . the intellectuals, students, et cetera, will turn on the government, as repressive and undemocratic in the not so distant future."[5] Kennedy would never learn the answer.

In the weeks leading up to the Diem coup, the president had been distracted by a brewing sex scandal that held the potential of exposing his relationship with a twenty-seven-year-old prostitute named Ellen Fimmel Rometsch.

Kennedy was no neophyte when it came to sordid sexual affairs. Throughout his marriage to Jacqueline Bouvier, he had taken up with a steady stream of chorus girls, movie actresses, and hookers to satisfy his voracious sexual appetite. "He had his father's attitude toward women—there was only one place for women and that was horizontal," noted one disapproving journalist. Indeed, the Ambassador had set the pattern early for his sons when he did little to hide the fact he was shamelessly cheating on their mother with a bevy of attractive mistresses, including most famously the Hollywood screen legend Gloria Swanson. "He was like a roped horse—rough, arduous, racing to be free," Swanson later said of their first sexual encounter.[6]

John Kennedy was cut from the same cloth. He never met a beautiful woman he didn't want to bed. "I get a migraine headache if I don't get laid every day," he insisted. Not even naïve interns were above his lascivious notice. Three decades before Bill Clinton had his infamous contretemps with Monica Lewinsky, Kennedy seduced Mimi Alford, a 19-year-old Wheaton College undergraduate who was working in the White House press office. Alford had been on the job for only four days in the summer of 1962 before the president made his advances. On the pretext he was giving her a private tour of the White House, Kennedy led her to the upstairs residential quarters, where he proceeded to pull down her underwear and touch her breasts in the same room where Jacqueline slept at night. They had sex soon thereafter. "Could I have done anything to resist President Kennedy?" Alford later wrote. "I doubt it: once we were alone in his wife's bedroom, he'd maneuvered me so swiftly and unexpectedly, and with such authority and strength that short of screaming, I don't think anything would have thwarted his intentions."[7]

Alford continued her liaison with Kennedy almost until the day he died eighteen months later. "Our sexual relationship was varied and fun," she claimed, "and we spent an inordinate amount of time taking baths together, turning his elegant bathroom into our own mini-spa." These watery excursions often bizarrely involved some yellow rubber ducks Kennedy had acquired. "Every time the President saw those rubber ducks, he'd become irresistibly playful," Alford recalled. "We named them after his family members, made up stories about them, and often set them racing from one end of the tub to the other. It was part of his charm that he was a serious, sophisticated man with extraordinary responsibilities, yet willing to be completely silly."[8]

The Rometsch affair was different. Originally a refugee from East Germany, Rometsch had come to America in 1961 after her husband, West German airman Rolf Rometsch, was assigned to his country's diplomatic mission in Washington. Taking up prostitution to underwrite her expensive tastes and lavish lifestyle, Rometsch became a favorite escort of many leading Democrats and Republicans on Capitol Hill, as her striking brunette looks and vivacious personality proved captivating. Kennedy certainly found this to be true when he had a mutual acquaintance arrange a number of trysts with her in the spring of 1963. "She spread a lot of joy in Washington," claimed Bobby Baker, the ethically challenged Senate Secretary who had formally employed Rometsch as a hostess at his exclusive Quorum Club in the Carroll Arms Hotel.[9]

That joy would turn to alarm by October, however, when the *Des Moines Register* got wind of the story and reported allegations that Rometsch had been carrying on with "White House officials" and "well-known persons in the legislative branch."[10] While Rometsch and her husband had been discreetly sent back to West Germany in August at the behest of Attorney General Robert Kennedy, who feared that Rometsch might pose a security risk (she had once belonged to Communist Party organizations in East Germany), this new development threatened to blow the lid off things and become another Profumo Affair. That scandal had helped bring down Harold Macmillan's British government earlier in the year when it was publicly revealed that his defense minister, John Profumo, had carried on an illicit sexual relationship with a prostitute who in turn had been sleeping with a Soviet naval attaché believed to be a spy.

Unwilling to see his administration stumble down a similar rabbit hole, John Kennedy begrudgingly sought the assistance of a man whom he had come to loathe during his presidency: J. Edgar Hoover. The longtime Federal Bureau of Investigation Director did not let him down. He approached Senate leaders from both parties and convinced them not to give in to growing political pressure to investigate the matter, as it would likely "taint Republicans as well as Democrats" due to Rometsch's bipartisan bed-hopping. The story died in the popular press, and Kennedy was able to breathe easier. Yet Hoover's help did not come without a price. Believing that Martin Luther King Jr. had fallen under the sway of communists, Hoover soon requested and received official approval from Robert Kennedy's Department of Justice office to wiretap the famed civil rights leader. Neither Kennedy nor his brother believed that King was a communist stooge, but they felt compelled to sign off on the request anyway. As the historian James W. Hilty relates, the Kennedys "now found themselves obligated to the director, dependent on his judgment, and like it or not, committed to him personally."[11]

Presidents since Calvin Coolidge had long turned to the taciturn Director in such times of deep personal and political crisis. Hoover was, after all, the man who kept the secrets, both official and otherwise, of Washington. His voluminous background files on nearly every figure of national importance were at once legendary and unsettling, for they contained tidbits of information that were often personally embarrassing, if not scandalous. Hoover already had a dense file on John Kennedy dating back to his passionate wartime romance with former Danish movie actress Inga Marie Arvad, whom the FBI had suspected of being a Nazi spy. While this concern ultimately proved unwarranted, several phone conversations between Kennedy and Arvad were nevertheless secretly recorded by Hoover's agents, revealing, among other things, that the then dashing naval intelligence officer possessed a cavalier attitude toward sex. "I heard you had a big orgy up in New York," Kennedy playfully informs Arvad in one of the calls. In 1962, Hoover learned that Kennedy had become intimately involved with Judith Campbell, a beautiful young California divorcee who was simultaneously carrying on an affair with Chicago underworld boss Sam Giancana. After apprising the President of the inappropriate nature of this relationship during a March 22 luncheon meeting at the White House, Hoover left it to Kennedy to cut all ties to Campbell, which he promptly did. "J. Edgar has Jack Kennedy by the balls," Lyndon Johnson said.[12]

The normally hyperbolic vice president was not exaggerating. Only Hoover prevented these affairs from becoming common knowledge. And this gave him immense power. "In theory and in practice," noted the journalist John Seigenthaler, "Hoover was a law unto himself." Presidents and administrations could come and go, but Hoover always remained the leader of his elite criminal investigative unit inside the Department of Justice, a fixed point in a sea of political uncertainty. "He is a pillar of strength in a city of weak men," Johnson said.[13] How he was able to achieve and maintain this position of great authority is a story of unbridled ambition, ruthless opportunism, and no small measure of luck.

Hoover entered the world on New Year's Day 1895 in Washington, DC, the youngest of four children of a striving middle-class family. "As a youth I was taught basic beliefs," he later said. "For instance, I was taught that no book was ever to be placed above the Bible. Children in my youth were taught the code of the American flag, and to defend it against any manner of desecration, as a symbol of life, liberty, and justice." Making sure he remained on the straight and narrow was his mother, the former Annie Marie Scheitlin, a proud descendant of a Swiss diplomatic family. She held young J. Edgar and his siblings to exacting standards of behavior while dispensing generous amounts of discipline. "She dominated the household," noted the biographer Curt Gentry. Hoover's father, Dickerson, took no issue with this arrangement. A clerk with the US Coast and Geodetic Survey, he suffered from debilitating bouts of personal depression that often left him detached from the day-to-day workings of home life. Indeed, so precarious was his state of mental health, he had to be institutionalized for a time at a local sanitarium. "It was a subject that was invisible," recalled one relative. "Even though we all knew, we were told not to talk about that. And we didn't. They said it was a breakdown. And that was all they said. It was a sad time, particularly for [J. Edgar]."[14]

To move beyond this sadness, Hoover buried himself in his studies, winning valedictorian honors for his high school class in 1913. He also became active in several student organizations, including the school's cadet corps. The equivalent to a modern-day junior ROTC program, Hoover was elevated to company commander status his senior year. The experience proved enormously formative, as it gave the formerly shy, socially awkward Hoover the confidence boost he needed to become more assertive. "The year has been a most enjoyable one," he reflected afterward, "for there is nothing more pleasant than to be associated with a company composed of officers and men who you feel are behind you heart and soul. The saddest moment of the year was . . . when I realized that I must part with a group of fellows who had become a part of my life."[15]

Hoover went on to George Washington University upon graduation and earned a law degree in 1916. He received a master's degree in law at the same institution a year later. As in high school, he evinced little interest in partaking in traditionally male adolescent pursuits like dancing or dating women. "He was slim, dark and intense," remembered a fellow GWU student. "He sat off by himself [in class] against the wall, and always had the answers. None of us got to know him very well."[16]

This standoffishness, especially toward members of the opposite sex, would eventually feed rumors that Hoover was a closeted homosexual who had a fetish for dressing up in women's clothing. Many speculated that he had a long-running affair with Clyde Tolson, the Associate Director of the FBI from 1930 to 1972. "Words are mere man-given symbols for thoughts and feelings, and they are grossly insufficient to express the thoughts in my mind and the feelings in my heart that I have for you," Hoover once wrote Tolson.[17]

Despite the obvious affection he had for his loyal subordinate and the fact the two frequently socialized and vacationed together, there remains no conclusive proof Hoover ever had a romantic relationship with Tolson or that he was a homosexual. "If they did have a homosexual relationship, as is widely believed though never established, it was discreet, stable, and disciplined, as was everything else about J. Edgar Hoover," Hoover biographer Kenneth D. Ackerman wrote. Hoover's actions over the years did suggest he was highly sensitive to such speculative gossip. He cashiered many Bureau employees for the mere suspicion of being gay. "Only one with a depraved mind could have such thoughts," he said.[18]

To help defray the costs of his college education, Hoover accepted a thirty-dollar-a-month file clerk position at the Library of Congress. While others might have found this work dull and demeaning, Hoover utterly reveled in it as he mastered the intricacies of the library's document indexing system, which closely resembled the more famous Dewey Decimal System. "He imagined how, with a few tweaks, he could use [the indexing system] to track anything he liked, even people," noted Ackerman. "He could use it to find anyone, even in a vast country of 105 million souls spanning the entire continent. He could use it to hide things, too, just by manipulating the code."[19] These were lessons that would prove invaluable when he became FBI Director a few years later and began creating his own "Official and Confidential" file system for the agency.

In 1917 Hoover passed the bar exam and accepted a position with the Department of Justice as a low-level clerk. It didn't take him long to impress his superiors. "From the day he entered the Department, certain things marked Hoover apart from scores of other young law clerks," observed one journalist. "He dressed better than most, a bit on the dandyish side. He had an exceptional capacity for detail work and he handled small chores with enthusiasm and thoroughness. He constantly sought new responsibilities to shoulder, and welcomed chances to work overtime. When he was in conference with an official of his department, his manner was that of a young man who confidently expected to rise."[20]

US Attorney General A. Mitchell Palmer soon tapped him to run the General Intelligence Division, a new Justice Department agency tasked with identifying and investigating radical and anarchist elements in American society. Hoover characteristically took on the assignment with great energy and enthusiasm, building up a network of undercover informants nationwide who tracked the movements of thousands of suspected subversives. Palmer, who had earlier survived an anarchist bomb attack on his home, used this information to launch a series of "Red Raids" to round up the individuals, many of them foreign nationals whose only perceived crime was that they held socialist beliefs. While Hoover later tried to distance himself from this "hysterical dragnet," which civil libertarians and legal scholars universally denounced as a violation of individual constitutional rights, contemporaries were quick to point out his culpability. "Hoover lies when he denies responsibility for the Red Raids," said Felix Frankfurter, a founding member of the American Civil Liberties Union and an Associate US Supreme Court Justice from 1939 to 1962. "He was in it—up to his ass."[21]

Irrespective of his controversial personal role, Hoover's career suffered no ill effects from the Red Raids. By 1924 the twenty-nine-year-old lawyer had become head of the Department of Justice's Bureau of Investigation, a small crime-fighting and domestic intelligence gathering agency that had been founded at the urging of President Theodore Roosevelt in 1908. It would later be rebranded the FBI in 1935. "Everyone says he's too young, but maybe that's his asset," mused Harlan Fiske Stone, Hoover's Department of Justice boss at the time of the appointment. "Apparently he hasn't learned to be afraid of the politicians, and I believe he would set up a group of young men as investigators and infuse them with a will to operate independent of congressional and political pressure."[22] Stone knew his man.

Undaunted by the bureaucratic challenges awaiting him, Hoover went about systematically building up the Bureau into a premier law enforcement outfit employing thousands and whose reputation for catching criminals would surpass that of Great Britain's celebrated Scotland Yard. His agents would be directly responsible for bringing to justice such high-profile gangsters as Charles Arthur "Pretty Boy" Floyd, John Dillinger, and Lester Gillis, alias "Baby Face" Nelson. He was able to accomplish these impressive feats by introducing a demanding new entrance exam for bureau personnel that produced higher-quality applicants along with a more professionalized workforce. He also took advantage of cutting-edge forensic methods like fingerprinting to make it easier for agents to identify crime suspects. "No one need erect a monument to you," an admirer later said. "You have built your own monument in the form of the FBI—for the FBI is J. Edgar Hoover and I think we can be rest assured that it will always be."[23]

The lavish praise obscured Hoover's obvious faults as Director, for as the years progressed and his public image as the country's leading G-man grew, he became increasingly more autocratic and rigid in his ways. "Listen," one of his agents later recounted, "Hoover was a bastard. He ruled by fear." He took even the slightest criticism of the Bureau as a personal affront upon his character. Dissent was not so much discouraged as it was banned altogether. "The most casual statement, the most strained implication, was sufficient cause for Mr. Hoover to write a memorandum to the Attorney General complaining, and impugning the integrity of its author," remembered Nicholas Katzenbach, Kennedy's Deputy Attorney General. An unhealthy sycophancy thus settled into the ranks. "Let's say you're an agent," confirmed one insider. "Go in there and tell him he looks better than ever, that you are inspired by his leadership, that he's saving America and you hope he lives forever. As soon as you

leave there will be a memo from the director saying, 'This man has executive ability.' A lot of agents have caught on."[24]

This sort of hubris led Hoover into making the most obvious failure of
his career. Despite reams of evidence indicating that organized crime had
existed and flourished in America since the 1920s, he steadfastly refused
to acknowledge there was such a threat. "No single individual or coalition of racketeers dominates organized crime across the country," he insisted. As to why Hoover exhibited this "curious myopia," his reasoning
is open to speculation. The most plausible explanation is that unlike the
Dillingers or Pretty Boy Floyds of the world, he felt the Mafia was simply
too big and powerful a criminal outfit to take on successfully. For sure,
Hoover's stature as the nation's "top cop" might have suffered an egre-
gious blow if he had tried. As Curt Gentry relates, "Maintaining a 96–98
percent conviction rate [in non–organized crime incidents] wasn't difficult when you were dealing with bank robberies, car thefts, kidnappings,
and white-slave cases—and could pick and choose which cases you
wanted to prosecute. But organized crime cases were hard cases, from
start to finish. Merely to indict a major mob figure might take hundreds
of agent hours and then, all too often, result in a hung jury or an acquittal.
An inveterate horse player, Hoover didn't like the odds."[25]

Hoover may not have also liked being blackmailed. According to
Meyer Lansky, the notorious underworld boss used photos of Hoover in
a sexually compromising position with Clyde Tolson as leverage to get
the FBI Director to back off the mob. But, as FBI chronicler Gil Reavill has
taken pains to point out, there is not a shred of evidence supporting this
claim. "No such photos have ever surfaced, even decades after Hoover's
death," Reavill wrote. "It's unlikely they ever existed." Nor was Lansky
above spreading outlandish falsehoods. The mobster, Reavill wrote,
"demonstrated himself over and over quite eager to muddy the waters
around his enemies with half-truths, outright lies, and indecent innuen-
dos."[26]

Hoover instead channeled the Bureau's energies and resources toward what he believed was the greatest danger facing the nation: the Red
Menace. "A disciplined Party of hard-core fanatical members is now at
work, with their fellow travelers, sympathizers, opportunists, and
dupes . . . to add America to Soviet Russia's list of conquests," he maintained. Laboring closely with the House Committee on Un-American Activities in the late 1940s and 1950s, Hoover attempted to cast a bright
spotlight on the internal communist threat. The results were mixed and
highly controversial. For every convicted atomic spy like Julius or Ethel
Rosenberg his agents were able to uncover, there were individuals like
renowned British-born screen actor and director Charlie Chaplin. Chaplin's chief offense in the eyes of Hoover was that he had frequently been
seen in the company of so-called dangerous left-wingers like Princeton
University physicist Albert Einstein, the author of the General Theory of

Relativity. For this perfidy, Chaplin had his reentry work permit to the United States revoked. "You have to remember that it was a small group that overthrew the Russian government, was [Hoover's] attitude," said Tom Clark, Attorney General for the Truman administration. "But most of the cases we had were squeezed oranges. I didn't think there was much to them."[27]

When Kennedy assumed the presidency in 1961, there were no indications of any looming rift with Hoover. His father had been a longtime friend and admirer of the Director, even going so far as to tout him as presidential timber back in 1956. "If that should come to pass," the Ambassador wrote Hoover, "it would be the most wonderful thing for the United States, and whether you were on a Republican or Democratic ticket, I would guarantee you the largest contribution that you would ever get from anybody and the hardest work by either a Democrat or Republican. I think the United States deserves you. I only hope it gets you." John Kennedy had also demonstrated his own measure of respect or fear for the lifelong Washington resident by reappointing him FBI Director in one of his first moves as president. Politics, of course, played a significant role here. It would have been unwise to dismiss Hoover, given his popularity among most Americans, especially after a close presidential contest. "I think [the President] made up his mind—'We're not going to rock the boat at this moment,'" explained longtime Kennedy aide Kenneth O'Donnell.[28]

Problems soon emerged, however. Much to the administration's displeasure, Hoover continued to resist efforts to confront domestic organized crime. Robert Kennedy, who had made a name for himself in the 1950s investigating the mob's influence on organized labor as Chief Counsel for the Senate Rackets Committee, found this stance especially perplexing. "Hoover didn't believe in the existence of the Cosa Nostra to the extent that he felt the bureau should not be expanding its manpower in what he regarded as essentially a problem for the local authorities," said Courtney Allen Evans, an Assistant Director of the FBI and liaison to the White House in the early 1960s. "He didn't want to dissipate his resources to investigate organized crime." Hoover didn't endear himself to the administration either by being slow to protect civil rights activists in the Deep South due to his own deep-seated prejudice against blacks. "Everybody knows that Negroes' brains are twenty percent smaller than white people's," he said. Nor did he show much enthusiasm for an administration edict requiring the Bureau to recruit and hire African Americans as field agents. "The FBI treated the civil rights movement as if it were an alien enemy attack on the United States," said Coretta Scott King, wife of Martin Luther King Jr.[29]

The foot-dragging infuriated the President and his brother Robert, who was officially Hoover's boss at the Department of Justice. "They were incensed at him from time to time," admitted Evans. "They felt he was wasting manpower investigating [domestic communist] cases." Robert demonstrated his contempt by openly speculating to aides that Hoover needed to "squat to pee." "Bobby was trying to take over the FBI, and run the FBI, water down the FBI to his own liking," charged longtime Hoover aide Cartha "Deke" DeLoach. "You might say, well, he was the Attorney General and therefore we were answerable to him; that's true. No doubt about that. But there also was—you just don't interfere with a machine that's going very well. He was trying to re-do the whole machine to his own liking, and he didn't have the experience or respect to command things like that . . . I did not like his own ambition, arrogance or viciousness." Believing the Director had become too old and inflexible to remain an effective administrator, both Kennedys gave earnest consideration to pushing him into retirement. "Hoover was really of no particular importance to [the president]," Robert Kennedy said.[30]

In reality, neither Kennedy was in a position to follow through on this threat. Hoover possessed considerable leverage over John Kennedy in the form of extensive dossiers on the President's affairs with Inga Arvad, Judith Campbell, and Ellen Rometsch. Kennedy would have been naïve politically to believe Hoover would not have leaked out details about

Figure 8.1.   Vice President John Nance Garner receives a hands-on lesson in law enforcement procedure from the Director. Reproduction Number: LC-DIG-hec-26298

these scandalous relationships to friendly members of the press if he were shown the door. The risks of public exposure, in terms of scandal and popular embarrassment, were simply too great. "Firing J. Edgar Hoover? Jesus Christ!" Nicholas Katzenbach later exclaimed. "I seriously question whether President Kennedy could have made a firing stick."[31]

While Hoover had expended considerable time and energy on monitoring the comings and goings of Kennedy's lovers, he failed to take an adequate accounting of the threat a twenty-four-year-old former American defector to Russia posed. For Lee Harvey Oswald was a very dangerous man. An emotionally unstable loner with an above-average intelligence, Oswald had spent his childhood skipping school and getting into minor scrapes. "He was quick to anger," a family acquaintance remembered. "He was vicious almost. . . . He was a bad kid."[32]

Experiencing fantasies "about being all-powerful and hurting people," the Louisiana native had been diagnosed by a psychiatrist as having a "personality pattern disturbance with schizoid features and passive-aggressive tendencies." "I dislike everybody," Oswald admitted. He dropped out of high school in 1955 and joined the Marine Corps as a way to see the broader world and to escape the smothering influence of his mother Marguerite, a widowed single parent who was financially struggling to make ends meet. "To him, military service meant freedom," his stepbrother John Pic said.[33]

As a Marine stationed overseas in Japan, Oswald continued his solitary ways, making no effort to connect with others. "We were trained to work as a team but Oswald seemed to be different," remembered one acquaintance. "He was always separate from most of the men and didn't have any close friends." Oswald also had difficulty taking orders from superior officers and was court-martialed twice for insubordinate behavior, including one incident where he accidentally shot himself with an unauthorized derringer pistol. Despite these setbacks, he did earn "marksman" status with the M-1 rifle and performed competently enough as a radio operator to earn a security clearance. But his general unpopularity among his fellow Marines (they derisively compared him to the "Ozzie Rabbit" cartoon character) and his growing disenchantment with military life ("All the Marines did was to teach you to kill, and after you got out of the Marines you might be good gangsters," he said) left him longing to return to civilian life. On September 11, 1959, his wish was granted as he received a hardship discharge from the corps. His mother had apparently been injured at work, and he was sent home to support her.[34]

However, his stay with Marguerite lasted only three days, as he made preparations to travel to Europe and eventually defect to the Soviet Union. "It is difficult to tell you how I feel," he wrote his mother in a departing note. "Just remember this is what I must do. I did not tell you about my plans because you could hardly be expected to understand." Os-

Figure 8.2. Hoover at the height of his power in 1940. Reproduction Number: LC-28438

wald's decision to defect had long been in the making. Since his teen years, he had become fascinated with communist philosophy and its searing critique of Western capitalism. He was particularly impressed with Karl Marx's 1867 opus, *Das Kapital*. "It was what I'd been looking for," he said. "It was like a very religious man opening the Bible for the first time." His stint in the Marine Corps did nothing to diminish his ardor for the revolutionary doctrine. He addressed colleagues with the appellation "Hello, Comrade," studied up on the Russian language, and was known to have a copy of *Das Kapital* at his fingertips. An open admirer of Fidel Castro and the Cuban revolution, he also began railing against what he saw as "American imperialism." "He kept referring to the Marines [at his base] as 'You Americans,' as if he were some sort of foreigner simply observing what we were doing," recalled a fellow Marine. "His tone was definitely accusatory."[35]

Upon reaching Russia in 1959, he renounced his US citizenship ("I have made up my mind. I'm through," he reportedly told an American embassy official in Moscow) and took up residence in Minsk, then capital of the Byelorussian Soviet Socialist Republic. "He was the most interesting defector I ever saw," said Priscilla Johnson, an American correspondent stationed in Moscow. "Of the three or four defectors I saw, he was the only ideological one . . . he talked in terms of capitalists and exploiters and he said something about he was sure that if he lived in the U.S. he couldn't get a job, that he'd be one of the exploited. He was like a babe in the woods, a lost child."[36]

Assigned by authorities to a low-skill job in a radio and television electronics factory, Oswald quickly became disillusioned with everyday life in the grim industrial city. His personal gloom was only relieved by a budding romantic relationship with Marina Nikolayevna Prusakova, a nineteen-year-old local pharmacist who caught his eye. "I want you to be my own girl," he had told her. Although Marina was initially cool to his advances, she was eventually won over by the flattering attention he gave her and the promise of a better life. Marina had grown up under tough economic circumstances, and she apparently was impressed that Oswald was gainfully employed with a comfortable apartment. "I've plenty of Russians to choose from," she told an acquaintance. "It's just that I like him and want to marry him."[37]

They tied the matrimonial knot in the spring of 1961, but Oswald's days as a member of the Soviet proletariat were drawing to a close. "The work is drab [and] the money I get is nowhere to be spent," he had complained earlier in his diary. "No nightclubs or bowling allys [sic] no places of recreation acept [sic] the trade union dances I have had enough." Feeling homesick, he applied for and received permission from the American Embassy to return to the United States with his new Russian wife. There were not many tears shed over their departure. Oswald "flits from side to side and is unhappy everywhere," noted one of Marina's family members. "People are tired of nursing him over here."[38]

Settling in the Dallas-Fort Worth, Texas, area, Oswald continued his path of general aimlessness. He bounced around from one low-paying job to another and expounded on his Marxist perspective of the world to anyone who cared to listen. "I think he was pretty satisfied with his view on of how life was, in the sense that he had it figured out," recalled Ruth Hyde Paine, a local housewife who befriended the Oswalds and opened her home to them. Bored with domestic life and increasingly withdrawn, Lee gave serious thought in the late summer of 1963 to hijacking a plane to Cuba with an Italian bolt-action rifle he had purchased by mail order. The US government had barred all travel to the Caribbean Island, but Oswald yearned to join Castro's communist revolution there as a volunteer. "He was preparing to go to Cuba," Marina later confirmed. "He very much wanted to go to Cuba and have the newspapers write that somebody had kidnapped an aircraft."[39]

Although his wife talked him out of taking such drastic action, Oswald's proclivity toward violence had already been established. The previous spring, he had used his Italian rifle in an assassination attempt upon the life of retired Army Major General and John Birch Society member Edwin A. Walker at the latter's Dallas home. According to Marina, her husband told her that Walker was a "fascist" for his extreme anticommunist views and therefore deserving of elimination. "He said if someone had killed Hitler in time it would have saved many lives," she later remembered. Like so many other endeavors in Oswald's failure-ridden life, this one proved equally unsuccessful. Walker escaped serious harm as his assailant's bullet deflected off the woodwork in the house. "I thought I'd shot General Walker," a disappointed Oswald said afterward.[40]

While he was fortunate at the time that no authorities linked him to the Walker assassination attempt, Oswald did not give up on the now-ingrained notion in his head that he needed to kill a figure of national importance. To this end, he briefly toyed with the idea of murdering former Vice President Richard Nixon when the latter came to Dallas on a business trip in late April. But he abandoned these plans when Marina, who was pregnant with their second child, got wind of them. "I can't take it all the time," she scolded him. "I could lose the baby and you wouldn't even care."[41]

Marina would not be so fortunate on November 22. After learning from local press coverage that Kennedy would be visiting Dallas on a political trip and that his presidential motorcade would pass by the Texas School Book Depository Building where he had recently accepted a job as a clerk, Oswald secretly decided to take action. Shortly before noontime, he improvised a sniper's nest on the sixth floor of the Depository before a large window overlooking Dealey Plaza, where Kennedy's open-air limousine would arrive half past the hour. Leading up to the trip, Kennedy had revealed a premonition of sorts to his old Senate colleague and friend George Smathers of Florida. "God, I hate to go out to Texas," he said. "I hate to go, I just hate like hell to go. I have a terrible feeling about going."[42] Now his worst fears were about to be realized.

Taking careful aim with his Italian rifle, Oswald managed to fire off three quick shots at the president, the last one delivering a skull-shattering, fatal blow to the back of Kennedy's head. "We saw pieces of bone and brain tissue and bits of his reddish hair flying through the air," recalled Kenneth O'Donnell, who was riding in the backup car behind the presidential limousine. "The impact lifted him and shook him limply, as if he was a rag doll, and then he dropped out of our sight, sprawled across the back seat of the car."[43]

His goal accomplished, an eerily calm Oswald jettisoned the assassination weapon among some book boxes before exiting through the Depository's front door. He was picked up less than two hours later by Dallas Police at a local movie theater showing a World War II adventure yarn called *Cry of Battle*, starring Liza Moreno and Van Heflin. In the interim between the assassination and his arrest, Oswald shot to death a local officer named J. D. Tippit with a pistol he was carrying in his belt. Tippit had stopped him on the street for routine questioning. "Poor dumb cop," Oswald exclaimed as he hurriedly departed the scene.[44]

In custody, Oswald, now sporting a badly bruised right eye from an arresting officer who had struck him, maintained an air of imperturbability. He told authorities they had the wrong man and claimed he had nothing against the late president personally. "They're taking me in because of the fact that I lived in the Soviet Union," he answered to the shouted questions of reporters. "I'm just a patsy." While Oswald maintained his innocence, one agitated local nightclub owner with mob ties had made up his mind that the "lousy Commie" was guilty. Jack "Sparky" Ruby was a lonely and insecure man who one acquaintance claimed "had to get into everything, including the excitement of that weekend Kennedy died." On the morning of November 24, he managed to sneak into the basement of the Dallas Police headquarters and gun down a handcuffed Oswald at point-blank range when the latter was being moved to an awaiting vehicle for transfer to the county jail. Ruby later claimed that he performed the deadly act to spare Jacqueline Kennedy the emotional anguish of having to appear at Oswald's trial. "I had the gun in my right hand pocket, and impulsively, if that is the correct word here, I saw him, and that is all I can say," he maintained. "And I didn't care what happened to me."[45]

The rapidity of these brutally tragic events caught J. Edgar Hoover off guard. And the FBI Director never liked to be surprised, especially when his agency bore so much of the responsibility. Simply stated, the Bureau had dropped the ball in allowing someone of Oswald's troubled personal background to get so near the President. Additionally, it failed to coordinate properly with Secret Service and local law enforcement personnel on the ground to alert them of the obvious threat the former Marine marksman posed. The Dallas Police even complained publicly that they had never heard of Oswald "until the shooting." "Such gross incompetency can't be overlooked," Hoover concluded after a secret internal FBI review of the assassination unearthed these glaring deficiencies. Beginning in 1959 when Oswald defected to Russia, Hoover and the FBI had kept tabs on him but neglected to put him on the Security Index, a listing of "potentially or actually dangerous" individuals who might pose a threat to the nation. "[Our agents] were worse than mistaken," Hoover said. "Certainly no one in full possession of all his faculties can claim Oswald didn't fall within this criteria."[46]

When Oswald returned to the United States with a new Russian wife, the spotty Bureau surveillance continued. After a local Dallas branch agent named James Hosty questioned Marina at her home about her husband's activities on two separate occasions in early November, an enraged Oswald left a signed note for his inquisitor at his office. "Let this be a warning," Oswald threatened. "I will blow up the FBI and the Dallas Police Department if you don't stop bothering my wife."[47]

Amazingly, there was no concerted follow-up that might have resulted in Oswald being removed or at least detained from the Texas School Depository by FBI officials on November 22. Hosty, who destroyed the note on the order of a supervisor after Oswald's death, later tried to downplay the significance of the event. But it is instructive to point out that Hosty admitted to a Dallas police officer in the aftermath of Kennedy's killing that the FBI believed Oswald "was capable of assassinating the President of the United States, but we didn't dream he would do it." A major opportunity to forgo a national tragedy was thus missed. For his actions or lack thereof, Hosty was formally censured and transferred to the Bureau's Kansas City, Missouri, office. Sixteen other Bureau employees were also disciplined, including an inspector at FBI Headquarters, for neglecting to exercise "sufficient imagination and foresight" to pass on incriminating background material about Oswald to the Secret Service. "There is no question in my mind [that] we failed in carrying through some of the salient aspects of the Oswald investigation," Hoover conceded behind closed doors. "It ought to be a lesson to all."[48]

But Hoover couldn't just leave the matter at that. Ever the wily bureaucrat, he realized that if official word got out about the Bureau's blunders, it might cause enough of a political firestorm to force him to be relieved of his duties as Director. "I think it would be very, very bad to have a rash of investigations on this thing," he said. To avoid such a scenario, Hoover resorted to an age-old tactic that has served modern Washington power brokers for decades: he covered up. Working closely with the Warren Commission, a special seven-member panel of upstanding private citizens and public officials appointed by President Lyndon Johnson to "uncover all the facts concerning the assassination of President Kennedy," Hoover largely succeeded in sweeping under the rug any suggestion that the FBI had been derelict in its duty.[49]

Some discerning federal officials were not so easily convinced, however. "Hoover, especially when he went on to his dotage, made a lot of mistakes," said Ray Cline, the Deputy Director of Intelligence for the CIA in the early 1960s. "What he did in the Warren Commission was to try to cover up the FBI mistakes; there were mistakes." Robert Kennedy was even more dismissive, privately calling the Hoover-influenced Warren investigation "a shoddy piece of craftsmanship." He had already been aggrieved by the offhand manner in which Hoover had first notified him of his brother's shooting by telephone. "I think it's serious. I'm endeavoring to get details," Hoover had told him. Kennedy complained afterward that Hoover's bland tone was "not quite as excited as if he were reporting the fact that he had found a Communist on the faculty of Howard University."[50]

With the Kennedy presidency over, Hoover managed to enjoy life under Lyndon Johnson, his accommodating new boss. The Bureau was given carte blanche authority to wiretap civil rights activists, disrupt anti–Vietnam War protest organizations, and to dig up dirt on administration opponents. "[Hoover] is a hero to millions of decent citizens and anathema to evil men," an appreciative LBJ said. "No other American now or in our past has ever served the cause of justice more faithfully or so well. No other American has fought so long or so hard for a safer and better national life." Johnson had known the Director for twenty years, dating back to when the two had been neighbors in the leafy suburbs of Washington, DC. "The Johnson daughters felt he was a rich uncle or something," remembered one observer. "Not that they'd see him that much, but in the old days he'd occasionally come over [to the Johnson home] for breakfast on Sunday." These mutual warm feelings had carried over to 1600 Pennsylvania Avenue. "I've got more confidence in your judgment than anybody in town," Johnson told Hoover upon assuming the presidency. To demonstrate this confidence, Johnson reappointed Hoover as Director in 1964 despite the fact that the latter was nearing seventy, the mandatory retirement age. "The nation cannot afford to lose you," explained Johnson. Johnson's unqualified endorsement may have also had something to do with the fact that Hoover had considerable dirt on his less-than-angelic private life, including his fondness for extramarital affairs. "[LBJ] personally feared J. Edgar Hoover," claimed Johnson press secretary Bill Moyers.[51]

Equally pleasing to Hoover was the fact that he no longer had to submit to the humiliation of having to answer a special Department of Justice "hotline" phone that Robert Kennedy had installed on the Director's desk. "Put that damn thing back on [longtime personal secretary and loyalist Helen Gandy's] desk where it belongs," Hoover thundered to a subordinate following Dallas. For his part, Kennedy knew immediately that the tables of power had turned against him. "Those people [in the FBI] don't work for us anymore," he said. Indeed, they worked for Kennedy's political archenemy, who relished the opportunity of using Hoover and his immense power as a means of marginalizing the attorney general. "Mr. Johnson at all times recognized strength and knew how to use strength," recalled DeLoach. "Hoover was riding the crest of the wave at the time and Mr. Johnson knew how to use him. They were not deep personal friends by any stretch of the imagination. There was political distrust between the two of them, but they both needed each other."[52]

His influence diminished, Robert Kennedy resigned from the Justice Department to mount a successful US Senate run in New York. All the while, his relationship with Hoover continued to remain antagonistic. When Kennedy entered the 1968 Democratic presidential race, Hoover leaked FBI documents to the press detailing how the former Attorney General had signed off on wiretapping Martin Luther King Jr. Kennedy didn't bat an eye when he realized the source of the embarrassing revelation. "There'll be a lot of that," he predicted. For sure, Hoover was alarmed at the prospect of Kennedy becoming president, knowing full well such an event would result in his removal as FBI Director. Better, he felt, to sabotage Kennedy's candidacy through unflattering disclosures like the King wiretap than to stand idly by as Kennedy lined up the necessary political support to reach the White House. Hoover's closest Bureau associates didn't require much prodding to reach a similar conclusion. To them, as Clyde Tolson revealed, Kennedy was a "little son of a bitch" who needed to be erased from the political picture.[53]

Kennedy's murder by a mentally deranged former stable boy named Sirhan Sirhan in Los Angeles, California, on June 6 thus did not dredge up any private feelings of remorse on Hoover's part. "I think that he felt . . . the Kennedys, although very sophisticated, intelligent, a wonderful education, a great family—nevertheless were very naïve in many respects, particularly Bobby," said DeLoach. "He thought they were very naïve as far as society was concerned. Also, Mr. Hoover, having been raised in a Quaker family, being a deeply religious individual—an elder in the Presbyterian Church—when he saw individuals more or less desecrating the law, in his opinion, or individuals in high places who acted improperly and didn't do anything about it, I am sure felt they were doing very wrong." In fact, outside the prying ears of reporters, Hoover took to mocking the late New York senator as a "Messiah of the generation gap." For public consumption, however, he embraced a more respectful tone. "We are all profoundly saddened over the tragic death of your husband and offer our deepest sympathy to you and your children," Hoover telegrammed Ethel Kennedy, Robert's widow. "His passing leaves a deep void in the hearts of the entire nation, and we pray that god's comforting hand will sustain you in your bereavement."[54]

While Hoover's loyalty to Johnson was unquestioned, his feelings toward the Texan's successor were less so. Hoover had first become acquainted with Richard Nixon in the late 1940s when the future Commander in Chief was an eager young congressman hoping to make a name for himself on the House Un-American Activities Committee. "[Nixon] looks to me as though he's going to be a good man for us," Hoover confided to a friend.[55] But the Director's initially high opinion of Nixon would sour by the early 1970s as the latter pushed for greater coordination between domestic and foreign intelligence agencies when it came to monitoring radical groups on these shores.

Dubbed the "Huston Plan" in honor of the junior White House aide who drew up the proposal, the top-secret initiative called for increased electronic surveillance of radicals and the establishment of a permanent interagency committee to oversee all logistical details. Fearing such a development might undermine the Bureau's influence, Hoover vigorously opposed the effort, claiming it to be "a terrible plan." "Hoover . . . didn't want his agents working with the CIA and other investigative agencies included in that plan," explained John Dean, Nixon's White House counsel. Frustrated by Hoover's response, Nixon formally scrapped the idea and unsuccessfully sought a way to ease his old friend

Figure 8.3.   Kennedy and his wife Jacqueline moments before Oswald's deadly shots were fired. Reproduction Number: LC-USZ62-134844

into retirement, a gesture Hoover greatly resented. "He should get the hell out of there," the president privately complained.[56]

Nixon also took the fateful step of setting up his own "Plumbers Unit" of clandestine political operatives inside the White House to deal with the perceived radical threat and other domestic opponents of his administration. This move would eventually result in the Watergate scandal—a botched break-in of the Democratic National Headquarters at the Watergate office building in Washington, DC, on June 17, 1972, that prompted Nixon's quitting the presidency two years later. Secretly leaking the details of the break-in and its attendant presidential cover-up to the press was the FBI's second-ranking official at the time, Mark Felt. Nicknamed "Deep Throat" by *Washington Post* reporters Bob Woodward and Carl Bernstein, this tall, blue-eyed Idaho native later wrote he felt a moral obligation to be a whistle-blower, as he believed the White House had engaged in acts of "widespread criminality."[57]

Whether Felt's old boss would have approved of this controversial course of action is a matter of speculation, as Hoover passed away from a heart attack two months before the Watergate scandal broke publicly. What is certain is that Hoover harbored no personal misgivings about the way he had conducted himself as FBI Director. He took special pride in the fact that he had acquired so many enemies over the years. As he once said, "If some of those people stop criticizing me, I'd be worried that somehow I wasn't doing my job right."[58]

No doubt John Kennedy felt the same about his own adversaries.

NOTES

1. Kennedy, "Transcript of Broadcast with Walter Cronkite Inaugurating a CBS Television News Program (September 2, 1962)," *Public Papers of the Presidents: John F. Kennedy 1963*, 652.

2. Anne E. Blair, *Lodge in Vietnam: A Patriot Abroad* (New Haven, 2014), 13; Richard Reeves, *President Kennedy, Profile in Power* (New York, 1993), 526–27.

3. Christopher Matthews, *Kennedy and Nixon: The Rivalry That Shaped Postwar America* (New York, 1996), 229.

4. William R. Rust, *Kennedy in Vietnam: American Vietnam Policy 1960-63* (New York, 1985), 168; Henry Cabot Lodge Oral History, John F. Kennedy Library (hereinafter cited as JFKL).

5. Michael O'Brien, *John F. Kennedy: A Biography* (New York, 2005), 864; John F. Kennedy, "Dictated Memoir Entry," November 4, 1963, President's Office Files, Presidential Recordings, JFKL.

6. Ralph G. Martin, *A Hero for Our Time: An Intimate Story of the Kennedy Years* (New York, 1963), 290; Gloria Swanson, *Swanson on Swanson* (New York, 1980), 356.

7. (Daily) *Mail Online*, February 10, 2012, http://www.dailymail.co.uk/news/article-2099498/Mimi-Alford-The-day-JFK-took-virginity-wifes-White-House-bed.html.

8. Ibid.

9. Mark Feldstein, *Poisoning the Press: Richard Nixon, Jack Anderson, and the Rise of Washington's Scandal Culture* (New York, 2010), 376.

10. *Des Moines Register*, October 31.

11. Michael Beschloss, *The Crisis Years: Kennedy and Khrushchev, 1960-1963* (New York, 1991), 616; James W. Hilty, *Robert Kennedy: Brother Protector* (Philadelphia, 1997), 256.

12. Burton Hersh, *Bobby and J. Edgar: The Historic Face-off Between the Kennedys and J. Edgar Hoover* (New York, 2007), 63; "Transcript Wiretap Conversation, Inga Arvad and John Kennedy, February 3, 1942, 11 P.M." in Athan Theoharis, ed., *From the Secret Files of J. Edgar Hoover* (Chicago, 1991), 21; Reeves, *President Kennedy*, 288.

13. Gerald S. Strober and Deborah H. Strober, *"Let Us Begin Anew": An Oral History of the Kennedy Presidency* (New York, 1993), 265; Richard Nixon, *RN: The Memoirs of Richard Nixon* (New York, 1978), 358.

14. Barry Denenberg, *The True Story of J. Edgar Hoover and the FBI* (New York 1993), 23-25; Curt Gentry, *J. Edgar Hoover: The Man with the Secrets* (New York, 1991), 63; Richard Hack, *Puppetmaster: The Secret Life of J. Edgar Hoover* (Beverly Hills, California, 2004), 43.

15. Richard Gid Powers, *Secrecy and Power: The Life of J. Edgar Hoover* (New York, 1987), 31–32.

16. Anthony Summers, *Official and Confidential: The Secret Life of J. Edgar Hoover* (New York, 1993), 27.

17. Ibid., 76.

18. Kenneth Ackerman, *Young J. Edgar: Hoover, the Red Scare and the Assault on Civil Liberties* (New York, 2007), 405; Powers, *Secrecy and Power*, 172.

19. Ackerman, *Young J. Edgar*, 43.

20. *New Yorker*, October 2, 1937.

21. *New York Times*, May 3, 1972; Summers, *Official and Confidential*, 39.

22. Altheus Thomas Mason, *Harlan Fiske Stone: Pillar of the Law* (New York, 1956), 150.

23. Denenberg, *The True Story of J. Edgar Hoover and the FBI*, 7.

24. Tim Weiner, *Enemies: A History of the FBI* (New York, 2012), 235; Summers, *Official and Confidential*, 171; *New York Times*, May 3, 1972.

25. Gentry, *J. Edgar Hoover*, 327–28.

26. Gil Reavill, *Mafia Summit: J. Edgar Hoover, The Kennedy Brothers, and the Meeting That Unmasked the Mob* (New York, 2013), 131.

27. J. Edgar Hoover, *Masters of Deceit: The Story of Communism in America and How to Fight It* (New York, 1958) 4; Summers, *Official and Confidential*, 163; Ovid Demaris, *The Director: An Oral Biography of J. Edgar Hoover* (New York, 1971), 121.

28. "Joseph P. Kennedy to J. Edgar Hoover," October 11, 1955, Amanda Smith, ed., *Hostage to Fortune: The Letters of Joseph P. Kennedy* (New York, 2001), 671; Summers, *Official and Confidential*, 274.

29. Strober and Strober, *"Let Us Begin Anew,"* 266; Lester David and Irene David, *Bobby Kennedy: The Making of a Folk Hero* (New York, 1986), 188; Denenberg, *The True Story of J. Edgar Hoover and the FBI*, 132.

30. Strober and Strober, *"Let Us Begin Anew,"* 266; Richard D. Mahoney, *The Kennedy Brothers: The Rise and Fall of Jack and Bobby* (New York, 2011), 98; Cartha DeLoach Oral History, Lyndon B. Johnson Library (hereinafter cited as LBJL); Edwin O. Guthman and Jeffrey Schulman, *Robert Kennedy in His Own Words: The Unpublished Recollections of the Kennedy Years* (New York, 1988), 134.

31. Strober and Strober, *"Let Us Begin Anew,"* 270.

32. Gerald Posner, *Case Closed: Lee Harvey Oswald and the Assassination of JFK* (New York, 1993), 9.

33. The New York Times Edition, *Report of the Warren Commission: The Assassination of President Kennedy* (New York, 1964), 29; Steven M. Gillon, *The Kennedy Assassination-24 Hours After* (New York, 2009), 153; Posner, *Case Closed*, 19.

34. Ibid., 30; The New York Times Edition, *The Report of the Warren Commission*, 30; Priscilla Johnson McMillan, *Marina and Lee* (New York, 1997), 77; Posner, *Case Closed*, 28.

35. *Life*, November 29, 1963; Posner, *Case Closed*, 29; Norman Mailer, *Oswald's Tale: An American Mystery* (New York, 1995), 391.

36. *Newsweek*, December 2, 1963; *Life*, November 29, 1959.

37. McMillan, *Marina and Lee*, 94, 101.

38. Posner, *Case Closed*, 61, 73.

39. Thomas Mallon, *Mrs. Paine's Garage and the Murder of John F. Kennedy* (New York, 2002), 29; Posner, *Case Closed*, 163.

40. Ibid., 116.

41. McMillan, *Marina and Lee*, 368.

42. Martin, *A Hero for Our Time*, 503.

43. Kenneth P. O'Donnell and David F. Powers with Joe McCarthy. *Johnny, We Hardly Knew Ye: Memories of John F. Kennedy* (Boston, 1972), 27–28.

44. Mailer, *Oswald's Tale*, 681.

45. "Lee Harvey Oswald declares 'I'm just a patsy,'" *YouTube Clip*, http://JFK-Archives.blogspot.com/2011/03/oswalds-patsy-lie.html; Posner, *Case Closed*, 376–77; The New York Times Edition, *Report of the Warren Commission*, 348; Mailer, *Oswald's Tale*, 756.

46. *Life*, December 6, 1963; Final Report of the Select Committee to Study Governmental Operations With Respect to Intelligence Activities, United States Senate, *The Investigation of the Assassination of John F. Kennedy: Performance of the Intelligence Agencies, April 23, 1976* (Washington, DC, 1976), 50; Tim Weiner, *Enemies*, 190; Final Report of the Select Committee to Study Governmental Operations With Respect to Intelligence Activities, United States Senate, *The Investigation of the Assassination of John F. Kennedy*, 51.

47. Ibid., 96.

48. Hersh, *Bobby and J. Edgar*, 421; *Time*, November 27, 1964; Final Report of the Select Committee to Study Governmental Operations With Respect to Intelligence Activities, United States Senate, *The Investigation of the Assassination of John F. Kennedy*, 52–53.

49. Michael Beschloss, *Taking Charge: The Johnson White House Tapes, 1963-1964* (New York, 1997), 51; The New York Times Edition, *Report of the Warren Commission*, 9.

50. Strober and Strober, *"Let Us Begin Anew,"* 464; *USA Today*, January 12, 2013; William Manchester, *The Death of a President: November 20-25, 1963* (New York, 1967), 196; *New York Times*, May 3, 1972.

51. Jay Robert Nash, *Citizen Hoover: A Critical Study of the Life and Times of J. Edgar Hoover and the FBI* (Chicago, 1972), 156; Powers, *Secrecy and Power*, 394; Beschloss, ed., *Taking Charge*, 58; Powers, *Secrecy and Power*, 394; *Newsweek*, March 10, 1975.

52. Powers, *Secrecy and Power*, 391; Helen O'Donnell, *A Common Good: The Friendship of Robert F. Kennedy and Kenneth P. O'Donnell* (New York, 1998), 321; Cartha D. DeLoach Oral History, LBJL.

53. Evan Thomas, *Robert Kennedy: His Life* (New York, 2000), 379; Gentry, *J. Edgar Hoover*, 606.

54. Strober and Strober, *"Let Us Begin Anew,"* 267; Weiner, *Enemies*, 275; Hersh, *Bobby and J. Edgar*, 483.

55. Demaris, *The Director*, 121.

56. Gerald S. Strober and Deborah H. Strober, *Nixon: An Oral History of His Presidency* (New York, 1994), *Nixon*, 225; Weiner, *Enemies*, 300.

57. Mark Felt with John O'Connor, *A G-Man's Life: The FBI, Being "Deep Throat," and the Struggle for Honor in Washington* (New York, 2006), 202.

58. Denenberg, *The True Story of J. Edgar Hoover and the FBI*, 111.

Acknowledgments

Hall of Fame baseball manager Casey Stengel was once asked how he was able to achieve championship success with the New York Yankees. "I couldna done it without my players," he responded.

While writing a book is in no way comparable to winning a World Series, I nevertheless feel I could not have accomplished this personal milestone without the support and encouragement of my many friends and colleagues.

Heading the list here are Dan Hammond and Chris Callely. Over the years we've been "The Three Amigos" and have mutually supported each other through thick and thin. As we hurtle toward the perils and uncertainty of middle age, it's heartening to know they'll always have my back and I theirs. The same goes for Steve Blumenkrantz and Don Clemenzi. They epitomize what true friendship is all about. I can't think of better people.

An equal debt of gratitude is owed Elizabeth Crowley, a marvelously gifted newspaper editor and writer who patiently offered advice on how to improve the book. She no doubt has made her old history professors at Harvard very proud.

It's been well over thirty years since I first laced up my running shoes for Fred Hammond, but my former coach and history mentor remains a constant source of inspiration and wisdom. He is a real-life Mr. Chips.

Sadly, fellow Boston historians Thomas H. O'Connor and Andrew Bunie are no longer around to compare notes with or swap stories. My scholarly work is clearly built on their wide shoulders.

Jon Sisk once again proved what a consummate professional he is in guiding this manuscript through the publication process. His good humor, tact, skill, and encyclopedic knowledge are much appreciated.

The staffs of the John F. Kennedy Library and Museum, the Massachusetts Historical Society, the Boston Public Library, the American Heritage Center at the University of Wyoming, and the Boston University Special Collections were all especially helpful and cooperative. Take a bow Steve Plotkin, Laurie Austin, Peter Drummey, Dennis Fiori, Anna Cook, and John Waggener.

Also deserving an appreciative shout-out are Chris Fahy, Andy Andres, Tom Testa, Jo Breiner, Mary Alston-Hammond, Wayne and Kris Ferrari, Scott Ferrera, Joseph and Kristin King, Bob Connors, Pat and Hillori Connors, Laureen Fitzgerald, Jodi Blumenkrantz, Bill and Nancy

Cook, Greg Dunne, Greg Morose, Natalie J. McKnight, Meg Tyler, Meghan Sullivan, Anita Cook, Joseph and Theresa Dever, Tracy Dimant, Yelizaveta Dimant, Alyse Bithavas-Glac, Stacy Godnick, Rebekah Hardeson, Ilda Hanxhari, Barbara Storella, Danielle Vinciguerra, Mary Tunney, Kira Jastive, John Lyons, Joshua Pederson, Bob Oresick, and Matt Dursin.

As for my students, space prohibits me from thanking each individually. But they have provided me with great intellectual stimulus over the years, and I again am reminded just how extremely fortunate I am to be in the teaching profession.

Last but certainly not least, I want to pay special tribute to my devoted friend Lady. An adorable white cat with striking green eyes and a playful disposition, she spent many an hour by my side as I prepared this manuscript. Her passing has left me sad but appreciative of her warm company and angelic nature. She will be greatly missed.

T. J. W.
Beverly, Massachusetts
August 2013

Selected Bibliography

Abel, Elie. *The Missile Crisis*. New York, 1966.

Ackerman, Kenneth. *Young J. Edgar: Hoover, the Red Scare and the Assault on Civil Liberties*. New York, 2007.

Ambrose, Stephen. *Nixon: The Education of a Politician, 1913–1962*. New York, 1988.

Andrew, Christopher. *For the President's Eyes Only: Secret Intelligence and the American Presidency*. New York, 1995.

Baker, Bobby with Larry King. *Wheeling and Dealing: Confessions of a Capitol Hill Operator*. New York, 1978.

Ball, George. *The Past Has Another Pattern: Memoirs*. New York, 1973.

Beatty, Jack. *The Rascal King: The Life and Times of James Michael Curley*. Reading, Massachusetts, 1992.

Beschloss, Michael. *Taking Charge: The Johnson White House Tapes, 1963–1964*. New York, 1997.

Beschloss, Michael. *The Crisis Years: Kennedy and Khrushchev, 1960–1963*. New York, 1991.

Bissell, Richard M. with Jonathan E. Lewis and Frances T. Pudlo. *Reflections of a Cold Warrior: From Yalta to the Bay of Pigs*. New Haven, Connecticut, 1996.

Blair, Anne E. *Lodge in Vietnam: A Patriot Abroad*. New Haven, Connecticut, 2014.

Blair, Joan and Clay Blair Jr. *The Search for J.F.K.* New York, 1976.

Bourne, Peter G. *Fidel: A Biography of Fidel Castro*. New York, 1986.

Bradlee, Benjamin C. *Conversations with Kennedy*. New York, 1975.

Branch, Taylor. *Parting the Waters: America in the King Years, 1954–63*. New York, 1988.

Brandt, Willy. *People and Politics: The Years 1960–73*. Boston, 1976.

Brauer, Carl. *John F. Kennedy and the Second Reconstruction*. New York, 1977.

Brinkley, Alan. *John F. Kennedy*. New York, 2012.

Brodie, Fawn M. *Richard Nixon: The Shaping of His Character*. New York, 1981.

Bryant, Nick. *The Bystander: John F. Kennedy and the Struggle for Black Equality*. New York, 2006.

Bundy, McGeorge. *Danger and Survival: Choices about the Bomb in the First Fifty Years*. New York, 1990.

Burner, David. *John F. Kennedy and a New Generation*. Boston, 1988.

Burner, David and Thomas R. West. *The Torch Is Passed: The Kennedy Brothers and American Liberalism*. New York, 1984.

Burns, James MacGregor. *John Kennedy: A Political Profile*. New York, 1960.

Carlson, Peter. *K Blows Top: A Cold War Comic Interlude Starring Nikita Khrushchev, America's Most Unlikely Tourist*. New York, 2009.

Caro, Robert. *Means of Ascent: The Years of Lyndon Johnson*. New York, 1990.

Caro, Robert. *The Path to Power: The Years of Lyndon Johnson*. New York, 1982.

Carter, Dan T. *The Politics of Rage: George Wallace, the Origins of the New Conservatism, and the Transformation of American Politics*. New York, 1995.

Casey, Shaun A. *The Making of a Catholic President: Kennedy vs. Nixon 1960*. Oxford, 2009.

Castro, Fidel. *Fidel Castro: My Life*. New York, 2009.

Chaute, David. *The Great Fear*. New York, 1978.

Chestnut Jr., J. L., and Julia Cass. *Black in Selma: The Uncommon Life of J. L. Chestnut Jr.: Politics and Power in a Small American City*. New York, 1990.

Cohn, Roy. *McCarthy*. New York, 1968.

Collier, Peter and David Horowitz. *The Kennedys: An American Drama*. New York, 1884.

Crowley, Monica. *Nixon off the Record: His Candid Commentary on People and Politics*. New York, 1996.

Dallek, Robert. *An Unfinished Life: John F. Kennedy*. Boston, 2003.

Dallek, Robert. *Lone Star Rising: Lyndon Johnson and His Times, 1908–1960*. New York, 1991.

David, Lester and Irene David. *Bobby Kennedy: The Making of a Folk Hero*. New York, 1986.

Denenberg, Barry. *The True Story of J. Edgar Hoover and the FBI*. New York, 1993.

Dobbs, Michael. *One Minute to Midnight: Kennedy, Khrushchev, and Castro on the Brink of Nuclear War*. New York, 2008.

Donovan, Robert. *PT-109: John F. Kennedy in World War II*. New York, 1960.

Eisenhower, Dwight D. *Mandate for Change: The White House Years, 1953–56*. New York, 1963.

Eisenhower, Dwight D. *Waging Peace: The White House Years 1956–1961*. Garden City, New York, 1965.

Eisenhower, Julie Nixon. *Pat Nixon: The Untold Story*. New York, 1986.

Feldstein, Michael. *Poisoning the Press: Richard Nixon, Jack Anderson, and the Rise of Washington's Scandal Culture*. New York, 2010.

Felt, Mark with John O'Connor. *A G-Man's Life: The FBI, Being "Deep Throat," and the Struggle for Honor in Washington*. New York, 2006.

Ferrell, Robert H., Ed. *The Eisenhower Diaries*. New York, 1981.

Frady, Marshall. *Wallace*. New York, 1968.

Fursenko, Aleksandr and Timothy Naftali. *Khrushchev's Cold War: The Inside Story of an American Adversary*. New York, 2006.

Gaddis, John Lewis. *The Cold War: A New History*. New York, 2005.

Gentry, Curt. *J. Edgar Hoover: The Man with the Secrets*. New York, 1991.

Geyer, Georgie Anne. *Guerrilla Prince: The Untold Story of Fidel Castro*. Boston, 1991.

Gibbs, Nancy and Michael Duffy. *The Preacher and the Presidents: Billy Graham in the White House*. New York, 2007.

Giglio, James N. *The Presidency of John F. Kennedy*. Lawrence, Kansas, 1991.

Gillon, Steven G. *The Kennedy Assassination—24 Hours After*. New York, 2009.

Goldman, Eric F. *The Crucial Decade—and After, America, 1945–1960*. New York, 1960.

Goldstein, Gordon M. *Lessons in Disaster: McGeorge Bundy and the Path to War in Vietnam*. New York, 2008.

Goodwin, Doris Kearns. *The Fitzgeralds and the Kennedys: An American Saga*. New York, 1987.

Goodwin, Doris Kearns. *Lyndon Johnson and the American Dream*. New York, 1991.

Gould, Lewis L. *Grand Old Party: A History of the Republicans*. New York, 2003.

Gould, Lewis L. *1968: The Election That Changed America*. Chicago, 1993.

Guthman, Edwin O. and Jeffrey Schulman, Eds. *Robert Kennedy in His Own Words: The Unpublished Recollections of the Kennedy Years*. New York, 1988.

Hack, Richard. *Puppetmaster: The Secret Life of J. Edgar Hoover*. Beverly Hills, California, 2004.

Halberstam, David. *The Fifties*. New York, 1993.

Hamilton, Nigel. *J.F.K.: Reckless Youth*. New York, 1992.

Harwood, Richard and Haynes Johnson. *Lyndon*. New York, 1973.

Hatch, Alden. *The Lodges of Massachusetts*. New York, 1973.

Hersh, Burton. *Bobby and J. Edgar: The Historic Face-off between the Kennedys and J. Edgar Hoover*. New York, 2007.

Hess, Stephen. *America's Political Dynasties*. Garden City, New York, 1960.

Higgins, Trumball. *The Perfect Failure: Kennedy, Eisenhower, and the CIA at the Bay of Pigs*. New York, 1989.

Hilty, James W. *Robert Kennedy: Brother Protector*. Philadelphia, 1997.

Holland, Max. *The Kennedy Assassination Tapes*. New York, 2004.

Hoover, J. Edgar. *Masters of Deceit: The Story of Communism in America and How to Fight It*. New York, 1958.

Hughes, Emmet John. *The Ordeal of Power: A Political Memoir of the Eisenhower Years*. New York, 1963.

Isaacson, Walter and Evan Thomas. *The Wise Men: Six Friends and the World They Made*. New York, 1986.

Kahn, Roger. *The Boys of Summer*. New York, 1972.

Katzenbach, Nicholas deB. *Some of It Was Fun: Working with RFK and LBJ*. New York, 2008.

Kennedy, Edward M. *True Compass: A Memoir*. New York, 2009.

Kennedy, Jacqueline. *Historic Conversations on Life with John F. Kennedy*. New York, 2011.

Kennedy, John F. *As We Remember Joe*. Privately published, 1945.

Kennedy, John F. "Commencement Address at American Universityin Washington" (June 10, 1963) in *Public Papers of the Presidents of the United States: John F. Kennedy, 1963*. Washington, DC, 1964, 461.

Kennedy, John F. *Prelude to Leadership: The European Diary of John F. Kennedy, Summer 1945*. Washington, DC, 1995.

Kennedy, Robert F. *Thirteen Days: A Memoir of the Cuban Missile Crisis*. New York, 1969.

Kennedy, Rose Fitzgerald. *Times to Remember*. New York, 1974.

Kenney, Charles. *John Kennedy: The Presidential Portfolio*. New York, 2000.

Kessler, Ronald. *The Sins of the Father: Joseph P. Kennedy and the Dynasty Founded*. New York, 1996.

Khrushchev, Nikita. *Khrushchev Remembers*. Boston, 1979.

Khrushchev, Sergei. *Khrushchev on Khrushchev: An Inside Account of the Man and His Era*. Boston, 1990.

Johnson, Rebekah Baines. *A Family Album*. New York, 1980.

Kornitzer, Bela. *The Real Nixon: An Intimate Biography*. New York, 1960.

Leaming, Barbara. *Jack Kennedy: The Education of a Statesman*. New York, 2006.

Leavy, Jane. *The Last Boy: Mickey Mantle and the End of America's Childhood*. New York, 2010.

Lesher, Stephan. *George Wallace: American Populist*. Reading, Massachusetts, 1994.

Levy, Shawn. *Rat Pack Confidential: Frank, Dean, Sammy, Joey, and the Last Great Showbiz Party*. New York, 1998.

Lincoln, Evelyn. *My Twelve Years with John F. Kennedy*. New York, 1965.

Lodge, Henry Cabot. *The Storm Has Many Eyes: A Personal Narrative*. New York, 1973.

Lukas, Anthony. *Common Ground: A Turbulent Decade in the Lives of Three American Families*. New York, 1986.

Mahoney, Richard D. *The Kennedy Brothers: The Rise and Fall of Jack and Bobby*. New York, 2011.

Mailer, Norman. *Oswald's Tale: An American Mystery*. New York, 1995.

Mallon, Thomas. *Mrs. Paine's Garage and the Murder of John F. Kennedy*. New York, 2002.

Martin, Ralph G. *A Hero for Our Time: An Intimate Story of the Kennedy Years*. New York, 1963.

Martin, Ralph G. *Seeds of Destruction: Joe Kennedy and His Sons*. New York, 1995.

Matthews, Christopher. *Jack Kennedy: Elusive Hero*. New York, 2011.

Matthews, Christopher. *Kennedy and Nixon: The Rivalry That Shaped Postwar America*. New York, 1996.

May, Ernest R. and Phillip D. Zelikow, Eds. *The Kennedy Tapes: Inside the White House During the Cuban Missile Crisis*. Cambridge, Massachusetts, 1990.

Mazo, Earl. *Richard Nixon: A Political and Personal Portrait*. New York, 1959.

McCarthy, Joe. *The Remarkable Kennedys*. New York, 1960.

McKeever, Porter. *Adlai Stevenson: His Life and Legacy*. New York, 1989.

McMillan, Priscilla Johnson. *Marina and Lee*. New York, 1997.

Miller, Merle. *Lyndon: An Oral Biography*. New York, 1980.

Miller, William J. *Henry Cabot Lodge: A Biography*. New York, 1967.

Mitchell, Greg. *Tricky Dick and the Pink Lady: Richard Nixon vs. Helen Gahagan Douglas—Sexual Politics and the Red Scare, 1950*. New York, 1998.

Moody, Anne. *Coming of Age in Mississippi*. New York, 1968.

Myers, Joan, Ed. *John F. Kennedy As We Remember Him*. New York, 1965.

Nash, Jay Robert. *Citizen Hoover: A Critical Study of the Life and Times of J. Edgar Hoover and FBI*. Chicago, 1972.

Nixon, Richard. *In the Arena: A Memoir of Victory, Defeat, and Renewal*. New York, 1990.

Nixon, Richard. *RN: The Memoirs of Richard Nixon*. New York, 1978.

Nixon, Richard. *Six Crises*. New York, 1990.

O'Brien, Larry F. *No Final Victories: A Life in Politics from John F. Kennedy to Watergate*. Garden City, New York, 1974.

O'Brien, Michael. *John F. Kennedy: A Biography*. New York, 2005.

O'Brien, Michael. *Rethinking Kennedy*. Chicago, 2009.

O'Connor, Thomas H. *The Boston Irish: A Political History*. Boston, 1994.

O'Donnell, Helen. *A Common Good: The Friendship of Robert F. Kennedy and Kenneth P. O'Donnell*. New York, 1998.

O'Donnell, Kenneth P. and David F. Powers with Joe McCarthy. *Johnny, We Hardly Knew Ye: Memories of John F. Kennedy*. Boston, 1972.

O'Neill, Thomas P. with William Novak. *Man of the House: The Life and Political Memoirs of Speaker Thomas P. Tip O'Neill*. New York, 1987.

Parmet, Herbert S. *Jack: The Struggles of John F. Kennedy*. New York, 1980.

Paterson, Thomas G., J. Garry Clifford, and Kenneth J. Hagen. *American Foreign Relations: A History Since 1895, Volume II*. Lexington, Massachusetts, 1995.

Perlstein, Rick. *Nixonland: The Rise of a President and the Fracturing of America*. Chicago, 1993.

Perret, Geoffrey. *Jack: A Life like No Other*. New York, 2002.

Posner, Gerald. *Case Closed: Lee Harvey Oswald and the Assassination of JFK*. New York, 1993.

Powers, Richard Gid. *Secrecy and Power: The Life of J. Edgar Hoover*. New York, 1987.

Rasenberger, Jim. *The Brilliant Disaster: JFK, Castro, and America's Doomed Invasion of Cuba's Bay of Pigs*. New York, 2011.

Reeves, Richard. *President Kennedy, Profile in Power*. New York, 1993.

Reisler, Jim. *The Best Game Ever: Pirates vs. Yankees: October 13, 1960*. New York, 2007.

Reston, James. *Deadline: A Memoir*. New York, 1991.

Rorabaugh, W. J. *Kennedy and the Promise of the Sixties*. New York, 2002.

Rust, William R. *Kennedy in Vietnam: American Vietnam Policy 1960–63*. New York, 1985.

Salinger, Pierre. *P.S.: A Memoir*. New York, 1995.

Saunders, Frank with James Southwood. *Torn Lace Curtain*. New York, 1982.

Schaap, Dick. *R.F.K.* New York, 1968.

Schlesinger, Arthur Jr. *A Thousand Days: John F. Kennedy in the White House*. Boston, 1965.

Schlesinger, Arthur Jr. *Journals, 1952–2000*. New York, 2007.

Schlesinger, Arthur Jr. *Robert F. Kennedy and His Times*. Boston, 1978.

Schoenbaum, Thomas J. *Waging Peace and War in the Truman, Kennedy, and Johnson Years*. New York, 1988.

Searls, Hank. *The Lost Prince: Young Joe, the Forgotten Kennedy*. New York, 1969.

Service, Robert. *A History of Twentieth Century Russia*. Cambridge, Massachusetts, 1997.

Sevareid, Eric, Ed. *Candidates 1960: Behind the Headlines in the Presidential Race*. New York, 1959.

Shesol, Jeff. *Mutual Contempt: Lyndon Johnson, Robert Kennedy, and the Feud That Defined a Decade*. New York, 1997.

Smith, Amanda, Ed. *Hostage to Fortune: The Letters of Joseph P. Kennedy*. New York, 2001.

Smith, Sally Bedell. *Grace and Power: The Private World of the Kennedy White House*. New York, 2004.

Smith, Thomas. *Showdown: JFK and the Integration of the Washington Redskins*. Boston, 2011.

Smyser, W. R. *Kennedy and the Berlin Wall*. Lanham, MD, 2009.

Sorensen, Ted. *Counselor: A Life at the Edge of History*. New York, 2009.

Sorensen, Theodore C. *Kennedy*. New York, 1965.

Stack, Robert with Mark Evans. *Straight Shooting*. New York, 1980.

Steiner, Jean and George Plimpton, Ed. *American Journey: The Times of Robert Kennedy*. New York, 1970.

Stern, Mark. *Calculating Visions: Kennedy, Johnson, and Civil Rights*. New Brunswick, New Jersey, 1992.

Strober, Gerald S. and Deborah H. Strober. *"Let Us Begin Anew": An Oral History of the Kennedy Presidency*. New York, 1993.

Strober, Gerald S. and Deborah H. Strober. *Nixon: An Oral History of His Presidency*. New York, 1994.

Summers, Anthony. *The Arrogance of Power: The Secret World of Richard Nixon*. New York, 2000.

Summers, Anthony. *Official and Confidential: The Secret Life of J. Edgar Hoover*. New York, 1993.

Swanson, Gloria. *Swanson on Swanson*. New York, 1980.

Szulc, Tad. *Fidel: A Critical Portrait*. New York, 1986.

Taubman, William. *Khrushchev: The Man and His Era*. New York, 2003.

The Boston Globe. *J.F.K.: The Man, the President*. Boston, 1979.

The New York Times Edition. *Report of the Warren Commission: The Assassination of President Kennedy*. New York, 1964.

Theoharis, Athan, Ed. *From the Secret Files of J. Edgar Hoover*. Chicago, 1991.

Thomas, Evan. *Robert Kennedy: His Life*. New York, 2000.

Thompson, William J. *Khrushchev: A Political Life*. New York, 1995.

Triay, Victor Andres. *Bay of Pigs: An Oral History of Brigade 2506*. Gainesville, Florida, 2001.

Unger, Irwin and Debi Unger. *LBJ: A Life*. New York, 1999.

Von Tunzelmann, Alex. *Red Heat: Conspiracy, Murder, and the Cold War in the Caribbean*. New York, 2011.

Walton, Richard J. *Cold War and Counterrevolution: The Foreign Policy of John F. Kennedy*. New York, 1972.

Wayman, Dorothy G. *David I. Walsh, Citizen-Patriot*. Milwaukee, WI, 1952.

Weiner, Tim. *Enemies: A History of the FBI*. New York, 2012.

Whalen, Thomas J. *A Higher Purpose: Profiles in Presidential Courage*. Chicago, 2007.

Whalen, Thomas J. *Kennedy versus Lodge: The 1952 Massachusetts Senate Race*. Boston, 2000.

White, Mark. Ed. *The Kennedys and Cuba: A Declassified Documentary History*. Chicago, 2001.

Williams, Juan. *Eyes on the Prize: America's Civil Rights Years 1954–1965*. New York, 1987.

Wilson, Robert A. *Character above All: Ten Presidents from FDR to George Bush*. New York, 1995.

Wofford, Harris. *Of Kennedy and Kings: Making Sense of the Sixties*. New York, 1980.

Woods, Randall B. *LBJ: Architect of American Ambition*. New York, 2006.

Wyckoff, Gene. *The Image Candidates: American Politics in the Age of Television*. New York, 1968.

Wyden, Peter. *Bay of Pigs: The Untold Story*. New York, 1979.

Young, Andrew. *An Easy Burden: The Civil Rights Movement and the Transformation of America*. New York, 1996.

Index

Wallace, George, 142; boxing, 142;
Carter, D. T., on, 144; childhood of,
142; as circuit judge, 144; on Civil
Rights Act of 1964, 152; on
Democratic Party, 152–153;
enlistment of, 142–143;
gubernatorial bid, 144–145; portrait
of, 154; reactionary themes of, 152;
Scammon on, 153; on segregation,
145, 153–154; shooting of, 153;
standing at schoolhouse door, x,
144, 146
Walsh, David I., 28
Warren, Earl, 77
Warren Commission, 175–176; Cline
on, 176; Kennedy, R., on, 176
Washington Redskins, 140
Watergate scandal, 90, 179
West Virginia, 56–57

Why England Slept (Kennedy, J. F.), 6
Wilford, Willy, 11
Wilkins, Roy, 148
Willkie, Wendell, 75
Wilson, Donald, ix
Wingert and Bewley, 74
winning, 2–3
Wofford, Harris, 82, 139
women's vote, 40
Woodward, Bob, 179
Wyckoff, Gene, 39

Yarborough, Ralph, 65
Year of the Veteran, 15
Yeomans, Henry A., 5
Young, Andrew, 151

Zapata Operation, 96

About the Author

Thomas J. Whalen is associate professor of social science at Boston University and author of *Kennedy versus Lodge, Dynasty's End, A Higher Purpose,* and *When the Red Sox Ruled.* An expert in modern American politics, American foreign policy, and the American presidency, Whalen's commentary has appeared in the *New York TImes,* the *Chicago Tribune,* ABCNews.com, the *Wall Street Journal, USA Today, The Washington Post, Politico, The Economist, the Huffington Post, La Presse,* NBCNews.com, the *Boston Globe,* the *Los Angeles Times,* and the Associated Press. He has also appeared on several national broadcast outlets including CNN, CNN-International, NPR, Reuters TV, BBC Radio, the Canadian Broadcasting Company, Fox News, and Voice of America-Moscow. He lives on Boston's North Shore.